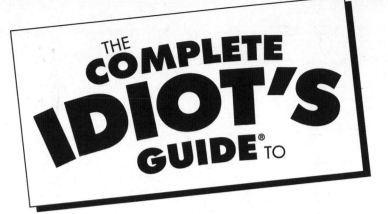

THE COMPLETE IDIOT'S GUIDE® TO

Grilling

by Don Mauer

ALPHA

A member of Penguin Group (USA) Inc.

I dedicate this book to Elizabeth Haynes Mauer Boyd, a.k.a., my mom. I wish she'd lived long enough to hold this book in her hands. She told me once how proud of me she was; I hope she knew how much that meant.

ALPHA BOOKS

Published by the Penguin Group

Penguin Group (USA) Inc., 375 Hudson Street, New York, New York 10014, U.S.A.

Penguin Group (Canada), 10 Alcorn Avenue, Toronto, Ontario, Canada M4V 3B2 (a division of Pearson Penguin Canada Inc.)

Penguin Books Ltd, 80 Strand, London WC2R 0RL, England

Penguin Ireland, 25 St Stephen's Green, Dublin 2, Ireland (a division of Penguin Books Ltd)

Penguin Group (Australia), 250 Camberwell Road, Camberwell, Victoria 3124, Australia (a division of Pearson Australia Group Pty Ltd)

Penguin Books India Pvt Ltd, 11 Community Centre, Panchsheel Park, New Delhi—10 017, India

Penguin Group (NZ), cnr Airborne and Rosedale Roads, Albany, Auckland 1310, New Zealand (a division of Pearson New Zealand Ltd)

Penguin Books (South Africa) (Pty) Ltd, 24 Sturdee Avenue, Rosebank, Johannesburg 2196, South Africa

Penguin Books Ltd, Registered Offices: 80 Strand, London WC2R 0RL, England

International Standard Book Number: 1-59257-481-5
Library of Congress Catalog Card Number: 2005937203

08 07 06   8 7 6 5 4 3 2

Interpretation of the printing code: The rightmost number of the first series of numbers is the year of the book's printing; the rightmost number of the second series of numbers is the number of the book's printing. For example, a printing code of 06-1 shows that the first printing occurred in 2006.

Printed in the United States of America

Note: This publication contains the opinions and ideas of its author. It is intended to provide helpful and informative material on the subject matter covered. It is sold with the understanding that the author and publisher are not engaged in rendering professional services in the book. If the reader requires personal assistance or advice, a competent professional should be consulted.

The author and publisher specifically disclaim any responsibility for any liability, loss, or risk, personal or otherwise, which is incurred as a consequence, directly or indirectly, of the use and application of any of the contents of this book.

Most Alpha books are available at special quantity discounts for bulk purchases for sales promotions, premiums, fund-raising, or educational use. Special books, or book excerpts, can also be created to fit specific needs.

For details, write: Special Markets, Alpha Books, 375 Hudson Street, New York, NY 10014.

Publisher: *Marie Butler-Knight*
Editorial Director: *Mike Sanders*
Senior Managing Editor: *Jennifer Bowles*
Acquisitions Editors: *Mike Sanders, Michele Wells, Renee Wilmeth*
Development Editor: *Christy Wagner*
Production Editor: *Megan Douglass*

Copy Editor: *Nancy Wagner*
Cartoonist: *Richard King*
Book Designer: *Trina Wurst*
Cover Designer: *Kurt Owens*
Indexer: *Heather McNeill*
Layout: *Ayanna Lacey*
Proofreading: *Mary Hunt*

Contents at a Glance

Contents

Foreword

Grilling is like throwing darts. Anybody can throw a dart, but hitting the bull's-eye is another story entirely. It's the same with grilling. Anybody can put food over a fire, but turning out a perfectly seared steak with a crisp crust and juicy interior takes a little more know-how. All too often, backyard grillmeisters get so excited about creating a big fire that they miss the target completely and turn out burnt, dry food that tastes like an ashtray.

Don Mauer can teach you how to grill with skill. He's a man who knows his meat and how to flame it right. I first met Don about 10 years ago after a cooking demonstration he did for his book *Lean and Lovin' It*. I was a cookbook editor at the time, and I'd been tasting lots of recipes for low-fat this and low-sugar that. During his demonstration, the very thought of choking down another dry, tasteless piece of "health food" made me cringe. But as I sat there rolling my eyes, Don's voice had a strange effect on me. He had a boylike wonder and enthusiasm for his subject. He was excited to talk about the food he loved. He was thrilled to share his culinary discoveries.

Don's positive attitude actually inspired someone like myself—a cynical, jaded food writer—to believe in this man's cooking and give it a shot. That night, I went home and tried Don's low-fat brownie recipe. To my amazement, the brownie tasted moist, chocolaty, and perfectly satisfying, despite its lack of fat.

In this grilling book, Don's attitude hasn't changed a bit. That same infectious enthusiasm is infused into every page. And he has a real knack for explaining the fine points of grilling in simple terms. Crack open the book to any page and start reading. In no time at all, you will have learned something you never knew before. Like the real difference between grilling and barbecuing. Or how to grill bison, one of the leanest meats, without drying it out. Skim the pages and pick up a few tips on what to look for when choosing a steak for grilling or how to grill the perfect burger. The book also includes a handy glossary of terms that explains things like how baby back ribs differ from your typical spareribs (hint: they're cut from a different area of the hog's rib section). And of course, it's packed with recipes for everything from chicken to beef to Moroccan ground lamb kabobs. Try a few recipes, and you'll soon be brining, rubbing, and basting your way to grilling heaven.

Even though grilling is one of the oldest cooking methods we know, we never stop mastering it. So fire up your grill and toss on some food. With this book in one hand and your trusty tongs in the other, you're sure to hit the grilling bull's-eye.

David Joachim
Author of *A Man, a Can, a Grill* and *Mastering the Grill*

Introduction

There are certainly more than a few books available filled to overflowing with complex and esoteric grilling recipes that assume you're already a "Grillmeister." Well, there are a heck of a lot more neophytes, beginners, and Saturday-afternoon grillers out there than "Grillmeisters." And all of us—I'm no "Grillmeister," either—want to know everything from how to buy the perfect grill, to how to select the right equipment, to how to grill something that tastes spectacular but doesn't cost half the budget of a third-world country and take so much time to prepare that you could write a short story about it—faster than actually doing it.

Grilling is fairly simple. Basically, it's just cooking food over a live fire until it's done. But simple is sometimes deceptive. Pasta, for example, is made from two ingredients (flour and eggs) and pie dough is made from three (flour, shortening, and ice water), and they're really hard to do. Simple may be as simple as simple seems.

Hopefully, I've taken all the work out of grilling for you. I've made the mistakes: burned food, gotten it stuck to the grill, accidentally broken food into pieces and seen it fall into the fire, and turned sweet barbecue sauce into a black crust—all so you won't have to.

I've surfed the web searching for sites that offer even more information about grilling and barbecuing from real enthusiasts who willingly and freely share their experiences with everyone. I've also located sources for kosher salt, grilling tools, charcoal, and meat that will let you focus on your grilling and not on finding what you need for your grill.

Essentially, this is also a book of recipes—tried and true, tested and retested recipes—that taste great and are also fun to make. Half of the fun is in the success, and the other half's in the eating. You should be able to find all the ingredients locally, right at your supermarket. So come on, get ready to fire up your grill.

How This Book Is Organized

This book is divided into seven parts:

Part 1, "Grilling and Barbecue Basics," explains the differences and similarities between grilling and barbecuing, because they are two similar but dissimilar live-fire cooking methods. You'll learn the roles of marinades, brines, and mops along with sauces and dry rubs. You'll find out how important cooking to a specified temperature is, and how to determine that temperature. Plus you'll find out how different grills work, how to create and use soaked wood chips to create smoke for tasty results, and what price you might expect to pay for different kinds and sizes of grills. You'll see a list of grilling equipment that's more than a list—it also explains things about that equipment. You'll get into technical stuff, too, like the differences between fire materials (briquettes versus lump charcoal and gas) and the pros and cons of different fire starters. And to keep you safe, I offer some notes on grill and food safety.

Part 2, "Rubs, Marinades, Brines, and Sauces," starts you down the road of flavor creation that can be as much fun as grilling itself. You'll learn how to find and buy fresh herbs and spices and mix them together to create and bring out flavor (more than the sum of its parts). Rubs are, for the most part, divided by what meat, poultry, or seafood they can season. Marinades are like a wet rub, with lots of flavors heading into what you're going to take out to the grill, and with right balance of acid and time can also tenderize. Brines help moisture and flavor migrate into meats and poultry and also tenderize, too. And sauces, like frosting on a birthday cake, add a flavor layer that's laid on last, but it's also the first to tease the palate.

Part 3, "Burgers and Other Bun Foods," is like opening up your own hamburger grill, where you can see how to make hamburgers in the classic style and then start to get a little wild by mixing and matching meats, poultry, condiments, buns, cheeses, and flavorings. And because sausage is a hand-mixed meat, like burgers, and similar to hot dogs (which is really a sausage, just not homemade), you'll discover how to take already-ground meats and poultry and combine them with seasonings, similar to rubs, to produce sausages that equal more than just the sum of their parts.

Part 4, "Beef, Bison, and Lamb," are three meats that belong on any grill. First up: steaks. You learn which ones work the best on the grill as well as how to prepare them to bring out their true and best flavor. Seasoning and temperature control are also highlighted to make their roles easier. There's more to beef than steaks, so you'll get into satay (beef on a stick); meaty, fall-off-the-bone short ribs and beef back ribs; as well as beef brisket and veal. Because bison's appeal is slowly but certainly growing, you'll discover how naturally lean bison is and how to grill it so it doesn't end up dry.

As you'll see in **Part 5, "Poultry and the Other White Meat—Pork,"** these meats are very well suited for grilling. You'll begin with whole, halved, and quartered chickens, including the now-famous (are you sure that's where you want to stick that?) "beer-can chicken." Next you'll easily glide into chicken and poultry pieces and parts, where you'll discover how to grill breasts, legs, thighs, and wings in ways that enhance each of their specific flavors and characteristics. And then there's pork, starting with (oh, I could eat some right now) ribs. Folks have different approaches to ribs, but I'll bet you find a rib recipe here that makes you the envy of your neighborhood. But ribs aren't the only thing that comes from a pig. There are chops and tenderloins, hams, and pork roasts, too. Because pork's been bred so lean, these recipes all show you how to cook pork till it's done but not overdone.

Part 6, "Seafood: Finfish and Shellfish," covers the creatures from the sea. Of all the protein sources, they're probably the healthiest, yet they can be a little tricky to grill. Part of the problem is how lean finfish and shellfish can be, but you'll learn how to work around that. You'll discover the best way to season fin fish and shell fish and how to deal with scallops and shrimp that can so easily fall though the grill grate and into the fire. You'll discover how glazes can add a flavor punch as well as a good-looking finish. You'll also turn salmon, a very popular fish, into a salmon burger that could, for a moment at least, make you forget about beef burgers.

Part 7, "Everything Else," describes so much more of what you can grill. If you've ever thought about making a pizza on the grill, here's where you learn how. You not only find out how to make a pizza from scratch and grill it but also how to work with premade pizza crusts to build and grill your pizza so it comes off the grill a golden disc of perfection. But that's not it for bread-based grilling. You'll also learn how to grill a grilled cheese sandwich that, with the added flavor of the grill, is better than any grilled cheese sandwich you've ever had. You'll also find out how to grill vegetables to perfection, with some tricks that make it easy to grill vegetables you didn't think could be grilled. Finally, you'll see how to grill fruit and then turn it into ethereal desserts, and at the very end you'll find a new twist on s'mores.

After the recipe chapters, some useful appendixes define all the terms used throughout the book for easy reference as well as places to find good charcoal, great equipment, or some good grilling ideas.

Extras

In every chapter and following nearly every recipe, you'll find boxes that share extra information, helpful tips, or just fun facts.

Flame Point _____

Be sure to read these boxes, as they point out things you'll need to know that might prove difficult or even danger-ous. After all, this is live-fire cooking.

Lean Note _____

From time to time, where appropriate, these notes appear to steer you away from too much fat or calories yet still maintain a recipe's integrity and flavor pro-file.

Barbecue Banter

Look to these boxes for tips, advice, and even stories covering interesting things about grilling that you may never have known before.

Grill Guide

These helpful boxes contain all the grilling jargon you need to know.

Acknowledgments

A cookbook is not born from the efforts of a single person. Many people play important roles along the way. For that assistance I wish to thank:

JoAnna Larson, for being an excellent friend who's helped guide me through some of the cookbook world's murkiest waters. Whenever I've asked her for assistance, she has offered it gladly. JoAnna was first asked to write this book, but due to other commitments could not, so she suggested that the next perfect person to do so might be me. You were right again. Thank you very much, JoAnna.

Marilyn Lewis, my agent, for putting all the pieces together that helped start this book down its road to completion.

Mike Sanders, Christy Wagner, Megan Douglass, Nancy Wagner, and Ellen Brown for their patience and insights. Without you, this book would never exist.

My brothers, Tom and Robert Mauer, for their love, guidance, and support through this and every cookbook I've written. I couldn't ask for two better brothers than you.

Bill Wurch, my long-time friend and personal legal adviser, whose wisdom, guidance, and friendship is truly priceless.

Deb Pankey, my *Chicago Daily Herald* editor and friend, who for many years, week after week, taught me more about food writing than anybody I know.

Mike and Cathy Fields and all the fine folks with whom I work during the day at P.S. International. I would never have been able to do this without your understanding and generous support.

Scott Davis, my friend and idea guy. Somehow you peer into the future and see what I cannot.

My mom, who's little (and sometimes not so little) culinary gifts throughout the years made it possible for me to own and use the equipment and books that allowed me to follow a different path. Mom, you've always been my loudest cheerleader, and I will never, ever, forget.

Special Thanks to the Technical Reviewer

The technical reviewer for *The Complete Idiot's Guide to Grilling* was Ellen Brown, a Providence, Rhode Island–based cookbook author, caterer, and food authority. The founding food editor of *USA Today*, she has written 10 cookbooks, including *The Complete Idiot's Guide to Slow Cooker Cooking*, *The Complete Idiot's Guide to Cooking with Mixes*, *The Complete Idiot's Guide to Smoothies*, and *The Complete Idiot's Guide to Cover and Bake Meals*. Her articles have appeared in more than two dozen publications, including *Bon Appétit*, *the Washington Post*, and *the Los Angeles Times*. *The Gourmet Gazelle Cookbook* won the IACP award in 1989, and she is a member of the prestigious "Who's Who of Cooking in America."

Trademarks

All terms mentioned in this book that are known to be or are suspected of being trademarks or service marks have been appropriately capitalized. Alpha Books and Penguin Group (USA) Inc. cannot attest to the accuracy of this information. Use of a term in this book should not be regarded as affecting the validity of any trademark or service mark.

Part 1

Grilling and Barbecue Basics

If I hadn't been such a "guy," and done the "guy thing"—only skim my gas grill's directions and assume I knew everything I needed to know—my first attempt at gas grilling would not have turned out to be "Chicken Ablaze."

That first gas grilling experience taught me important lessons: review the basics, familiarize myself with every piece that makes up the whole, and when I have a "real and true" understanding of how to grill, only then do I jump on in.

Part 1 is all about basics—grilling and barbecue basics, that is. You'll find everything from what separates grilling from barbecue, to what equipment is really necessary, and finally how to safely put all the pieces together and start grilling.

Chapter 1

Grilling and Barbecue Defined

In This Chapter

- Discovering how grilling came to be (probably)
- Understanding the differences between grilling and barbecuing
- Making the most of flavor enhancers such as marinades, brines, mops, rubs, and more

I don't know what it is, but I've seen it time and time again: almost all men and many women not only want to cook outdoors over a live fire, but they also can hardly contain their excitement for doing so. And for some reason, they believe they know how to do it with little or no instructions.

In fact, that's how I started—I incinerated an unfortunate chicken on my backyard gas grill. I set that whole chicken on fire, and because I didn't check on it soon enough, it was in serious, inedible condition by the time I did.

At that moment, I decided I'd learn as much about grilling as I could and become my neighborhood grilling expert. That was 25 years ago, and I'm still learning—but I haven't burned up a single chicken since! If you read this book, follow the suggestions in it, and prepare the recipes you'll never have to worry about incinerating a chicken or anything else you cook on a grill over a live fire.

Let's get grilling!

Grilling's Humble Beginnings

People have been grilling, or cooking over a *live fire*, for so long that no historical documents or even cave drawings exist to pinpoint when they first began. As with most other discoveries and inventions, the act of grilling was probably an accident that went something like this:

One night, a very long time ago, a terrible storm rolled across the countryside, bringing with it lots of lightning and thunder. One lightning bolt struck a tall, old pine tree, setting it ablaze. The flames and heat set nearby trees on fire, and soon flames leapt high into the night's sky and then slowly turned to embers. Later that night, the rains came, putting out the fire.

At sunrise, a group living near the forest set out to see what had happened the night before and found a forest animal killed by the blaze. The animal's unfamiliar form confused the group, at which point some adventurous spirit poked at it with a stick. A chunk of cooked meat fell away. The group, except for the adventurous one, immediately took two steps back and began to murmur.

When the adventurous one brought his stick up to wipe it off, he noticed its enticing aroma. He wiped off the end of his stick with his hand and then licked his fingers. His eyes lit up, and he said to the others, "This is good! I want more." The group didn't need to hear another word. When nothing remained of the charred critter, they all agreed that they, too, wanted more. Unfortunately, they needed to wait for another lightning storm–started forest fire—or learn to start their own fire.

Grill Guide

You'll see the wonderfully descriptive phrase "**live-fire** cooking" throughout this book. Live-fire cooking describes cooking over the flames and heat of a variety of fires, charcoal, gas, or wood. The heat that rises up from the flames seems almost alive. No two fires are ever alike, which seems to create the impression that each one has a life its own.

Today we start our own mini-forest fire—the grill—and grill and barbecue count-less meals over a live fire whenever we want to. Grilling and barbecuing can both be done using a grill, but they're very different live-fire cooking methods.

The Skinny on Grilling

In a "turtle and the hare" analogy, grilling is the hare of live-fire cooking. It uses direct, high to medium-high heat, produced by either charcoal or gas, to cook the food fast. It might even be considered the first "fast food."

The high heat quickly creates a crust of caramelized proteins and sugars on the food's exterior. The technical term for this is searing. Searing, or quickly cooking the exterior, does many things, but sealing in the juices is, unfortunately, not one of them. The best way to retain moisture in any piece of meat is to keep the time it spends over the heat to a minimum, while, at the same time, cooking it sufficiently.

Barbecue Banter _____

Justus von Liebig, a nineteenth-century German scientist, came up with the idea that high temperatures coagulate proteins at the surface of a piece of meat, which, in turn produces a protective shell that should trap the meat's juices inside. Unfortunately, Liebig didn't thoroughly test his theory, but still, his theory caught on and became a fact—without proof. In the early 1900s when someone did try to prove the theory, they found that seared meat lost more moisture than unseared meat.

The searing-created crust (sometimes helped along with a dry rub—more on that later) greatly enhances the flavor of the grilled food. And when you bite into that burger, steak, or whatever you grilled, you taste the flavor added from the smoke pro-duced by juices that drip down into the fire.

Grilling over a high-heat, live fire is speedy. A thin pork chop is usually done—seared and cooked through—in about 6 total minutes. But grilling's not limited to pork chops. Grilling over a live fire is perfect for hamburgers, sausages, steaks, fish, pizza, shellfish, fruit, and ham steaks.

Basic Grill Setup

In an ideal setup in a charcoal grill, one side of the grill has a pile of briquettes built up and banked three high for high heat. The other side has a sparse, single-briquette layer. This dual-heat setup gives you control over cooking temperatures.

Barbecue Banter _____

For more on the technical aspects of grills and grilling, see Chapters 2 and 3.

Most gas grills, except for the very smallest, have two or more separate burners that you can adjust to create two temperatures in the same grill: high heat for quick searing and medium to medium-low heat to slow down the cooking so the inside can cook completely without charring the outside.

Taking Your Grill's Temperature

Today many gas grills and some charcoal grills have a thermometer built in the lid so you know the grill's exact temperature. Well, that's the idea, but that's not exactly correct. Unlike in an oven, which holds a fairly constant temperature, the thermometer on a grill lid gives a reading of the air near the top of the lid, not the temperature on the grilling surface.

The best way to judge your grill's surface temperature is with your hand. After your fire's started, place your hand, palm side down, about 4 to 5 inches above the cooking rack. If you can hold your hand there without pulling away for 1 to 2 seconds, you've got a high-heat fire. If you can hold your hand there 3 to 4 seconds, that's a medium fire. Holding your hand there for 3 to 5 to seconds indicates a low fire.

Knowing the heat of your fire helps you judge how long something will take to cook. Obviously, the higher the heat, the faster the food will cook; the lower the heat, the slower.

How You Know It's Done

If you're cooking hamburger or chicken, you can check its doneness in one of two ways. The first uses an instant-read thermometer, of which there are several good brands, such as Maverick Redi-Chek Food Probe Thermometer or a Polder Cooking Thermometer (both around $30). Any one of the different instant-read thermometers functions in the same way. At one end is a pointed metal probe, that's what's inserted to the center of any piece of cooking meat. The probe is connected to a digital read-out that quickly tells the temperature wherever the point of the probe reaches. Read your thermometer's instructions carefully. Every recipe will give you the proper temperature at which to pull the food off the grill.

The second method of testing doneness is by pressing the food with your finger, tongs, or spatula. Let's use a hamburger as the example. If you press down on the center of a hamburger with your finger or tongs and it gives easily, maybe squirting some juice, it's rare slowly heading toward medium. If you press and there's some resistance, it's probably medium-rare to medium. If you press and there's almost no give and a lot of resistance, your hamburger is medium-well to well done.

> **Barbecue Banter** _____
>
> Although you'll lose some precious juices, you can cut open a steak, hamburger, or lamb chop to see how done it is. At very rare, the center will be blood red. If it's rare, it should have a deep pink color all the way through. If it's medium-rare, it's pink in the center and the edges are starting to turn gray. For medium, the gray edges will have expanded more into the pink. If it's gray all the way through, it's medium-well. At well done, the center will not only be gray but dry and very firm.

The Basics of Barbecue

If grilling's the hare—hot and fast—then barbecuing's the tortoise—low and slow with indirect heat. Barbecue also requires an enclosed cooking area—a cover on the grill. Because the food is cooked with the lid closed, the flavor of smoke greatly affects barbecued foods.

Where thin chops and steaks rule in grilling, thick slabs of ribs, briskets, roasts, larger chunks of meat, and whole turkeys dominate barbecue. If barbecuing used the same higher-heat levels of grilling, the outside of your dinner would be burned while the inside wouldn't be cooked enough. Slow and long, that's the drill in BBQ.

In this book, you'll learn how to create excellent barbecue, but because most of us don't have a barbecue pit in the backyard—or the patience and time to keep loading our grills with charcoal for hours—I've created shortcuts in the recipes that follow which produce almost the same results to great "Q," with significantly lowered hassle factors.

Flavor Enhancers

Regardless of whether grilling or barbecuing is your game, you'll want to know how to enhance the flavor of your food with some "extras." Some are specific to grilling—marinades, brines, and rubs—and some are good for the slow cooking of barbecue—sauces and rubs. Whatever your pleasure, these tips will make whatever you're cooking taste that much better.

On the Grill

Grilled meats, poultry, and fish are good. Marinated or brined grilled meats, poultry, and fish go to a whole other flavor level.

Try using some of these flavor enhancers when you are grilling:

A *marinade* is a flavorful liquid that can be made from a combination of many ingredients such as wine, beer, buttermilk, liquor, vinegar, fruit juice, soy sauce, herbs, spices, and fruits or vegetables. Highly acidic marinades, such as those made with lots of vinegar or citrus juice, shorten grilling times.

Flame Point

Highly acidic marinades actually react with the meat, almost as if it's being cooked, and the meat will, if left in a high-acid marinade long enough, turn an unappetizing gray.

Barbecue Banter

Large barbecue operations use cotton kitchen mops with long handles to "mop" the pork and other grilling meats with a flavored vinegar solution and then also to "mop" on the sauce at the end, hence the name.

Brines are also liquid, but have a very different makeup and purpose. A basic brine is made from carefully balanced amounts of water, sugar, and salt. Buttermilk, wine, or beer can also be made into brine. Black pepper, bay leaves, brown sugar, honey, and even vanilla can be used to season brine. Brines add water to the food being brined. A chicken that goes into brine will come out weighing about 10 percent more than when it went in because of it's "water gain." A brine's saltiness makes the food being brined absorb water as well as the flavors in that water.

A brine changes protein in a positive way, making meat, poultry, or fish more tender. Think of protein as little springs. Brining forces those protein springs to unwind, to relax.

Mops work extremely well with grilling. A mop is a highly seasoned vinegar-based liquid, sometimes sweet and hot and other times just hot or just sweet. Because of the acidity of the vinegar, the meat or poultry mopped during grill time absorbs the liquid, adding flavor and if not adding moisture, at least helping keep moisture loss low.

On the Barbecue

Barbecue is made for sauces and dry rubs. Therefore, I offer a lot of rubs and sauces in this book because they're real flavor-makers. If you're brushing sauce on anything while grilling, you do so at the very end, in the last few minutes on the grill. Most sauces contain sugars (natural and added) that don't caramelize into a glaze but quickly burn and blacken at grilling's higher temperatures. Barbecue's low temperatures and indirect heat make brushing on sauce an excellent addition.

That's also true for dry rubs—mixtures of herbs, spices, sugars, salt, and pepper. The flavor of a dry rub slowly penetrates the meat before and during the barbecue. When grilling, there's just not enough time to allow for the transportation of those flavors.

Either way—gas or charcoal, grilling or barbecuing—you're headed down a path of easy-to-prepare, flavor-filled meals.

Barbecue Banter

When barbecuing large cuts of meat, you can use brines to help the meat retain its moisture. The brining or soaking process takes longer for full penetration in the thicker piece of meat, but a brined and barbecued brisket will be deliciously moist at the end.

The Least You Need to Know

- The idea of cooking meats and other foods over a live fire probably originated by accident, thanks to Mother Nature and some lighting.
- Grilling is hot and fast. Barbecuing, the more laid-back of the two, is slow and low.
- Grilling or barbecuing, whatever your pleasure, you can enhance the flavor of your foods by employing sauces, rubs, mops, and more.

Chapter 2

Grills and Grilling Equipment

In This Chapter

- ◆ Looking at charcoal grills and gas grills and how both work
- ◆ Understanding how smoke influences the flavor of the grilled food
- ◆ Deciding what to spend on your grill
- ◆ Checking out grill "accessories"

In the past 15 years or so, we have seen something of a grilling revolution. In 1989, more households owned charcoal grills (59 percent) than gas grills (41 percent). By the beginning of the twenty-first century, those numbers reversed, with gas grill owners beating out charcoal grill owners, 56 percent to 43 percent, respectively.

Some of these families own both a charcoal and a gas grill, and for good reason. Although both produce heat and both cook with their covers open or closed, each grill type produces different flavors, cooks at different rates, and has very different methods of heat control.

In this chapter, I present both charcoal and gas grills as well as the equipment for each. You will be surprised at how much information there is to cover.

Charcoal Grills

In the early 1950s, George Stephen invented the covered kettle charcoal grill first known as "George's Kettle," which shortly thereafter became the "Weber Kettle" and ultimately morphed into what we now know as the famous "Weber Grill." This reasonably priced charcoal grill fired up people's enthusiasm for backyard grilling that's been growing ever since.

Barbecue Banter

The man who created and manufactured the Model T Ford automobile—Henry Ford—also invented the charcoal briquette.

How They Work

Basically, charcoal grills have two grill grates, an upper and a lower. The lower grate holds the charcoal beneath the food, and the upper grate holds the food above the heat. Charcoal briquettes or hardwood charcoal rest on the lower grill, and when they're lit, you can move them around to create the required heat pattern for proper cooking.

The upper grill grate is usually larger to accommodate the food. The tell-tale brown striped grill marks you see on grilled food come from this grate. Those brown or dark brown lines are more than just decoration, though. Those lines indicate that proteins and sugar in the food have caramelized and turned brown, which adds that classic grill flavor to the food.

Flavoring With Wet Wood Smoke

Smoke adds flavor to the cooked food, too. To charcoal grills, you can add damp oak, hickory, cherry, apple, or mesquite wood chips to the charcoal fire so that when covered, the grill fills with flavored smoke. That smoke, in turn, creates a wonderful depth of flavor in the grilled foods.

Most experienced grillers use 2 to 3 cups of oak, hickory, or mesquite wood chips, available from a variety of sources, that have been soaked in warm water for 30 minutes or so. Dampening wood chips keeps them from bursting immediately into flames when placed on the hot coals, producing fire, not smoke.

Here's how it works: dampened chips are placed directly on the hot coals just before food is placed on the grill and then the grill is covered to hold most of the smoke inside the grill near the food. Think of it as bathing the food in smoke while it cooks. Some grillers like to use large chunks of wood to produce smoke, but they are mostly used when slowly barbecuing so the grill doesn't have to be frequently uncovered.

Producing smoke in a gas grill is a little different. You start with 2 or 3 cups of dry wood chips in a foil packet to produce smoke. Just as in a charcoal grill, you need to keep the cover closed for the smoke to penetrate and season the grilled food. Either way, beef, pork and chicken, as well as strong flavored fish, like salmon, all benefit from the addition of smoke while grilling.

You can easily use a charcoal grill to barbecue (remember the tortoise analogy from Chapter 1?) because you can control the coals for lower, slower heat levels. Plus many charcoal grills, either through the use of hinged grates or grates with large holes on either end, offer fairly easy access to the coals and to the addition of charcoal or damp wood chips for increased cooking times and deeper flavor notes.

Barbecue Banter

European grillers go beyond wood and use chunky sprigs of fresh herbs, like rosemary or sage to flavor the smoke, and where available, grape vines left over after grape harvests can also add their unique flavor notes carried by their smoke. Where available, consider these for your own grilling.

Flame Point

When selecting wood chips to add to your grill, I strongly suggest you avoid using pine. Although pine needles smell good during December holidays, pine wood smoke does not make food taste good.

Prices

Portable charcoal grills range in price from less than $50 to around $400. To recommend one grill over another is beyond the scope of this book. However, you can check sources such as *Consumer Reports* and *Cook's Illustrated* magazines online or at your local library if you want insightful and accurate advice on choosing the right grill for you. You can also talk to your friends, relatives, and co-workers about their grills and experiences.

Gas Grills

It appears that gas grill owners owe a debt of thanks to the Chicago Combustion Corporation (now Lazy Man, Inc.) and its founder, Louis McGlaughlin, who, according to their corporate website was the father (both literal and figurative) of the gas grill. As the story goes, McGlaughlin introduced the first gas-fired broiler at the 1939

World's Fair in New York. In 1954, Louis' son Don Sr. adapted a 20-pound propane cylinder to an outdoor-fired gas barbecue and the gas grill was born. Don Sr. had the right idea, because there are plenty of gas grills around today, as evidenced by back-yards across the nation,

How They Work

Early gas grills mirrored charcoal grills in design—essentially a closed, vented box. These grills were rectangular, heavy-duty aluminum boxes with hinged covers. Inside on the bottom was one gas burner; above that was a lower metal grill grate covered in a single layer of ceramic briquettes; topping everything was an upper metal grill grate used for cooking. The design works so well that grills just like this setup are still being manufactured and sold today.

However, most of today's gas grills don't use ceramic briquettes. Instead, under-neath the two to five gas burners sit sloping metal plates that reflect the heat upward and allow the melting fats to drip down into a metal container below for easy disposal. And usually above the gas burners, inverted V-shaped metal shields disperse the heat generated by the burners, turn dripping liquids into smoke, and protect the burners from dripping liquids or fat. The cooking grate above the shields is made of stainless steel, ceramic coated or chromed steel, or, less frequently, iron.

There are two types of gas used to produce flames in a gas grill: natural gas (if already available in your home), which is brought to a fixed position grill by metal pipes (this is professional plumber's work, not a weekend project for amateurs) or liquid propane (LP) from portable, returnable tanks that use a universal fitting that, with a few twists, easily connects to the grill. Be certain that you following all manu-facturers' instructions for use of either and pay special attention to the warnings written on the side of portable propane tanks. Use the same caution using LP gas as you would natural gas, and be sure children do not think of a gas grill as something to play with.

With propane tanks, it is especially important to check that no connection ever leaks, and the instructions for checking for leaks come with every gas grill and are also on the side of every LP tank.

Flavoring With Dry Wood Smoke

Using smoke to enhance flavor with a gas grill is different from a charcoal grill. Instead of the damp wood chips used in charcoal grills, on a gas grill you use about 2 cups *dry* wood chips. Place them in the center of a large (12- by 18-inch) piece of heavy-duty aluminum foil; then bring up the foil on all sides and roll the ends together to create and seal the packet. Poke several small holes in the top of the packet. Once the grill is hot, place the wood chip packet under the grate across the burner shields. Smoke comes out of the holes and will fill the closed grill with flavorful smoke.

Prices

Prices for portable gas grills begin at less than $150. Some of the larger and higher-end gas grills with fancy features can go up to more than $4,000. *Consumer Reports* magazine rates gas grills, so stop by their website (www.consumerreports.org) to see their latest ratings. And as with charcoal grills, check with friends and family to see what brand or size they have and like, or check online for gas grill pictures, descriptions and specifications. Several stores (Lowe's, The Home Depot, etc.) have gas grills set up and although you can't actually cook a burger on one, you can give them a thorough visual going-over as part of your decision-making process.

Pros and Cons of Gas Grills

More than half of the USA's grillers use gas grills, so there must be some pros to using gas grills over charcoal:

- Gas grills are cleaner to work with (no charcoal handling).
- Gas grills are quicker to begin cooking (10 to 15 minutes versus 20 to 30 minutes for charcoal).
- Gas grills can quickly change heat levels.
- Gas grills are better equipped to cook large pieces of meat (no need to keep adding charcoal).
- Larger gas grills now come with a stovetop-style side burner (or two).

Gas grills do have some disadvantages, however:

- The gas used in gas grills produces less flavor than charcoal (although grills with ceramic briquettes come close).
- Gas grills are more time-consuming to clean.
- Gas grills' heat source and cooking grates are in fixed positions, reducing flexibility.
- LP (liquid propane) tanks for gas grills are filled, under pressure, with propane. Definite safety precautions are necessary when using an LP tank. All hose connections should regularly be checked for leaks, and be sure your LP tank is completely turned off after each use. Read and follow all the instructions and warnings on the side of the tank that come with the grill.

No matter what grill you choose, always read and follow the instructions, and be aware of the warnings enclosed with any grill or piece of grilling equipment before using it.

Choosing the Perfect Grill for You

Charcoal or gas, ultimately, the grill you purchase has to fit your needs, including size, price, etc. But these general guidelines should help you in your selection:

- Check your budget to determine what you can comfortably spend on a charcoal or gas grill.
- Look for a well-built grill, with a cover sufficiently high to accommodate a whole average-size turkey or a whole chicken cooked vertically in the middle.
- The grill should have easily washable or cleanable surfaces.
- Once charcoal burns, it produces white ash that accumulates underneath the charcoal grate. Be certain the charcoal grill you purchase has an easy-to-use system for collecting and discarding those ashes.
- Consider a charcoal grill's ventilation system. Vents in the top and the bottom allow air to circulate through the grill to make it easier to start the fire (allowing lots of air in), trap smoke (reducing air flow by partially closing vents), or putting the fire out (covering the grill and closing all the vents). The vents on top and underneath should all be adjustable and make sense to you.

The purchase and use of a vinyl grill cover to protect your new grill from inclement weather will lengthen your new grill's life.

Grill "Accessories"

You've found and purchased your perfect grill, fired it up, and now you're ready to do some grilling. It's time to throw the meat on the grill and get started, right? Not quite. As any fashion diva will tell you, you need to accessorize. No, I'm not talking about jewelry and shoes. I'm talking *grill accessories*. (I doubt you'll mind going shopping for some of these pieces.)

Whether you're a newbie or very experienced, every backyard chef needs a few things to go along with their grill:

Chimney charcoal lighter. A chimney charcoal lighter is a formed sheet-metal tube with a handle on the side, a grate inside, and holes around the bottom. You insert folded newspaper into the bottom of the chimney, place it on the grill's charcoal grate, and pour charcoal in the top of the chimney. When you light the newspaper, it burns slowly, starting the charcoal and using up-drafting, chimney-effect air movement to ignite everything in the chimney. I like both charcoal chimneys and electric starters, but I give the nod to chimneys.

Flame Point

Always use just enough charcoal lighter fluid, and always use it with caution. Never squirt on "a little more" after the fire is lit—even if it's just smoking and not burning. The heat or a spark from the charcoal can ignite the lighter fluid stream, shooting it back up along that stream and potentially explode the container.

And never, never use gasoline, kerosene alcohol, or any other highly combustible fluids to light a charcoal fire.

Electric charcoal lighter. An electric lighter is like a toaster in that the heating element glows red, except this element is much thicker. You set the electric rod on a layer of charcoal and then pile charcoal on and over the rod. The rod is attached to an electric cord, which you then plug into an electric outlet. Eight to ten minutes later, when some of the coals are gray and some glowing red, you unplug the starter and remove it from the pile of half-started charcoal. Then you can arrange the charcoal and allow it to fully ignite (another 10 minutes or so).

You can also find "hybrid" grills that start charcoal using LP gas but don't use the gas for cooking once the charcoal's lighted.

Self-starting charcoal briquettes. These don't require starter fluid, a chimney, or an electric starter. However, some folks believe they can taste the petroleum-based starter fluid embedded in the briquettes in their cooked food.

Fire extinguisher. Keep a fire extinguisher near your grill in case flames in or around your grill get out of control.

Spring-loaded stainless-steel tongs. You'll need long-handled tongs for moving lit briquettes around as well as for moving food around on the grill. Be sure the weight and ease-of-use fit your personal abilities and needs.

Spatula. A long-handled spatula makes flipping hamburgers and moving other foods easy. Be sure the spatula feels comfortable in your hands.

Basting brushes. You'll need something to baste on the sauces! One or two brushes are pretty standard. One with a 12- to 18-inch handle is especially handy. You don't need anything fancy, though. I use unfinished, wood-handled, natural bristle 1- to 1½-inch brushes from a hardware or paint store.

Drip pans. Check your grill and measure the area needed for a drip pan; then head to the supermarket, where you'll find a wide variety of inexpensive, disposable aluminum pans, one of which should fill your requirements.

Grill brush. Used a grill brush to clean the food grill grate of burned-on stuff, including barbecue sauce which can be hard to get off. My favorite grill brush that seems to work best and lasts from season to season is the *Grill Wizard*. It comes with either a heavy-duty plastic or hardwood handle and uses replaceable stainless-steel pads for cleaning. Grill Wizards are available in some stores as well as online (see Appendix B).

Hinged wire basket. Some folks can't live without this basket and use it to hold fish or multiple hamburger patties, etc.

Instant-read thermometer. I don't know what I'd do without mine. The first time you take an expensive piece of meat off your grill at just the right time and temperature, this thermometer will have paid for itself. I give you temperatures for almost all my recipes so you know when, using your instant-read thermometer, your food's done.

Metal and bamboo skewers. When buying metal skewers, get flat-bladed skewers, not round ones. Food has less of a tendency to spin when turned on a flat blade than a round one. If you use bamboo skewers, be sure to soak them for half an hour before using them on the grill to reduce their tendency to burn. Skewers come in various lengths, including 8, 10, and 12 inches. It's good to have some of each size on hand.

Flame Point

When using a wood plank, be sure the wood used to make the plank has never been treated and was created expressly for cooking. You don't want to use any old scrap piece of lumber.

Grilling planks. Generally, these thick 15×7-inch pieces of cedar, oak, or hickory boards have been soaked in water and preheated on the grill. Then you can arrange fish, poultry, or veggies on top, and close the grill. The food cooks, picking up the flavor of the wood. Plus, it's reusable.

Spray bottle. Use a spray bottle to send a water stream or wide spray to put out charcoal flame-ups, promote steam or smoke, or moisten food. These are inexpensive and easy to find.

Grilling skillet. These look just like a skillet with a handle except with small holes across the bottom and around the sides to let heat, flames, and smoke through. Some are stainless steel; others are nonstick. They're great for cooking a wide variety of vegetables as well as for fish that can easily fall apart and then fall through a grill. Grilling skillets are both inexpensive and handy.

You won't need to run out and buy everything I've listed here. However, a spatula, tongs, grill brush, and thermometer, as well as any safety item or items that keep you out of harm's way should be available for your use from the beginning. Then, start grilling easy foods such as hamburgers and hot dogs (as we'll be doing shortly), see where your curiosity and interest takes you, and then acquire the appropriate tools or equipment.

The Least You Need to Know

- ◆ Understanding the ins and outs of charcoal grills versus gas grills and how each works helps you decide which is better for you.
- ◆ When grill shopping, choose a well-built grill that fits both your needs—and your budget.
- ◆ Whether you choose a charcoal or gas grill, be sure to pick up some wood chips, too, as the resulting smoke can enhance the flavor of your grilled food.
- ◆ Man (or woman) cannot live by grill alone. You've gotta have accessories, too!

Technical Stuff

In This Chapter

- ◆ Understanding fire starters
- ◆ Lighting the fire
- ◆ Practicing grill safety
- ◆ Practicing food safety

Some technical stuff is always necessary to consider when it comes to cooking, and that's especially true with grilling. After all, we're talking live-fire cooking here. No two live fires are alike (save perhaps gas fires), and you need to consider several things before any food lands on your grill.

Let's start at the very beginning of live-fire cooking: what's burning.

Briquettes vs. Hardwood Charcoal vs. Gas

The most common and popular combustible used in grilling are charcoal briquettes. Invented by Henry Ford, the original car guy, charcoal briquettes are made of low-quality, powdered charcoal and binders (a fancy word for "glue") that are compressed and molded into those black pillow-shapes with which we are all so familiar. Charcoal briquettes may also contain additives such as sawdust or sodium nitrate that aid in their lighting.

There are also briquettes that contain small chips of aromatic mesquite wood. The mesquite burns along with the briquette and doesn't produce smoke, and grilled food spends so little time on the grill above the briquettes, so the mesquite leaves little if any traces of added flavor to grilled food.

In addition to charcoal briquettes, you could also use hardwood charcoal to start some fires. Hardwood charcoal is created by burning hardwood in a closed and controlled environment (such as a furnace), using very little oxygen. A piece of hardwood charcoal is almost pure carbon—no glue, no additives.

Hardwood charcoal is easier to light and burns faster, cleaner, and a touch hotter than briquettes. It also responds with greater sensitivity to changes in oxygen levels, which gives you better heat control. Burning cleaner is good (remember, your food sits just above it), but burning faster isn't (you've got to add more charcoal sooner to keep the fire at the same level). Charcoal's oxygen sensitivity also makes it easier and quicker to extinguish the fire when you're done cooking.

A gas grill using natural or LP gas for heat and flames is a fairly efficient fire. It's easy to start, especially with electronic ignition, easy to control (turning a knob clockwise or counterclockwise), and easy to end (cut off the gas, and it's out). For these reasons, gas grills have become more popular than charcoal grills.

Starting a Charcoal Fire

You can get your charcoal fire started and ready to cook over in three main ways, each of which has advantages and disadvantages. We'll start with charcoal lighter fluid, which I believe is the most dangerous method, with few if any advantages. Then we'll look at lighting charcoal with a chimney starter, using newspaper for heat (newspaper's cheap, so your biggest expense here is the purchase of the chimney). And finally, we'll check out electric charcoal lighters that you plug into the wall and can use, like the chimney, over and over, year after year.

Barbecue Banter

When a recipe calls for two different heats (one high and one medium, for example), always build a big enough fire so you have enough coals to build two good-size fires.

Lighter Fluid

The most common way to light charcoal briquettes is with charcoal lighter fluid—an easily ignitable, petroleum-based product:

1. For a 22½-inch-diameter standard-size charcoal grill, you'll need to start about 25 briquettes for covered indirect cooking and 60 briquettes for uncovered direct cooking. Arrange your charcoal in a pyramid shape, with a large base that you build up almost to a point.
2. Spray the coals evenly all over with charcoal lighter fluid until they are saturated.
3. Close the lighter fluid container tightly, and set the container away from the grill.
4. Using a long match or long-handled butane lighter, light the fluid-saturated briquettes in several spots, watching to see that the flames leap to other charcoal until the entire stack is burning. Let it burn until the flames go out.

As this point do not, *do not*, *do not* (did I mention *do not?*) spray more lighter fluid on the smoldering briquettes. The lighter fluid's stream could easily ignite, head up the stream of fluid to the bottle, and explode.

Instead, give the coals that have started to ignite more air. To speed up ignition I use an old, thin aluminum cookie sheet to gently fan the briquettes until I see blue flames in different spots. Let those burn for a while, and then repeat the fanning process a few times.

There'll be an obvious point when the briquettes are taking care of themselves and will ultimately form a nice gray ash. At this point, your fire's ready! With tongs, redistribute the briquettes for whatever fire you require.

Always follow the lighter fluid maker's directions for use and safety precautions.

Barbecue Banter

Ever hear the phrase "fanning the flames"? That's exactly what you're doing here. You're adding oxygen to get your briquettes flaming.

Charcoal Chimney Lighter

A charcoal chimney starter is essentially a metal tube, usually steel, with a handle on the side. Inside is a grate to hold the briquettes and to keep them above the crumpled newspaper, which goes in under the charcoal and is what starts the briquettes. Ventilation holes ring the bottom of the tube.

Here's how it works:

1. Roll up one or two sheets of newspaper and form into a doughnut-shaped ring. Roll up one or two more sheets of newspaper and form into a large doughnut-shaped ring. Fit the newspaper rings into the circular bottom of the chimney, leaving a small hole in the middle to create a draft. Place the chimney in the center of your grill, and pour briquettes from the bag into the chimney.

2. Light the newspaper using a match or lighter, (you may need to tilt the chimney slightly to light the newspaper from underneath). The chimney effect takes the newspaper's flames up through the briquettes and lights them. The heat from the starting charcoal makes the air in the chimney rise, which in turn pulls more air in through the chimney's bottom.

3. When a white ash forms on the briquettes, pour the lighted coals out onto the charcoal grate and, with tongs, distribute the briquettes for whatever fire you require.

Always follow the chimney maker's directions for use and safety precautions.

Barbecue Banter

You can also find self-lighting charcoal briquettes. With these, all you do is pile the briquettes on your grill, light them with a match or butane lighter, and voilà—you have an almost-instant fire. After that, they're just like regular briquettes. Some grillers like to use self-starting charcoal to easily and quickly get 10 to 12 briquettes going, and then after those are well started, place additional regular briquettes on top to get them going.

Note, however, that chimney starter manufacturers indicate in the information they supply with their chimneys that self-starting briquettes and chimney starters do not mix.

Electric Charcoal Lighter

Electric charcoal lighters look like an elongated outline of a Ping-Pong paddle. That outline is the lighter element loop that, when plugged in, glows like the heating elements in a toaster.

Here is how you use it.

1. Arrange a layer of briquettes on the grill's charcoal grate slightly larger than the area of the starter's element.

2. Place the lighter element on the charcoal, arrange additional charcoal in a pyramid shape on and over the loop, and plug in the lighter.

3. After 8 to 10 minutes, when the coals around the element are glowing red, pull the lighter from the briquettes and carefully set it in a heat-safe place to cool down. Then, with tongs, redistribute the briquettes for whatever fire you require.

Always follow the electric charcoal lighter maker's directions for use and safety precautions.

Barbecue Banter

Igniting hardwood charcoal is the same as igniting briquettes. However, hardwood charcoal lights faster, and the resulting fires burn hotter and quicker, so be prepared to start with more and add more as you go to keep the same fire level.

Extinguishing Your Charcoal Fire

Stopping your fire is just as important as starting it. It's easier to extinguish your fire if your grill comes with a cover. When you're done cooking, using proper protection for your hand, carefully close your grill's bottom vents. Then, place the cover securely on your grill and close the cover's vent or vents. This deprives the fire of oxygen, which will efficiently put out the fire. Assume it will take at least 1 hour for your fire to go out and your grill to cool down.

If your charcoal grill doesn't have a cover, you'll need to let your fire burn itself out, which could take an hour or two or more.

There is no ON or OFF switch with a charcoal fire. Always be cautious about making any assumptions about when your fire is completely out. It's better to be safe than sorry—and burned.

Location, Location, Location

It's important to place your charcoal grill in a safe location for starting the fire, as well as cooking. Some cities, by law, don't allow a lighted grill to be closer to a building than 10 feet. If it's a windy day, I'd increase that margin of safety to 15 to 20 feet. Be especially careful about what your grill sits on, too. Be aware that a wooden deck, if hot "live" coals land on it, can quickly start a fire. For optimal placement, set up your grill on a concrete pad or other "safe" location.

Starting and Stopping a Gas Grill

Starting a modern gas grill is easy:

1. Open the grill cover.

2. Open the gas valve (natural or LP).

3. One at a time, turn the controls to High and ignite the corresponding burner with either a long butane lighter, long matches, or the newest battery-charged electronic ignition.

Barbecue Banter

Some folks like to clean their food racks with a grill cleaning tool before turning them off, which will leave them clean for next use. Others like to finish cooking, turn their burners to high, close the cover, and leave the grill on for 15 minutes before shutting down, using the grill's heat to clean the grill's interior, similar to how a self-cleaning oven works.

4. Close the cover and wait 10 to 15 minutes for your grill to reach it's highest heat.

Stopping a gas grill is nearly as easy, if not more so:

1. Turn off each burner.

2. Close the gas valve (natural or LP).

3. Turn one of the burners on High for 15 seconds to bleed any gas remaining in the line, turn that burner off, and close the cover.

It will take at least 1 hour for your gas grill to cool completely.

Grill Safety

Grilling isn't rocket science, but because you're using open flames and sometimes a flammable gas and other combustible materials, you should always be careful. Remember this list of basic grill safety.

- Never assume everything's fine and leave your lighted barbecue unattended, not even for a moment.

- Always have a hose, bucket of water, or fire extinguisher nearby in case the fire gets out of control.

- Always keep clothing, towels, and hot pads away from flames.

- Use long-handled utensils to avoid burns.

- Use charcoal lighter fluid *sparingly* and *with caution*.

- Always discard spent briquettes and warm ashes in a *metal* can far away from combustibles (such as the deck or siding). Briquettes can stay hot for hours after the fire is extinguished and burn through paper bags or plastic buckets. Wait 1 full day before removing used briquettes from the barbecue.

- Store unused briquettes in a dry place and away from potential ignition sources and other combustible materials.

- At every change of propane tanks/bottles, follow the manufacturer's directions for checking the fittings to insure proper seal and fit.

- Keep young children away from grills—even if you're there to remind them to stay away—especially when you're done cooking and the grill's still hot. And never leave children unattended near the grill.

- Keeps pets away from all hot surfaces, especially when you're not there to remind them.

- Be certain nothing close to your grill can catch fire. A good rule of thumb to follow: in your mind, draw a 10-foot safety circle around your grill.

Keep It Clean

Always keep your whole grill clean so your grilled food doesn't pick up any off flavors. Especially always clean your grill's grate before the food lands there. And over time, the inside of your grill cover can accumulate soot and other things that, when closed, can permeate the flavor of whatever's cooked under it. So keep it clean, even if you have to use a brush and hot soapy water.

The best time to clean your food cooking rack is just before putting out the fire. As it goes out, your fire will continue to burn off any small food particles that remain and leave your grill rack ready for your next cookout.

The "Always" of Basic Food Safety

Zero compromise should "always" exist when it comes to keeping food safe for consumption. Always follow these rules:

- *Always* wash your hands with warm, soapy water; rinse them well; and dry them on a clean paper towel, especially after going to the bathroom or after handling raw meat.

- Always be sure everyone who is handling food with you washes his hands with warm, soapy water; rinses them well; and dries them on clean paper towels.

- Always keep all raw and fresh foods below 40°F.
- Always keep hot foods above 140°F.
- Always use at least two cutting boards: one exclusively for meats and poultry, the other for fresh vegetables.
- Always keep cutting boards spotlessly clean, and never use the meat board for veggies or the veggie board for meats. The same goes for other tools and utensils that come in contact with raw meat.
- Always take a close look at every food you're preparing before you start. Does it look good? Does it smell good? Does anything look or appear questionable or off? If so, throw out that item and change your menu.
- Raw and cooked meats should never come in contact with one another. I solve this problem by lining the tray I take the meat out to the grill on with two layers of foil. Raw meat (or poultry or fish) sits on the first layer of foil and heads out to the grill. When all the meat's been removed to the grill, I crumple up the top layer of foil, leaving the clean second layer of foil on which I can put my cooked meat.
- Play it safe with meat marinades: a marinade that's had raw meat in it should either be discarded immediately after use or poured into a sauté pan and brought to a full boil for 4 to 5 minutes before brushing it on cooking food or passing around the table.

If you've been able to absorb all the information in this and the previous two chapters, you should be ready to grill outdoors well and safely, even if it's your first time. You may be a little reticent to get started, trying to remember everything, but be confident that each time you start up your grill, cook food, and put out the fire, you'll find the next time even easier.

The Least You Need to Know

- Whether you use charcoal or gas, with the right combustibles, you'll get the right fire.
- Be sure to allow plenty of time for the fire to extinguish and your grill and any charcoal to cool.
- Always practice good grill safety. Fire isn't something to play with.
- Always practice good food safety. Always. You don't want your diners to ever get sick from what you cooked!

Part 2

Rubs, Marinades, Brines, and Sauces

The act of cooking meat alone creates flavor. That's part of the magic of mixing heat and protein in the right proportion to brown the outside. However, you can do a lot more to affect the final flavor of any grilled meat, poultry, or seafood. That's where rubs, marinades, brines, and sauces come in. Each affects the final flavor in a different way.

The alchemy of blending together just the right kind and amount of herbs, spices, and flavorings such as sugar and salt and rubbing those dry ingredients onto steak or ribs turns "okay" into "exciting." A marinade's goal is to accomplish the same thing—improve the final flavor—but it does it with wet ingredients instead of dry. Brines are balanced salty solutions that transport flavor and change the texture of meat so it holds more moisture and is more tender. Sauces are the finishing touch—the frosting on the cake, so to speak—adding a wide variety of unexpected flavors.

Chapter 4

Rub-a-Dub Rubs

In This Chapter

- Getting the rub on rubs
- Sharing kitchen secrets on making rubs easily
- Storing leftover rubs

Just a few years ago, the majority of backyard grilling and barbecue enthusiasts never heard of a rub being applied to a piece of meat before it headed for the heat. Today the use of rubs is so common that you can buy specialized rubs for steak or fish or chicken at your local supermarket, all mixed up and ready to go.

That's convenient, but that's also someone else's creativity and tastes in those bottles. I've heard many grillers say, "I like that new rub from Bob's Blistering Rubs, but it'd sure taste better if it didn't contain _____." The only way a rub can meet all your specifications is if you make it yourself. True, someone else created the rub recipes in this chapter (me!), whose tastes may differ from yours. But you can use my recipes here, make adjustments, tweak the balances, and create rubs that are all your own.

Rubs: More Than a Massage

Spice rubs contain three fairly common ingredients: sugar, salt, and paprika.

> **Grill Guide**
>
> **Turbinado sugar** works better than any other form of sugar in a rub. If you want to try it, you can sometimes find it in 1-pound packages at your local supermarket, or you can purchase it from most health and natural food stores. It looks like very light brown sugar; unlike brown sugar, though, it's free flowing but with larger crystals.

The best sugar to use in a rub is *turbinado sugar*, a less-refined, large-crystal sugar, because it melts slower than granulated sugar. However, because there's no guarantee you can find or buy turbinado sugar, you can use granulated sugar instead, and that's what I call for in the recipes. If you can find and buy turbinado sugar, substitute it equally in the rubs for granulated sugar.

Salt is frequently found in many rubs, and you'll see the words *kosher salt* used a lot in the recipes that follow. Kosher salt is different from table salt; it's fluffier. Kosher salt is produced differently, has less sodium by volume, dissolves quicker, and is not "iodized" (it has no iodine added). Kosher salt is available in most supermarkets.

The third rub ingredient is paprika. Ahhh, paprika. At one time you probably saw your mom sprinkle paprika over mashed potatoes or potato salad to add color. Although it is a beautiful bright red, paprika is so much more than color. Paprika delivers exquisite flavor notes, similar to what a fresh red sweet pepper tastes like. Made of dried and ground paprika peppers, there's sweet paprika and hot paprika (the latter of which can be almost as incendiary as cayenne), and each has its own use. Hungarian paprika is relatively inexpensive and can easily be found in red tins in the spice section of most supermarkets.

> **Barbecue Banter**
>
> Herbs and spices require air-tight containers stored in a cool, dry, low- or no-light place. Stored properly, most herbs and spices last 6 months to a year before landing on your "To buy" list.

In addition, a rub is made up of a wide variety of dried herbs and spices. The level and combination of these is what really makes each rub unique. When it comes to herbs, I have a simple rule: if your herbs have lost their bright color and turned a drab grayish green and your spices have lost their aroma, always throw them away and buy new. Few things are more disappointing than having something taste odd because old herbs and spices were used and didn't deliver.

A Very Handy Piece of Equipment

I've found, over the time I've been making rubs, that a wire mesh strainer is about the handiest piece of equipment I could ever ask for. Most rubs include brown sugar, and if you've ever worked with brown sugar, you know it lumps and clumps together. This clumping doesn't work well with a rub.

So after I have my rub ingredients in a bowl, I grab another bowl, pour the rub into my wire mesh strainer, and, with the back of a wooden spoon, work the rub (read: brown sugar) through the strainer into the empty bowl until nothing's left in the strainer. A quick stir, and my rub is ready to use and perfectly mixed—with no clumps!

Storing Rubs

The rub recipes that follow make fairly good-size quantities. That way, you make the rub once, use some of it, and store the rest. Then the next time you grill, all you have to do is light the grill and grab the leftover rub mix.

The best way I've found to store rubs is in the freezer. You'll need two, zipper-lock reclosable plastic sandwich bags and a marking pen. On the first bag, mark the name of the rub, what you used it for (pork, chicken, etc.), and the date. Pour the leftover rub in the bag, push out as much air as possible, and seal the bag. Roll up the bag, put it into the second bag, press out the air, seal, roll up the second bag, and put in the freezer. The next time you want that rub, it'll be in perfect condition with all the flavor it had today. Rubs can stay good in the freezer for at least 3 months.

Flame Point _____

One important note about making rubs: after you've mixed and either used or stored a rub, especially those that are hot or spicy, be sure to wash your hands thoroughly with hot soapy water to remove any "hot" spice residue.

Spicy Hot Steak Dry Rub

Yield: about 1 cup
Prep time: less than 5 minutes

½ cup salt

¼ cup plus 2 TB. chili powder

¼ cup fresh-ground black pepper

1. In a medium mixing bowl, thoroughly combine salt, chili powder, and black pepper.

2. Use 1 tablespoon rub for both sides of any steak.

Sweet and Hot Baby Back Rib Dry Rub

Yield: just over ¾ cup
Prep time: 5 minutes

¼ cup sweet paprika

¼ cup firmly packed light brown sugar

¼ cup kosher salt

4 tsp. ground cayenne

2 tsp. dry mustard

1. In a medium mixing bowl, thoroughly combine paprika, light brown sugar, kosher salt, cayenne, and dry mustard.

2. Rub both sides of a rack of spareribs or two racks of baby back ribs with a thick coat of rub. Then follow your favorite basic barbecued baby back rib recipe.

Barbecue Banter

It can be fun to grow cayenne peppers for yourself and your neighbors (one plant will likely be enough for all of you). In the fall, you can string, hang, and dry any of the last of the unused peppers. Store dried peppers in reclosable plastic freezer bags and freeze for 1 year, or trim the tops, split and remove the seeds, and grind them in a spice grinder to make your own ground cayenne that looks and tastes like no one else's.

Charles Harrison's Dry Rib Rub

½ cup fresh-ground black pepper

½ cup sweet paprika

½ cup granulated sugar (Charles recommends turbinado sugar)

2 TB. kosher salt

4 tsp. dry mustard

2 tsp. ground cayenne

> **Yield:** almost 1¼ cups
> **Prep time:** 5 to 7 minutes

1. In a medium mixing bowl, thoroughly combine black pepper, paprika, granulated sugar, kosher salt, dry mustard, and cayenne. (If you're using turbinado sugar, grind it together with the salt in a spice grinder until powdered.)

2. Rub both sides of a rack of spareribs or baby back ribs with a thick coat of rub. Place ribs in a plastic bag, and refrigerate overnight. Then follow your favorite basic barbecued rib recipe.

Barbecue Banter

An electric spice or coffee grinder makes quick work of breaking up hard dried rosemary or chewing up bay leaves for a rub. Consider having a dedicated spice grinder used exclusively to grind herbs and spices and nothing else so your spices won't pick up any other flavors from your grinder.

Fire and Spice Rib Rub

2 TB. sweet paprika

2 TB. kosher salt

4 tsp. garlic powder

2 tsp. cracked black pepper

2 tsp. crushed red pepper flakes

2 tsp. ground cayenne

2 tsp. onion powder

1 tsp. dry mustard

½ tsp. celery salt

½ tsp. chili powder

½ tsp. ground cumin

> **Yield:** ½ cup
> **Prep time:** 6 minutes

1. In a medium mixing bowl, thoroughly combine sweet paprika, kosher salt, garlic powder, black pepper, crushed red pepper flakes, cayenne, onion powder, dry mustard, celery salt, chili powder, and ground cumin.

2. Rub both sides of a rack of ribs with a thick coat of rub. Place ribs in a plastic bag, and refrigerate overnight. Then follow your favorite basic barbecued rib recipe.

Barbecue Banter

Rubs can really create a lot of flavor. They start by penetrating the meat during the initial rub and then continue while the meat rests in the refrigerator. The rub penetrates further as the ribs bake. And finally, the grill's heat intensifies the flavor when the rub mixes with the meat's juices and fats.

Dry Spice Poultry Rub

Yield: ½ cup
Prep time: 10 to 12 minutes

3 TB. sweet paprika

2 TB. dried tarragon, crumbled

2 TB. fresh-ground black pepper

1 TB. garlic powder

1 TB. dried oregano, crumbled

1½ tsp. rubbed sage, crumbled

1½ tsp. dried thyme, crumbled

1½ tsp. ground cayenne

1½ tsp. salt

Barbecue Banter

If you have access to fresh herbs, you can easily substitute fresh for dry herbs by doubling the quantity. For example, substitute 2 teaspoons fresh oregano leaves for 1 teaspoon dry.

1. In a medium mixing bowl, thoroughly combine sweet paprika, dried tarragon, black pepper, garlic powder, dried marjoram, rubbed sage, dried thyme, ground cayenne, and salt.

2. Rub inside, outside, and under the skin of a whole or split chicken. Place chicken in a plastic bag, and refrigerate 4 hours or overnight. Then follow your favorite basic grilled chicken recipe.

Aromatic and Savory Beef Rib Rub

2 to 3 medium bay leaves

2½ TB. firmly packed light brown sugar

2 TB. sweet paprika

1 TB. dry mustard

2 tsp. onion powder

2 tsp. garlic powder

1½ tsp. dried basil, crumbled

¾ tsp. ground coriander

¾ tsp. coarse-ground black pepper

¾ tsp. ground white pepper

¾ tsp. dried thyme, crumbled

½ tsp. kosher salt

¼ tsp. ground cumin

Yield: ¾ cup
Prep time: 15 minutes

1. Using an electric grinder, grind bay leaves as close as possible to a powder.

2. In a medium mixing bowl, thoroughly combine 1 teaspoon ground bay leaves, brown sugar, sweet paprika, dry mustard, onion powder, garlic powder, dried basil, coriander, black pepper, white pepper, dried thyme, kosher salt, and cumin.

3. Place a wire mesh strainer over another bowl, and pour rub mixture into the strainer. Using the back of a wooden spoon, press mixture, especially brown sugar, through the strainer until all that remains in the strainer are small pieces of bay leaf. Return bay leaf pieces to rub mixture.

4. Use ½ rub mixture to coat 3 pounds beef back ribs. Then, follow your favorite basic barbecued beef rib recipe.

Barbecue Banter

White pepper is actually made from naked black peppercorns that are soaked in water to soften their black skin and the skin's removed. Soaking creates a unique fermented flavor note of it's own.

Full-Flavor Lamb Rub

6 TB. chopped fresh rosemary leaves or 2 TB. dried rosemary

1 TB. plus 1½ tsp. salt

2 large cloves garlic, peeled and minced, or pushed through a *garlic press*

1 tsp. fresh-ground black pepper

Finely grated zest of 1 lemon

Yield: about ½ cup
Prep time: 8 to 10 minutes

1. In a medium mixing bowl, thoroughly combine rosemary, salt, garlic, black pepper, and lemon zest.

2. Use 1 tablespoon per shoulder lamb chop, 1 teaspoon per side for rib lamb chops, or ¼ cup for a 4- or 5-pound leg of lamb. Place lamb in a plastic bag, and refrigerate 4 hours. Then follow your favorite basic barbecued lamb recipe.

> **Grill Guide**
> A **garlic press** is a dandy metal kitchen tool that works by squeezing or "pressing" a peeled garlic clove through small holes, producing instantly what would otherwise take a minute or two with a knife and cutting board. If you cook with a lot of garlic, a garlic press can be a real time-saver.

Fresh Fish Rub

Yield: about ½ cup
Prep time: 10 minutes

6 TB. chopped fresh dill or 2 TB. dried dill, crumbled

2 TB. sweet paprika

1 TB. grated *lemon zest*

1 TB. salt

1 TB. fresh-ground black pepper

¾ tsp. ground cayenne

1. In a medium mixing bowl, thoroughly combine dill, sweet paprika, lemon zest, salt, black pepper, and cayenne.

2. Rub 1 teaspoon or more in each side of fish fillet before grilling. Then follow your favorite basic barbecued fish recipe.

> **Grill Guide**
> **Lemon zest** is the yellow part of a lemon peel, packed with lemon oil and a real flavor-booster. A standard box grater, using the next-to-the smallest grate, makes grating lemon or lime zest quick and easy. Be careful not to grate the white part under the zest, called the pith, because it's bitter.

Tex's Dry Beef Rib Rub

4 TB. kosher salt

3 TB. sweet paprika

2 TB. fresh-ground black pepper

2 TB. chili powder

1 TB. *celery salt*

1 TB. ground cayenne

1 TB. dry mustard

1½ tsp. ground white pepper

1½ tsp. garlic powder

Yield: almost 1 cup

Prep time: 5 minutes

1. In a medium mixing bowl, thoroughly combine kosher salt, paprika, black pepper, chili powder, celery salt, cayenne, dry mustard, white pepper, and garlic powder.

2. Rub a generous amount on beef back ribs or beef short ribs. Then follow your favorite basic barbecued beef rib recipe.

 Grill Guide

Celery salt is a blend of ground celery seeds and table salt. You've probably tasted it in tuna salad without knowing it.

Kansas City–Style Sweet Rub

2 cups granulated sugar

½ cup kosher salt

¼ cup sweet paprika

1 TB. coarse-ground black pepper

1 TB. chili powder

1 tsp. garlic powder

1 tsp. ground cayenne

Yield: about 2¾ cups

Prep time: 8 minutes

1. In a medium mixing bowl, thoroughly combine granulated sugar, kosher salt, sweet paprika, black pepper, chili powder, garlic powder, and cayenne.

2. Use a ½ cup rub to generously coat pork spareribs, front and back. Place ribs in a plastic bag, refrigerate 4 hours or overnight. Then follow your favorite basic barbecue sparerib recipe.

 Barbecue Banter

Don't be surprised that as ribs sit with this KC rub on that the ribs throw off more water than some other rubs.

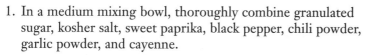

Hot and Sweet Southern Barbecue Rub

Yield: about ⅔ cup
Prep time: 5 minutes

¼ cup firmly packed light brown sugar

2 TB. coarse-ground black pepper

2 TB. hot paprika

1 TB. kosher salt

1 TB. garlic powder

1½ tsp. onion powder

1 tsp. ground cayenne

½ tsp. dry mustard

1. In a medium mixing bowl, thoroughly combine brown sugar, black pepper, hot paprika, kosher salt, garlic powder, onion powder, cayenne, and dry mustard.

2. Rub 1 teaspoon or more in each side of a fish fillet before grilling.

Chapter 5

Marinade Magic

In This Chapter

- ◆ Flavoring with marinades
- ◆ Handling marinades safely
- ◆ Uncovering lime juice's hidden abilities

Marinades, those wonderfully flavored liquids and sauces used to soak foods, are a great way to add flavor to any food, whether it will eventually head to the grill or not. For the most part, marinades exist to add flavor, not necessarily to tenderize. And if handled properly, marinades are also good to baste on the grill, for yet more flavor.

Timing can be everything with a marinade. In general, the smaller the piece of food, the faster it marinates; a whole chicken, for example, will take longer. Also, be aware that fish and chicken usually should spend less time in a marinade than beef, lamb, or pork.

The most common marinade bases are, not in any particular order, soy sauce, beer, vegetable oil, and lime juice.

Marinades don't take a lot of preparation, and with reclosable 1 gallon bags, marinating and cleanup is a cinch. Once you see how easy and flavorful marinating is, you'll want to marinate all the time!

Marinade Safety Rules

You usually place raw, uncooked meat, poultry, or fish into a marinade and then let it sit in the refrigerator to absorb all the flavor it can. Even though you kept the marinade and meat cool, practice caution with anything that comes into contact with raw meat, poultry, or fish. After you have removed the meat from the marinade, throw out the bag and the marinade, because it is unsafe for any other use.

If you want to use some of the marinade to baste the meat, set some aside *before* you add the meat. Never assume that because the grill's hot and will cook away any germs, that you can use the marinade that came in contact with the meat. The only safe way to reuse a marinade after it has touched raw meat is to pour the marinade into a saucepan, bring it to a boil, lower the heat and simmer it for 10 minutes before using or consuming. Cooked marinade doesn't have the same flavor as uncooked and because it loses some water, the flavors intensify, which is why it's better (and easier) to reserve some at the beginning.

What's the Deal with Lime Juice?

Lime juice is so acidic it actually creates the appearance of cooked meat or fish—without any applied heat! Ceviche, a wonderful Spanish dish made from fish that's never seen heat or flame, is actually "cooked" in lime juice, meaning the flesh turns opaque and, if removed on time, firms up. A marinade can have lime juice in it, but be careful of the time because if left in too long such marinades produce gray and mushy meat.

Spicy Beef-and-Beer-Flavored Marinade

3 fresh tomatoes, rinsed, cores removed, seeded and chopped

3 medium bay leaves, crushed

1 cup full-flavored beer

1 cup canned beef broth

1 TB. Worcestershire sauce

1 TB. fresh lemon juice

2 tsp. hot pepper sauce

1 tsp. fresh-ground black pepper

½ tsp. dried thyme, crumbled

> **Yield:** about 4 cups, enough for 1 to 2 large steaks or 3 to 4 small steaks
>
> **Prep time:** 10 minutes

1. To a 1-gallon reclosable plastic bag, add tomatoes, bay leaves, beer, beef broth, Worcestershire sauce, lemon juice, hot pepper sauce, black pepper, and dried thyme. Seal the bag, and shake it until ingredients are combined.

2. Open the bag, and add 4 beef tenderloin steaks, 1 flank steak, 1 tri-tip steak, 4 chuck eye steaks, or 4 cube steaks into marinade. Squeeze as much air out of the bag as possible before closing, and then refrigerate for 2 to 6 hours. Discard marinade, and grill meat using your favorite recipe.

Flame Point

When using beer as an ingredient in a marinade or brine, don't use a light beer because the beer's flavor will get lost in the flavors of the other ingredients. A stronger, bigger-flavored beer boosts the final flavor of a marinade or brine in a positive way.

Kansas City–Style Beef Marinade

Yield: about 2¾ cups, enough for 2 large steaks, 3 to 4 medium steaks or 5 to 6 small steaks

Prep time: 7 to 8 minutes

1 cup mild-flavored vegetable oil

¾ cup soy sauce

½ cup fresh lemon juice

¼ cup Worcestershire sauce

¼ cup yellow mustard

1 TB. coarse-ground black pepper

1 TB. seasoned salt

2 cloves garlic, peeled and minced, or pushed through a garlic press

1. Add vegetable oil, soy sauce, lemon juice, Worcestershire sauce, yellow mustard, black pepper, seasoned salt, and garlic to a blender, and blend until smooth.

2. Place steaks and marinade in a plastic bag, and marinate for 4 to 24 hours, turning meat occasionally. Remove steaks from marinade, discard marinade, and grill steaks using your favorite recipe.

Barbecue Banter _____

When a marinade calls for yellow mustard, you can still use another type of mustard if you don't have yellow. Think about your ending flavor notes before you do so, but try using a different mustard than the one you always use. It'll probably work great, and you'll have a new recipe.

Beer and Vinegar Beef Brisket Marinade

Yield: about 3 cups, enough for 1 small whole or ½ large brisket

Prep time: 7 to 8 minutes

1 (12-oz.) can full-flavored beer

½ cup white vinegar

½ cup mild vegetable oil

1 yellow onion, peeled and chopped

1 TB. firmly packed dark brown sugar

1 TB. liquid smoke flavoring

1 tsp. kosher salt

1 tsp. ground *cayenne*

1 tsp. fresh-ground black pepper

1. Add beer, white vinegar, oil, onion, brown sugar, liquid smoke flavoring, kosher salt, cayenne, and black pepper to a 1-gallon reclosable plastic bag. Close the bag, and shake until ingredients are combined. Pierce brisket all over both sides with the tines of a dinner fork, open the bag, and add brisket to marinade. Push out as much air as possible, close the bag, and refrigerate at least 4 and up to 24 hours.

2. Remove brisket from the bag, and discard all but 1½ cups marinade and the bag. Add marinade and brisket to a roasting pan, cover, and roast brisket in a 250°F oven for 3 to 4 hours or until brisket becomes tender. Finish brisket on grill over a low fire, basting with liquid from the bottom of the roasting pan and using your favorite recipe as a guide.

Grill Guide

Cayenne is made from dried and ground cayenne peppers, which produce 10 times the amount of heat as a jalapeño pepper but only ¹⁄₁₀ the heat of a habañero pepper.

Beer and Mustard Beef Marinade

1 cup full-flavored beer
½ cup Dijon mustard
½ cup honey mustard
½ cup olive oil
½ medium yellow onion, peeled and finely chopped

3 cloves garlic, peeled and minced, or pushed through a garlic press
2 tsp. dried rosemary, crumbled
½ tsp. kosher salt
½ tsp. fresh-ground black pepper

Yield: about 3 cups
Prep time: 8 to 10 minutes

1. To a 1-gallon reclosable plastic bag, add beer, Dijon mustard, honey mustard, olive oil, onion, garlic, dried rosemary, kosher salt, and pepper. Seal the bag, and shake until ingredients are combined.

2. Open the bag, and add 6 to 8 beef tenderloin steaks, 1 flank steak, 1 tri-tip steak, 6 to 8 chuck eye steaks, or 6 to 8 cube steaks. Squeeze as much air out of the bag as possible before closing, and refrigerate for 2 to 6 hours.

3. Remove meat from the bag, and discard marinade and the bag. Grill meat using your favorite recipe.

Barbecue Banter

Fresh rosemary leaves work very well with this marinade. But because fresh herbs aren't as strong as dried herbs, increase the amount of fresh rosemary to 2 tablespoons.

Cuban-Style Pork Marinade

Yield: about 1¼ cups marinade, enough for 4 to 6 pork chops, 2 pork tenderloins, 1 split slab pork spareribs, or 1 split slab baby back ribs

Prep time: 18 to 20 minutes plus cool-down time

Barbecue Banter

You can find fresh mint leaves as well as other flavorful herbs, too, in most supermarket produce sections.

½ cup olive or good-quality vegetable oil

8 cloves garlic, peeled and minced, or put through a garlic press

½ cup not-from-concentrate orange juice

½ cup fresh lime juice (from about 4 limes)

½ cup chopped fresh mint leaves

1½ tsp. kosher salt

1 tsp. ground cumin

½ tsp. fresh-ground black pepper

½ tsp. dried oregano, crumbled

1. In a medium saucepan, heat oil over medium heat. Add garlic and cook until golden, about 3 to 4 minutes. Add orange juice and lime juice (be careful, it might spatter), and simmer 2 minutes. Remove the saucepan from the heat, and add mint, kosher salt, cumin, pepper, and oregano. Cool to room temperature, and then refrigerate.

2. When cool, pour marinade into a 1-gallon reclosable plastic bag, and add pork chops, pork tenderloin or ribs. Squeeze as much air out of the bag as possible before closing, and refrigerate for 2 to 6 hours.

3. Remove meat from the bag, and discard marinade and the bag. Grill meat using your favorite recipe.

Classic Jamaican Fire-Breathing Jerk Marinade

1 medium yellow onion, peeled and chopped

4 cloves garlic, peeled and minced, or pushed through a garlic press

6 green onions, green and white parts, finely chopped

6 habañero chili peppers, seeds and ribs discarded, and finely chopped (see Flame Point)

½ cup olive oil

½ cup red wine vinegar

4 TB. soy sauce

4 TB. dark rum

2 TB. ground ginger

2 TB. fresh lime juice (from about 1 lime)

2 TB. firmly packed dark brown sugar

2 TB. dried thyme, crumbled

1 TB. plus 1 tsp. ground allspice

1 tsp. kosher salt

1 tsp. ground nutmeg

1 tsp. ground cinnamon

1 tsp. coarse-ground black pepper

> **Yield:** about 2¾ cups marinade, enough for 4 to 6 pork chops; 2 pork tenderloins; 1 split slab pork spareribs; 1 split slab baby back ribs; 1 whole chicken, split in half; 6 to 8 chicken breasts; or 8 to 10 chicken pieces
>
> **Prep time:** 20 to 25 minutes

1. To a 1-gallon reclosable plastic bag, add yellow onion, garlic, green onions, habañero chili peppers (or substituted jalapeño or serrano peppers), olive oil, red wine vinegar, soy sauce, dark rum, ginger, lime juice, brown sugar, thyme, allspice, kosher salt, nutmeg, cinnamon, and black pepper. Seal the bag, and shake until ingredients are combined.

2. Open the bag, and add 4 to 6 pork chops; 2 pork tenderloins; 1 split slab pork spareribs; 1 split slab baby back ribs; 1 whole chicken, split in half; 6 to 8 chicken breasts; or 8 to 10 chicken pieces. Squeeze as much air out of the bag as possible before closing, and refrigerate for at least 2 and no more than 6 hours.

3. Remove meat from the bag, and discard marinade and the bag. Grill meat using your favorite recipe.

Variation: If you can't find or don't feel comfortable working with habañero peppers, substitute an equal amount of milder, but still hot, jalapeño peppers (with their seeds) or even livelier serrano chili peppers.

Flame Point

Habañero peppers are some of the hottest in the world. Use inexpensive disposable rubber gloves when handling and cutting them to protect your skin from the burning heat in the oil. When you're done handling the habañeros, carefully remove and discard the gloves and wash your hands thoroughly.

Lemon, Soy Sauce, and Onion–Flavored Steak Marinade

Yield: ¼ cup, enough to marinate 1 large steak or 2 to 3 small steaks

Prep time: 7 to 9 minutes

¼ cup vegetable oil

2 TB. fresh-squeezed lemon juice

2 TB. soy sauce

2 TB. chopped green onion, white and green parts

1 tsp. coarse-ground black pepper

1 tsp. celery salt

½ tsp. garlic powder

1. To a 1-gallon reclosable plastic bag, add vegetable oil, lemon juice, soy sauce, onion, black pepper, celery salt, and garlic powder. Seal the bag, and shake it until ingredients are combined.

2. Open the bag and place a beef flank steak, a tri-tip steak, chuck eye steaks, or even cube steaks into marinade. Squeeze as much air out of the bag as possible before closing, and then refrigerate for 2 to 6 hours. Discard marinade, and grill meat using your favorite recipe.

Barbecue Banter

It's easy to halve and then squeeze the juice from lemons or limes using a lemon reamer. Squeezing your own juice is worth the effort because fresh juice has a better flavor than bottled and the end results in your grilled meats and other meals will be improved, too.

Chapter 6

Flavor-Enhancing Brines

In This Chapter

- ◆ Defining brines and the brining process
- ◆ Learning some easy brining methods
- ◆ Checking out brine do's and don'ts

Tasting a piece of chicken or meat that has been soaked in brine (a salt-water and sugar solution) and then grilled can almost seem to be a magical experience. The chicken or meat comes off the grill full of flavor, dripping with moisture, and tender as can be. That, my friend, is the magic of brines.

"Brining" might sound intimidating if you've never tried it, but actually, it's a very easy process. Couple a brine with your favorite grilling recipe, and you've got an unbeatable combination.

What's a Brine and How It Works Its Magic

A basic brine is a mixture of salt, sugar, and water. Kosher salt is often used in brines because it hasn't been iodized, or had the bitter iodine added, as most salt has. Plus kosher salt dissolves quickly, even in cold water.

Here's how a brine works: when the ratio of salt to water is correct (usually ½ cup Diamond Crystal kosher salt, 6 tablespoons Morton kosher salt, or 4 tablespoons regular table salt for each 1 quart water), whatever food soaks in the brine will absorb about 10 percent of its weight of the salted brine water. So if a 4-pound chicken goes into a brine bath, it'll come out weighing 4 pounds, 6 ounces. The meat will lose some of this moisture during grilling, but it'll hang on to some of it, too, and the end result after grilling will be tender and moist.

It's in the Bag: An Easy Brining Method

As in Chapter 5 with marinades, using plastic bags is perfect for brines—no mess and a quick cleanup! Using a 1- or 2-gallon reclosable, plastic bag to hold whatever you're brining works really well. All you have to do is dump the brine into the bag, add the chicken or roast, squeeze out as much air as you can, seal the bag and keep it cold for no less than 1 and no more than 8 hours (1 hour per pound). That's all it takes, and you're ready to go. When you're done, discard the brine and the bag. That's it!

A Brine Caution

You can leave a whole 3-pound chicken in a brine made from 1 cup Diamond Crystal brand kosher salt, 1 cup granulated sugar, and 2 quarts water for up to 3 hours. Longer than that won't change much, except it may make the chicken too salty.

It's easy to think, *The longer that chicken's in there, the better it will be.* Nope. A chicken, as all meats, will absorb only so much and then stop. Soaking longer than recommended isn't … well … recommended.

Simple Chicken Brine

1 cup Diamond Crystal kosher salt, ¾ cup Morton kosher salt, or ½ cup ordinary table salt

1 cup granulated sugar

2 qt. water

Yield: 2 quarts, enough for 1 whole or split 3- to 4-pound chicken or 3 to 4 pounds chicken pieces

Prep time: 5 to 6 minutes

1. In a 1-gallon reclosable plastic bag, add salt, sugar, and water. Seal the bag, and shake until salt and sugar are dissolved.

2. Rinse chicken halves or pieces under cold water, and add to the bag. Squeeze out as much air as possible before closing, and refrigerate for 3 (for a 3-pound chicken) to 4 (for a 4-pound chicken) hours.

3. Remove chicken from the bag, and discard brine and the bag, rinse chicken under cold water, and pat dry with paper towels. Grill chicken using your favorite recipe.

Flame Point _____
Use good quality, reliable reclosable plastic bags. Cheap bags can open, and take the word of someone who's cleaned it up; it's no fun trying to remove very salty, sugary water from a carpet.

Buttermilk Chicken Brine

½ cup chopped onions

8 to 10 cloves garlic (2 TB.) peeled and minced, or pushed through a garlic press

¼ cup Diamond Crystal kosher salt, 3 TB. Morton kosher salt, or 2 TB. ordinary table salt

¼ cup granulated sugar

1 TB. ground cumin

1 qt. low-fat or fat-free buttermilk, well shaken

2 tsp. fresh-ground black pepper, plus more to taste

Yield: about 1 quart, enough for 1 whole chicken, split; 5 pounds chicken thighs; or 5 pounds chicken breasts

Prep time: 8 to 10 minutes

1. Add onions, garlic, salt, sugar, cumin, and buttermilk to a 1-gallon reclosable plastic bag. Close the bag and shake until combined. Open the bag and add chicken or chicken pieces.

Barbecue Banter

Buttermilk naturally tenderizes chicken and adds an excellent flavor note. But the name is a little misleading. The only butter in buttermilk is the name on the carton.

Squeeze out as much air as possible before closing, and refrigerate for 24 hours, turning the bag every once in a while.

2. Remove chicken from the bag, and discard brine and the bag. Rinse chicken under cold water, pat dry with paper towels, and grind on black pepper to taste. Grill chicken using your favorite recipe.

Brown Sugar, Black Pepper, and Cayenne Beef Brine

Yield: 1 quart, enough to brine 1 (1½- to 2-pound) beef flank steak or 6 pork chops

Prep time: 4 to 5 minutes

1 qt. bottled water

½ cup Diamond Crystal kosher salt, 6 tablespoons Morton kosher salt, or 4 tablespoons ordinary table salt

½ cup firmly packed light brown sugar

10 to 15 black peppercorns

½ tsp. ground cayenne

1 bay leaf

1. To a 1-gallon reclosable plastic bag, add water, salt, brown sugar, peppercorns, cayenne, and bay leaf. Seal the bag, and shake until salt and sugar are dissolved. Add steak or pork chops to the bag. Squeeze out as much air as possible before closing, and refrigerate for 24 hours.

2. Remove steak or chops from the bag, and discard brine and the bag. Rinse meat under cold water and dry with paper towels. Grind on black pepper to taste, and grill meat using your favorite recipe.

Flame Point

Brines are not made for beef steaks such as T-bone, strip, or filet; burgers; or anything that is already tender. They won't add much if anything to such meats.

Louisiana Turkey Brine

8 cups cold water

1 cup firmly packed dark brown sugar

1 cup Diamond Crystal kosher salt, ¾ cup Morton kosher salt, or ½ cup ordinary table salt

¼ cup gin (any brand)

¼ cup coarse-ground black pepper

1½ tsp. ground allspice

1 tsp. dried thyme, crumbled

1 tsp. ground cloves

2 medium bay leaves

Yield: 2 quarts, enough for 1 small turkey or 2 whole chickens

Prep time: 6 to 8 minutes

Cook time: 10 minutes + cooling time

1. To a medium-size saucepan add 4 cups water, brown sugar, salt, gin, black pepper, allspice, thyme, cloves, and bay leaves. Bring to a boil over high heat, reduce heat to low, and simmer 10 minutes, stirring occasionally. Remove the saucepan from the heat, add remaining 4 cups water, and cool to room temperature.

2. Pour cooled brine into a 2-gallon reclosable plastic bag, and add 1 small turkey. Squeeze out as much air as possible before closing, and refrigerate at least 1 hour for every pound of turkey or up to 24 hours.

3. Remove turkey from the bag, and discard brine and the bag. Rinse turkey under cold water, and pat dry with paper towels. Barbecue turkey using your favorite recipe.

Barbecue Banter

When grilling or barbecuing a turkey, you can catch and reserve the juices that drip off as it cooks and use them later to make a smoky-flavored gravy or use as a terrific base for a no-ham split-pea soup.

Chapter 7

Boss Barbecue Sauces

In This Chapter

- Making your own barbecue sauce
- Introducing the stars of barbecue sauce: sugar, honey, tomatoes, and vinegar
- Watching the clock: time to slather on the sauce

With so many barbecue sauces lining supermarket shelves today, why would anyone want to make his own barbecue sauce at home? Three little words: *it'll taste better*.

When you make your own barbecue sauce, you get to choose which brand or type of ingredients you put into your sauce, which can definitely make it taste better. We used dried herbs in the dry rubs, because they are just that—dry. Due to their natural moisture, fresh herbs are difficult if not impossible to use in a dry rub. But since barbecue sauces are already wet, you can easily utilize fresh herbs, which can make a big flavor difference. (Most bottled sauces use dry herbs.)

What's Sugar Got to Do with It?

Sugar is a key component in most barbecue sauces whether you see "sugar" in the ingredient list or not. Many barbecue sauces contain ketchup, and although most ketchups produced today have little of any "sugar," they contain high-fructose corn syrup, which isn't made from sugar cane, but corn. But it doesn't matter what you name it, they're both sugar.

Most barbecue sauces also have "added" sugar, such as granulated sugar or brown sugar. Granulated sugar is neutral in flavor—it's just sweet. Brown sugar, however, is rich with flavors that come from the molasses that either hasn't been refined out or has been added back. Molasses on its own may taste great, but swirl it with refined sugar and—*wow*—flavor!

Honey, even though it comes from bees, is still a form of sugar. Some barbecue sauces add honey for two reasons: it's sweet (like sugar) but has flavor, sometimes complex (unlike sugar).

It doesn't matter where it comes from; sugar in all its forms makes barbecue sauces a sweet delight.

Tomato ... No Tomato

Tomatoes are the second ubiquitous barbecue sauce ingredient. Tomatoes bring their own natural sugar as well as flavor to a sauce.

Rarely are fresh tomatoes added to a barbecue sauce, though. Tomatoes enter a barbecue sauce in one of three forms: ketchup (most common), tomato sauce (much less common), and tomato paste (even less common).

It's a Blessing: Vinegar

Vinegar is often used in sauces to balance sugar's sweetness. It creates an edge that sharpens sugar's softness. The most commonly used vinegar is distilled "white" vinegar. The good news about distilled vinegar: it's always the same. Every bottle you pick up has the same flavor and the same level of acidity because it's all controlled in the production process.

Cider vinegar is used less frequently than distilled vinegar, but it has more flavor notes. "Cider vinegar" is shorthand for "apple cider vinegar." Natural cider vinegar has many different flavor notes—apple being the most prominent.

Finally, rice vinegar is becoming more common thanks to availability and is appearing in some barbecue sauces. Rice vinegar is made from—what else?—fermented rice. You can find it in seasoned and unseasoned varieties. Sugar and salt are the most common rice vinegar "seasonings." Unseasoned rice vinegar has a light, clean taste and aroma, and seasoned or unseasoned, rice vinegar is lower in acid than American distilled "white" vinegar, which makes it smoother tasting than regular distilled vinegar.

Flame Point _____

Beware: some vinegars available today have the word *cider* on the label but have never seen or touched an apple. Look closely, and you'll see the word *flavored* in small type. Even the color may be added.

Take a minute to stop and read vinegar labels and see what they contain.

Timing Is Everything

Making your own barbecue sauces is great fun—and they make terrific gifts! Barbecue sauce can be used as a condiment, like ketchup, on hamburgers, baked chicken, broiled pork chops and even hot dogs. But the main end use of a barbecue sauce is to slather it all over grilled or barbecued beef, pork, chicken, fish, and even vegetables.

Here's where timing gets tricky. Many folks who are somewhat new to grilling or barbecuing want to add the sauce at the beginning, right after they slap the meat on the grill. The problem with this, though, is because barbecue sauce contains so much sugar, natural and added, that by the time the chicken or other meat is done, the sauce has turned black because the sugar in it has burned.

There's an easy solution, though: be patient, and wait to add the barbecue sauce until almost the end of the cooking time. If put on just before the end, the sauce will turn to a wonderful glaze and actually deliver more flavor than it originally had before it went on. How's that possible? The heat changes the sauce, improving and deepening its flavor. So never brush on barbecue sauce any sooner than 10 minutes before the meat's done cooking.

What about leftover sauce? Because of its high acid content (just like ketchup), as long as it hasn't come in contact with raw meat, leftover barbecue sauce can be transferred to a clean glass bottle, covered, and refrigerated to be used at another time.

Barbecue Banter _____

Most homemade barbecue sauces will keep for several weeks if you properly cover and store them in the refrigerator.

Beginner's BBQ Sauce

Yield: about 2½ cups
Prep time: 10 minutes
Cook time: 25 to 30 minutes
Serving size: 1 to 2 tablespoons

2 TB. vegetable oil

1 medium onion, peeled and finely chopped

3 cloves garlic, peeled and minced, or pushed through a garlic press

1½ cups ketchup

⅓ cup granulated sugar

½ cup apple cider vinegar

¼ cup Worcestershire sauce

1 TB. chili powder

1 tsp. ground cayenne or to taste

1. In a medium saucepan over medium heat, heat vegetable oil. When hot, add onion and cook, stirring occasionally, for 5 to 6 minutes or until onion is soft. Add garlic and cook for 1 minute or until fragrant. Add ketchup, sugar, cider vinegar, Worcestershire sauce, chili powder, and cayenne. Reduce heat and simmer, partially covered, until sauce thickens slightly, about 15 to 20 minutes.

2. Brush on chicken, pork, beef, or hamburgers during the last 10 minutes of grilling. If desired, reheat and pass additional sauce.

Barbecue Banter

Cooking onions and garlic in oil makes them sweeter. It also helps to concentrate the flavor because onions and garlic are 89 percent water. By cooking them in oil, the water evaporates, which intensifies the flavor.

Excellent Barbecue Rib Sauce

Yield: about 2½ cups
Prep time: 7 to 8 minutes
Cook time: about 20 minutes
Serving size: 1 to 2 tablespoons

3 TB. vegetable oil

1 TB. peeled and minced garlic (about 4 medium cloves)

½ cup firmly packed dark brown sugar

½ cup canned, fat-free chicken broth

½ cup unseasoned rice vinegar

½ cup ketchup

3 TB. Dijon mustard

2 TB. soy sauce

1 TB. crushed red pepper flakes

1. In a small, heavy saucepan over medium-low heat, heat olive oil. Add garlic, and cook about 3 minutes or until softened.

2. Stir in brown sugar, chicken broth, rice vinegar, ketchup, Dijon mustard, soy sauce, and crushed red pepper flakes. Bring to a simmer, reduce heat to low, and cook, stirring occasionally, until mixture thickens, about 15 minutes.

Barbecue Banter

Simmering a barbecue sauce for even 15 minutes allows the flavors to merge.

3. Brush on pork or beef ribs during the last 10 minutes of grilling. If desired, reheat and pass additional sauce.

So-Good-You'll-Lick-Your-Fingers BBQ Sauce

1 medium yellow onion, peeled and chopped

2 TB. unsalted butter

1 tsp. peeled and minced garlic (from 1 medium clove) or ½ tsp. garlic powder

1 tsp. fresh sage leaves, minced or ½ tsp. rubbed sage, crumbled

2 cups ketchup

1 cup full-flavored beer

¾ cup firmly packed dark brown sugar

¼ cup plus 2 TB. fresh lemon juice (from 1 large or 2 medium lemons)

2 TB. soy sauce

1½ TB. Worcestershire sauce

1 TB. steak sauce

1½ tsp. hot pepper sauce

1 tsp. kosher salt

1 tsp. celery seed

½ tsp. fresh-ground black pepper

2 TB. bottled grated horseradish or to taste

Yield: 4½ cups
Prep time: 10 to 12 minutes
Cook time: about 25 minutes
Serving size: 1 to 2 tablespoons

1. In a medium saucepan over medium heat, cook onion in butter 7 to 8 minutes or until onion wilts and is golden around the edges. Add garlic and sage, and cook until fragrant, about 30 seconds. Add ketchup, beer, brown sugar, lemon juice, soy sauce, Worcestershire sauce, steak sauce, hot pepper sauce, kosher salt, celery seed, and black pepper. Bring to a boil, reduce heat and simmer, uncovered, for 15 minutes, stirring occasionally. Cool.

2. Transfer cool sauce to a blender, and blend until smooth. Stir in horseradish.

3. Brush on chicken, pork, or beef during the last 10 minutes of grilling. If desired, reheat and pass additional sauce.

Barbecue Banter

Without horseradish, some things just wouldn't taste right. Many commercial creamy cabbage slaws include horseradish in the dressing, and you'd miss it if it wasn't there. It also does nice things for a barbecue sauce—besides taking your breath away and clearing your sinuses, I mean.

Charles Harrison's Chicken Barbecue Sauce

Yield: about 7 cups
Prep time: 13 to 15 minutes
Cook time: 25 minutes
Serving size: 1 to 2 tablespoons

3 cups ketchup

1 cup minced onion

1 cup dry red wine

1 cup *Chinese oyster sauce*

½ cup soy sauce

½ cup firmly packed dark brown sugar

3 large cloves garlic, peeled and minced, or pushed through a garlic press

2 TB. peeled and grated fresh ginger

2 TB. Worcestershire sauce

2 TB. Dijon mustard

1 tsp. hot pepper sauce

1 tsp. ground coriander

½ tsp. fresh-ground black pepper or to taste

1. In a medium saucepan over medium heat, stir together ketchup, onion, red wine, Chinese oyster sauce, soy sauce, brown sugar, garlic, ginger, Worcestershire sauce, mustard, hot pepper sauce, coriander, and black pepper until combined. Bring to a boil, reduce heat to low, and simmer, stirring occasionally, until it thickens, about 20 minutes. Cool.

2. Brush on chicken at the end of grilling or serve on the side.

Grill Guide

Chinese oyster sauce, an extract of oysters blended with salt, sugar, soybeans and sometimes MSG, is used in many Chinese recipes, especially dishes found in Chinese restaurants. Its distinctive flavor is worth finding to add to this sauce. You can find it in the Asian food section of your supermarket or at local Asian markets.

Sweet and Hot Chicken BBQ Sauce

1½ cups ketchup

¾ cup firmly packed dark brown sugar

¾ cup red wine vinegar

¾ cup full-flavored beer

½ cup fresh lemon juice (from about 2 or 3 lemons)

¾ cup *chili sauce*

¼ cup steak sauce (your favorite)

2 TB. hot pepper sauce or to taste (you can always add more)

2½ TB. yellow mustard

2 TB. Worcestershire sauce

1 TB. fresh-ground black pepper

1 TB. vegetable oil

1½ tsp. soy sauce

1½ tsp. dry mustard

Yield: about 6 cups
Prep time: 10 minutes
Cook time: 20 minutes
Serving size: 1 to 2 table-spoons

1. In a medium saucepan over medium heat, stir together ketchup, brown sugar, red wine vinegar, beer, lemon juice, chili sauce, steak sauce, hot pepper sauce, yellow mustard, Worcestershire sauce, pepper, vegetable oil, soy sauce, and dry mustard until combined. Bring to a boil, reduce heat to low, and simmer, stirring occasionally, for 15 minutes, or until it thickens. Cool.

2. Brush on chicken at the end of grilling or serve on the side.

Note: Like fine wine, this sauce gets better with age. Two days in the refrigerator does this sauce a world of good.

Grill Guide

Chili sauce is made from tomato purée, vinegar, sugar or high fructose corn syrup, onion, garlic, sometimes green peppers. It's commonly seasoned with paprika, cinnamon, allspice, nutmeg, and sometimes cayenne.

A Honey of a Barbecue Sauce

Yield: about 4¾ cups
Prep time: 8 to 10 minutes
Cook time: 18 to 20 minutes
Serving size: 1 to 2 tablespoons

¼ cup olive oil

4 TB. unsalted butter

¾ cup chopped yellow onion

1 clove garlic, peeled and minced, or pushed through a garlic press

1 cup ketchup

1 cup clover (or other mild) honey

1 cup good-quality red wine vinegar

½ cup *Worcestershire sauce*

1 TB. dry mustard

1½ tsp. kosher salt

1 tsp. coarse-ground black pepper

1 tsp. dried marjoram, crumbled

½ tsp. dried thyme, crumbled

Grill Guide

Worcestershire sauce is used quite often in grilling, but no one, except the manufacturer, knows *exactly* what's in it?

1. In a medium saucepan over medium heat, heat olive oil and butter until butter melts. Add onion and cook, stirring occasionally, about 6 to 7 minutes, or until soft. Add garlic and cook, stirring, for 1 minute or until fragrant. Add and stir together ketchup, clover honey, red wine vinegar, Worcestershire sauce, dry mustard, kosher salt, black pepper, marjoram, and thyme. Bring to a boil, reduce heat to low, and simmer, stirring occasionally, for 10 minutes. Remove from heat and cool completely.

2. Brush on chicken, pork, or beef during the last 10 minutes of grilling. If desired, reheat and pass additional sauce.

Kansas City-Style Barbecue Sauce

Yield: about 3 cups
Prep time: 10 minutes
Cook time: 40 minutes
Serving size: 1 to 2 tablespoons

1 TB. olive oil or vegetable oil

½ cup finely chopped onion

2 cloves garlic, peeled and minced, or pushed through a garlic press

1 cup ketchup

¾ cup apple juice

¼ cup apple cider vinegar

2 TB. firmly packed light brown sugar

2 TB. molasses (not black-strap)

1 TB. sweet paprika

1 TB. prepared horseradish

1 TB. Worcestershire sauce

1 tsp. salt

1 tsp. celery seed

½ tsp. fresh-ground black pepper

¼ tsp. ground cayenne

1. In a medium saucepan over medium heat, heat olive or vegetable oil. Add onion and garlic, and cook, stirring occasionally, about 5 minutes or until onion is tender. Stir in ketchup, apple juice, vinegar, brown sugar, molasses, paprika, horseradish, Worcestershire sauce, salt, celery seed, black pepper, and cayenne. Bring to a boil, reduce heat to low, and cook uncovered at a low simmer, stirring occasionally, about 30 minutes or until thicker. Remove from heat, and cool completely before using.

2. Brush on chicken, pork, or beef during the last 10 minutes of grilling. If desired, reheat and pass additional sauce.

Flame Point
Blackstrap molasses has too strong a flavor for barbecue sauce. Although it's a form of sugar, blackstrap molasses has a very bitter flavor when tasted alone.

Texas-Style Yee-Haw Barbecue Sauce

1 TB. vegetable oil
1½ cups chopped yellow onion
2 cloves garlic, peeled and minced, or pushed through a garlic press
2 jalapeño chili peppers, stem cut off, seeds and ribs discarded, and finely chopped
2 TB. chili powder

1 (12-oz.) can tomato paste

1 (12-oz.) can full-flavored beer

1 cup ketchup

½ cup firmly packed dark brown sugar

½ cup fresh lime juice (from 4 small or 3 medium limes)

1 TB. Worcestershire sauce

Yield: about 6 cups
Prep time: 10 to 11 minutes
Cook time: 15 minutes
Serving size: 1 to 2 tablespoons

1. In a medium saucepan over medium heat, heat vegetable oil. Add onion, garlic, and jalapeño pepper and cook about 5 minutes or until tender. Add chili powder and cook, stirring, 1 minute. Add tomato paste, beer, ketchup, brown sugar, lime juice, and Worcestershire sauce. Bring to a boil, stirring constantly. Reduce heat and simmer 5 minutes, stirring occasionally. Remove from heat and cool completely.

2. Brush on chicken, pork, or beef during the last 10 minutes of grilling. If desired, reheat and pass additional sauce.

Barbecue Banter
Juicing lemons or limes by hand can be quick and easy. I like to use a wooden lemon reamer. To juice, cut the lemon or lime in half, push the pointed end of the reamer into the center of the lemon or lime and, over a measuring cup to catch the juice, squeeze and twist and the juice streams down into the cup.

Tennessee-Style All-Purpose Barbecue Sauce

Yield: about 2½ cups
Prep time: 10 minutes
Cook time: 40 minutes
Serving size: 1 or 2 table-spoons

1 TB. vegetable oil

1 medium yellow onion, peeled and finely chopped

1 clove garlic, peeled and minced, or pushed through a garlic press

½ tsp. crushed red pepper flakes

½ cup ketchup

½ cup not-from-concentrate orange juice

½ cup dark molasses (not blackstrap)

½ cup whiskey

1 TB. firmly packed light brown sugar

1 tsp. dry mustard

1 tsp. Worcestershire sauce

1 tsp. grated orange zest

1. Heat oil in a medium saucepan over medium heat. Add onions, garlic, and red pepper flakes, and cook, stirring occasionally, 5 minutes or until softened. Add and combine ketchup, orange juice, molasses, whiskey, brown sugar, dry mustard, Worcestershire sauce, and orange zest. Bring to a low simmer, and simmer for 30 minutes, stirring occasionally. Remove from heat and cool to room temperature.

2. Brush on chicken, pork, or beef during the last 10 minutes of grilling. If desired, reheat and pass additional sauce.

Barbecue Banter _____

When grating orange zest, first rinse the peel under cold running water, and then dry it well with a clean paper towel. Using the finest side on your box grater, just take the orange part, not the white part—the pith—underneath. The pith is bitter.

Old Kentucky Barbecue Sauce

2 TB. unsalted butter

½ cup chopped yellow onion

2½ cups water

½ cup apple cider vinegar

2 TB. Worcestershire sauce

1 TB. granulated sugar

2½ tsp. fresh-ground black pepper

2 tsp. chili powder

1 tsp. kosher salt

1 tsp. dry mustard

½ tsp. hot pepper sauce

1 clove garlic, peeled and minced, or pushed through a garlic press

Yield: 3¾ cups
Prep time: 10 minutes
Cook time: 20 minutes
Serving size: 1 to 2 table-spoons

1. In a medium saucepan over medium heat, melt butter. Add onions and cook, stirring occasionally for 5 minutes or until soft. Add water, vinegar, Worcestershire sauce, sugar, black pepper, chili powder, kosher salt, dry mustard, hot pepper sauce, and garlic. Bring to a low simmer, and simmer for 10 minutes, stirring occasionally. Remove from heat and cool.

2. Brush on chicken, pork, or beef during the last 10 minutes of grilling. If desired, reheat and pass additional sauce.

Barbecue Banter _____

Unsalted butter has a better flavor than salted butter. And brand to brand, there's no way to be sure how much salt has been added. Using unsalted or sweet butter, you add the salt, if any, and you know how much you add. Sweet butter is more fragile than salted butter and is best kept in the freezer.

North Carolina No-Tomato Grillin' Sauce

Yield: about3 cups
Prep time: 5 minutes
Cook time: 14 to 15 minutes
Serving size: 1 to 2 tablespoons

1 cup apple cider vinegar

1 cup distilled white vinegar

1 TB. crushed red pepper flakes

1 TB. granulated sugar

1 TB. fresh-ground black pepper

1 TB. hot pepper sauce

2 tsp. salt

1. In a medium saucepan over medium heat, combine cider vinegar, white vinegar, crushed red pepper flakes, sugar, black pepper, hot pepper sauce, and salt and bring to a boil. Lower heat and simmer slowly for 10 minutes, stirring occasionally.

2. Brush on pork of any kind or grilling chicken during the last 10 minutes. If desired, reheat and pass additional sauce.

Barbecue Banter

North Carolina barbecue sauces are known for their big flavor but thin consistency. This sauce is similar to Kentucky barbecue sauces, especially because it uses no tomato or tomato products at all.

Asian-Style Barbecue Sauce

Yield: about 2 cups
Prep time: 8 to 10 minutes
Cook time: 15 minutes
Serving size: 1 to 2 tablespoons

¾ cup *hoisin sauce*

⅔ cup minced shallot

⅔ cup granulated sugar

¼ cup unseasoned rice vinegar

2 TB. *Asian fish sauce*

2 TB. soy sauce

2 TB. clover (or other mild)

honey

2 TB. peeled and minced fresh ginger

4 cloves garlic, peeled and minced, or pushed through a garlic press

¼ tsp. Chinese five-spice powder

1. In a medium saucepan over medium heat, combine hoisin sauce, shallot, sugar, rice vinegar, Asian fish sauce, soy sauce, honey, ginger, garlic, and Chinese five-spice powder. Bring to a simmer, and simmer for 10 minutes. Remove from heat and cool.

2. Brush on chicken, pork, or beef during the last 10 minutes of grilling. If desired, reheat and pass additional sauce.

Grill Guide

Hoisin (rhymes with *moisten*) **sauce** is a thick, spicy-sweet Asian sauce made from sugar and soybeans, seasoned with sesame seed paste, garlic, and chili pepper. It's used as both a seasoning and a dipping sauce. **Asian fish sauce** is an extremely pungent, strong-flavored, and salty liquid made from fermented anchovies, water, and salt. It's lighter in flavor and in color than soy sauce and is used as a condiment, sauce, and seasoning ingredient.

Black Jack Brown Sugar Barbecue Sauce

2 cups strong brewed coffee (the stronger, the better)

1 cup Jack Daniel's black label whiskey (or your favorite whiskey)

1 cup firmly packed light brown sugar

1 cup soy sauce

¼ cup cider vinegar

2 tsp. Worcestershire sauce

Yield: about 2 cups
Prep time: 10 minutes
Cook time: approximately 30 minutes
Serving size: 1 to 2 tablespoons

1. In a medium, heavy-bottomed saucepan over medium heat, combine coffee, whiskey, brown sugar, soy sauce, vinegar, and Worcestershire sauce. Simmer, uncovered, stirring occasionally, about 30 minutes or until reduced to about 2 cups. Sauce will not be thick. Cool to room temperature.

2. Brush on chicken, pork, or beef during the last 10 minutes of grilling. If desired, reheat and pass additional sauce.

Homemade Teriyaki Sauce

Yield: ¾ *cup*
Prep time: 7 to 8 minutes
Cook time: 7 to 8 minutes
Serving size: 1 tablespoon

½ cup soy sauce

½ cup granulated sugar

1 tsp. grated fresh ginger

2 medium cloves garlic, peeled and minced, or pushed through garlic press

1 TB. whiskey (can be bourbon, sour mash, or Scotch)

½ tsp. cornstarch

1. In a small saucepan over medium heat, combine soy sauce, sugar, ginger, and garlic.

2. In a small bowl, stir together whiskey and cornstarch until cornstarch dissolves. Stir cornstarch mixture into soy sauce mixture.

3. Bring sauce to a boil, stirring occasionally, until syrupy, about 4 minutes. Remove from the heat, and cover to keep warm.

4. Brush on chicken, pork, or beef during the last 10 minutes of grilling. If desired, reheat and pass additional sauce.

Barbecue Banter

No brand of bottled teriyaki sauce tastes nearly as good as homemade, so it's worth the (minor) effort to make it at home. But if you must purchase teriyaki sauce, try Annie Chun's All Natural Teriyaki Sauce or Soy Vay Veri Veri Teriyaki.

Charles Harrison's Favorite Barbecue Sauce

Yield: about 4 cups
Prep time: 10 minutes
Cook time: 20 minutes
Serving size: 1 to 2 tablespoons

2¼ cups ketchup

2¼ cups water

1 cup apple cider vinegar

3 TB. firmly packed dark brown sugar

1 TB. fresh lemon juice (from half of a lemon)

1 TB. chili powder

2 tsp. instant beef broth or 2 beef bouillon cubes

2 tsp. Worcestershire sauce

1¼ tsp. dry mustard

1 tsp. fresh-ground black pepper

½ tsp. garlic powder

¼ tsp. ground cayenne

½ tsp. liquid smoke

2 dashes hot pepper sauce

1. In a medium saucepan over medium heat, combine ketchup, water, vinegar, brown sugar, lemon juice, chili powder, beef broth granules or bouillon cubes, Worcestershire sauce, dry mustard, black pepper, garlic powder, cayenne, liquid smoke, and hot pepper sauce. Bring to a boil, reduce heat to low, and simmer, stirring occasionally, for 15 minutes.

2. Brush on chicken, pork, or beef during the last 10 minutes of grilling. If desired, reheat and pass additional sauce. If not using immediately, cool and refrigerate.

Barbecue Banter

When I first began working on the recipes for this book, I headed straight to North Carolina born-and-bred Charles Harrison, banker, grill master, and barbecue-guy extraordinaire. I don't know anyone in North Carolina who enjoys grilling and barbecuing on 30 square feet of *hot* grill more than Charles. Charles was not only kind enough to share some grill time and tips with me, but also generously shared his lip-smackin', tried-and-true recipes. I promised Charles that in exchange for his generosity, I would give him the credit he so justly deserves.

Docta Peppa Barbecue Sauce

2 cups tomato sauce

¾ cup Dr Pepper carbonated soda

¾ cup cider vinegar

¾ cup chili sauce

¼ cup yellow mustard

¼ cup bottled steak sauce

3 TB. fresh lemon juice (from about 1 lemon)

¼ cup Worcestershire sauce

1 TB. vegetable oil

1½ tsp. soy sauce

1½ tsp. hot pepper sauce

¾ cup firmly packed dark brown sugar

1 TB. fresh-ground black pepper

1 TB. garlic salt

1½ tsp. dry mustard

Yield: 6 cups
Prep time: 12 to 14 minutes
Cook time: 35 to 40 minutes
Serving size: 1 to 2 tablespoons

Barbecue Banter

Using your favorite brand of steak sauce and other favorite condiments helps insure you'll be pleased with the final results.

1. In a medium saucepan over medium heat, combine tomato sauce, Dr Pepper, vinegar, chili sauce, yellow mustard, steak sauce, lemon juice, Worcestershire sauce, vegetable oil, soy sauce, and hot pepper sauce. Stir well and bring to a simmer. Add brown sugar, pepper, garlic salt, and dry mustard, and stir until combined. Return to a simmer, reduce heat to low, and simmer, uncovered, stirring occasionally, for about 30 minutes or until flavors are well blended. Cool to room temperature.

2. Brush on chicken, pork, or beef during the last 10 minutes of grilling. If desired, reheat and pass additional sauce.

Zippy Tartar Sauce

Yield: 2 cups

Prep time: 12 minutes

Serving size: 1 to 2 tablespoons

1¾ cups mayonnaise (reduced-fat or light mayonnaise may be substituted)

¼ cup finely chopped fresh parsley leaves

2 TB. Dijon mustard

2 TB. sweet pickle relish

2 TB. chopped fresh dill

1 TB. chopped green onion, white part only

1 tsp. Worcestershire sauce

½ tsp. cayenne

½ tsp. reduced-sodium soy sauce

½ tsp. hot pepper sauce

1. In a medium mixing bowl, combine mayonnaise, parsley, Dijon mustard, pickle relish, dill, green onion, Worcestershire sauce, cayenne, soy sauce, and hot pepper sauce. Stir sauce until well combined.

2. Place in a bowl or jar, cover, and refrigerate for a few hours to allow the flavors to blend.

Barbecue Banter

A piece of fried or grilled fish doesn't seem to taste as good without the real thing: homemade tartar sauce.

Part 3

Burgers and Other Bun Foods

When you have the basics under control and know how to affect flavor in a variety of ways, you'll want to take that knowledge and put it into practice. My first gas grilling experience was like trying to run before I could walk. I should have started with something I really enjoyed and wasn't so complex, like hamburgers. That's what we start with in Part 3: hamburgers: one of the best things to grill. Try the basic "All-American" hamburger, or select one of nearly 30 other burgers, some made with beef, some with pork, turkey, or chicken.

In addition, hot dogs and sausages taste better when they've been cooked on a grill. So in Part 3, you also discover how to grill a classic hot dog, with some tasty variations, as well as delicious ways to make your own sausages and then finish them perfectly by heading out to the grill.

Chapter 8

D'Best All-Beef Burgers

In This Chapter

- ◆ The gold standard: all-American beef hamburger
- ◆ Flavor: grilling vs. griddles and pan-frying
- ◆ Hamburgers 101

No sandwich (except maybe for hot dogs) has ever reached the worldwide popularity of the all-American beef hamburger. No doubt about it, with billions—possibly trillions—eaten, it ranks number one, and for good reason.

The Secrets of a Great Burger

If you start with high-quality ground beef, if you cook them properly, and if you serve them up on fresh buns with quality condiments, burgers taste great.

To my way of thinking, there's only one way to cook a hamburger: on a hot grill. Unfortunately, because griddles and pans fry hamburgers in their own grease, they produce—what else?—a greasy burger. However, cooking over charcoal or gas flames allows melting fat to drip off (sometimes causing flare-ups), which, if controlled and correctly timed, produce a flavorful, crusty exterior while not overcooking the interior.

Grilling over an open fire is only part of the secret to producing a great burger—the quality and type of ground meat makes an enormous difference. A great hamburger starts with freshly ground, choice-grade beef. Frozen beef is not recommended because it loses water as it defrosts—so long juiciness.

The best hamburger comes from *ground chuck* (80 percent lean), and needs to be labeled as such—not just "ground beef (70 percent lean)," for example. *Ground beef* can be beef from any cut, flavorful or not so flavorful. Ground chuck must come from the chuck, an exceptionally flavorful beef part.

Barbecue Banter _____

What's the difference between **ground chuck** and **ground beef?** Ground beef is cheaper than ground chuck, but that's due to its extra fat. Ground beef is usually 70 percent lean or 30 percent fat. That's almost 5 ounces fat in 1 pound ground beef. Cooking a burger on a grill with that much fat causes numerous grill flame flare-ups, which will char a burger's outside long before the inside's done. Ground beef may contain some ground chuck, but it doesn't have to; it can contain beef from anywhere on a steer, like some areas that are far less flavorful than the chuck.

Ground chuck's 80 percent leanness makes a bigger difference than it might seem. Twenty percent fat equals 3.2 ounces—almost 2 ounces per pound less than ground beef. Less fat equals far fewer flare-ups, so the burger will brown nicely on the outside while the inside gets fully cooked.

Good-quality name-brand condiments also make a difference. If you've been buying your ketchup, mustard, or relish by price, that may be why your homemade burgers just don't equal the flavor level of others you've tasted. You wouldn't skimp on the beef; so don't skimp on the condiments, either.

The bun that makes your hamburger into a sandwich should never be described as "fluffy." If you make "juicy" hamburgers, you'll need a bun with enough substance to absorb some of that juice and not fall apart. Although they have a "nuttier" flavor note, whole-grain hamburger buns have what it takes to hang together until the last bite.

To Sear, with Love

At one time, we thought that cooking meat over high heat seared the outside and, therefore, sealed in the juices: pure fallacy. Food scientists have proven beyond any doubt that searing does *not* seal in the juices.

However, searing plays a key flavor role in cooking meat, whether you're grilling a hamburger or a lamb chop. Beginning the cooking process over high heat starts the release of the meat's juices, which are made of water, protein, and fat. That heat changes the chemical makeup of those juices in a positive way (you'll know the chemical change occurred because the meat browns) and creates the flavor of grilled meats we all love.

Hamburgers 101

Here are a few more quick tips for grilling the best hamburgers:

- Make all hamburgers the same size. They'll cook at the same rate, and there'll be less guess work on the cooking times.

- To keep from compressing the burgers, handle the raw hamburger as little as possible. You'll tell the difference in the moist results.

- Salt a hamburger's exterior after grilling, not before, to keep the cooked hamburger as moist as possible. Salting after cooking helps keep the moisture from being pulled to the surface.

- Never, never, never (did I mention never?), press down on a hamburger with your spatula while grilling. This only helps to squeeze out more moisture.

- To produce great flavor, first cook hamburgers over a high-heat fire on the grill for 1 to 2 minutes per side. This helps create that dark brown surface and actually creates and boosts flavor.

- To keep grill-cooked hamburgers juicy, turn them every 1 to 2 minutes. This keeps the water in the burger from quickly heading up and out.

- Use an instant-read thermometer to check for doneness; burgers should be 150°F to 155°F when properly cooked. Let cooked burgers rest off the grill before serving. Their heat will diminish and when that happens the burgers firm up and hold more juice.

Flame Point

Grilling hamburgers over a very high fire and extreme heat often produces charred, not crusty, exteriors and dry, over-cooked interiors.

Great All-American Hamburger

Serves: 6
Prep time: 10 minutes
Cook time: 13 to 16 minutes
Serving size: 1 hamburger

2¼ lb. fresh ground chuck (or 80 percent lean ground beef)

2 tsp. salt

1 tsp. fresh-ground black pepper

6 whole-grain hamburger buns

Ketchup

Mustard

Pickles or pickle relish

Onion slices

Tomato slices

Lettuce leaves

Mayonnaise

1. Fire up the grill:

   For a charcoal grill: Open the bottom vents. Ignite 6 quarts or 2½ pounds charcoal briquettes or hardwood charcoal. When the coals are hot, set up for a two-level fire: one side high heat (so you can hold your hand 1 to 2 inches above the cooking rack only 1 to 2 seconds), and the other medium heat (so you can hold your hand 1 to 2 inches above cooking rack only 4 to 5 seconds).

   For a gas grill: Turn each burner to high and ignite. Cover the grill. When hot, leave half the burners on high heat, and set the other half on medium heat.

Barbecue Banter

Toasting the buns adds flavor. Your nose will tell you when the buns are probably done—or burnt—but it's also okay to flip them over and take a look.

2. While the grill heats, place ground chuck in a large mixing bowl, season with salt and black pepper and, with clean hands, lightly mix seasonings into meat. Gently shape into 6 (½- to ¾-inch-thick) patties, being careful not to press too hard.

3. Grill burgers, uncovered, over high heat for 1 to 2 minutes per side. *On a charcoal grill:* move burgers to medium heat, and grill for 10 to 12 minutes total, turning every 2 minutes, until medium-done (155°F). *On a gas grill:* move burgers to medium heat, and grill 5 to 6 minutes, covered. Turn and grill 5 to 6 minutes more, covered, until medium-done (155°F). Remove burgers from the grill and let rest for 5 minutes.

4. While hamburgers rest, lightly toast cut sides of hamburger buns on high heat, about 1 to 2 minutes. Place hamburgers on buns, and serve immediately, passing ketchup, mustard, pickles, onion slices, tomato slices, lettuce leaves, and mayonnaise.

Outside-In Cheeseburger

2¼ lb. fresh ground chuck (or 80 percent lean ground beef)

6 oz. (about 1½ cups) grated American or mild cheddar cheese

1½ tsp. salt

1 tsp. fresh-ground black pepper

6 good-quality hamburger buns

Ketchup

Mustard

Pickles or pickle relish

Onion slices

Tomato slices

Lettuce leaves

Mayonnaise

Serves: 6
Prep time: 10 minutes
Cook time: 13 to 16 minutes
Serving size: 1 hamburger

1. Fire up the grill:

   For a charcoal grill: Open the bottom vents. Ignite 6 quarts or 2½ pounds charcoal briquettes or hardwood charcoal. When the coals are hot, set up for a two-level fire: one side high heat (so you can hold your hand 1 to 2 inches above the cooking rack only 1 to 2 seconds), and the other medium heat (so you can hold your hand 1 to 2 inches above cooking rack only 4 to 5 seconds).

   For a gas grill: Turn each burner to high and ignite. Cover the grill. When hot, leave half the burners on high heat, and set the other half on medium heat.

2. While grill heats, place ground chuck, cheese, salt, and black pepper in a large mixing bowl. With clean hands, lightly mix cheese and seasonings into meat. Gently shape into 6 (½- to ¾-inch-thick) patties, being careful not to press too hard.

3. Grill burgers, uncovered, over high heat for 1 to 2 minutes per side. *On a charcoal grill:* move burgers to medium heat, and grill for 10 to 12 minutes total, turning every 2 minutes, until medium-done (155°F). *On a gas grill:* move burgers to medium heat, and grill 5 to 6 minutes, covered. Turn and grill 5 to 6 minutes more, covered, until medium-done (155°F). Remove burgers from the grill, and let rest for 5 minutes.

4. While hamburgers rest, lightly toast cut sides of hamburger buns on high heat, about 1 to 2 minutes. Place hamburgers on buns, and serve immediately, passing ketchup, mustard, pickles, onion slices, tomato slices, lettuce leaves, and mayonnaise.

Barbecue Banter

You can mix in any one of your favorite cheeses in these burgers. Shredded Swiss, brick, provolone, or even grated Parmesan work well.

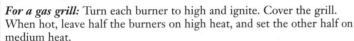

Holy Jalapeño Burger

Serves: 6
Prep time: 10 minutes
Cook time: 13 to 16 minutes
Serving size: 1 hamburger

2¼ lb. fresh ground chuck (or 80 percent lean ground beef)

6 oz. (about 1½ cups) grated pepper Jack cheese

1½ tsp. salt

1 tsp. fresh-ground black pepper

6 hamburger buns

Charles Harrison's Favorite Barbecue Sauce (recipe in Chapter 7) or a bottled sweet and smoky flavored barbecue sauce

Thinly sliced sweet onion rounds

1. Fire up the grill:

 For a charcoal grill: Open the bottom vents. Ignite 6 quarts or 2½ pounds charcoal briquettes or hardwood charcoal. When the coals are hot, set up for a two-level fire: one side high heat (so you can hold your hand 1 to 2 inches above the cooking rack only 1 to 2 seconds), and the other medium heat (so you can hold your hand 1 to 2 inches above cooking rack only 4 to 5 seconds).

 For a gas grill: Turn each burner to high and ignite. Cover the grill. When hot, leave half the burners on high heat, and set the other half on medium heat.

Grill Guide

Jalapeño peppers are small, green—and red hot!—peppers. Most of the heat is in the seeds, which is why the jalapeño pepper seeds (ouch) aren't mixed into cheese.

2. Place ground chuck, cheese, salt, and black pepper in a large mixing bowl. With clean hands, lightly mix cheese and seasonings into meat. Gently shape into 6 (½- to ¾-inch-thick) patties, being careful not to press too hard.

3. Grill burgers, uncovered, over high heat for 1 to 2 minutes per side. *On a charcoal grill:* move burgers to medium heat, and grill for 10 to 12 minutes total, turning every 2 minutes, until medium done (155°F). *On a gas grill:* move burgers to medium heat, and grill 5 to 6 minutes, covered. Turn and grill 5 to 6 minutes more, covered, until medium-done (155°F). Remove burgers from the grill, and let rest for 5 minutes.

4. While hamburgers rest, lightly toast cut sides of hamburger buns on high heat, about 1 to 2 minutes. Place hamburgers on buns, and serve immediately, passing barbecue sauce and onion rounds.

Reuben Sandwich-Style Burger

1½ lb. ground chuck (or 80 percent lean ground beef)

1 tsp. salt

½ tsp. garlic powder

½ tsp. fresh-ground black pepper

6 slices lean bacon, finely chopped

1 small onion, peeled and finely chopped

1 (16-oz.) pkg. refrigerated sauerkraut, rinsed under cold water, and well drained

8 slices seeded or seedless rye bread

4 (1-oz.) slices Swiss cheese

Thousand Island or Russian salad dressing

Serves: 4
Prep time: 18 to 20 minutes
Cook time: 13 to 16 minutes
Serving size: 1 hamburger

1. Fire up the grill:

> *For a charcoal grill:* Open the bottom vents. Ignite 6 quarts or 2½ pounds charcoal briquettes or hardwood charcoal. When the coals are hot, set up for a two-level fire: one side high heat (so you can hold your hand 1 to 2 inches above the cooking rack only 1 to 2 seconds), and the other medium heat (so you can hold your hand 1 to 2 inches above cooking rack only 4 to 5 seconds).
>
> *For a gas grill:* Turn each burner to high and ignite. Cover the grill. When hot, leave half the burners on high heat, and set the other half on medium heat.

2. Place ground chuck in a large mixing bowl, and season with salt, garlic powder, and black pepper. With clean hands, lightly mix seasonings into meat. Gently shape into 4 (½- to ¾-inch-thick) patties, being careful not to press too hard.

3. Place a large skillet over medium-high heat. Add bacon, and cook until translucent, about 5 minutes. Drain all but 1 tablespoon bacon fat from the skillet. Add onion and cook, stirring, until onion is translucent and bacon is browned, about 4 to 6 minutes. Add sauerkraut, mix well with onion and bacon, and stir until heated through, about 3 minutes. Cover and keep warm.

4. Grill burgers, uncovered, over high heat for 1 to 2 minutes per side. *On a charcoal grill:* move burgers to medium heat, and grill for 10 to 12 minutes total, turning every 2 minutes, until medium-done (155°F). *On a gas grill:* move burgers to medium heat, and grill 5 to 6 minutes, covered. Turn and grill 5 to 6 minutes more, covered, until medium-done (155°F). Remove burgers from the grill, and let rest for 5 minutes.

Barbecue Banter

Sauerkraut sold refrigerated in plastic bags tastes much better than canned sauerkraut. However, refrigerated sauerkraut isn't always available, so canned sauerkraut will do in a pinch. You'll need to rinse and drain canned sauerkraut well, too, before using it.

5. While hamburgers rest, lightly toast rye bread slices on high heat, about 1 to 2 minutes. Place hamburgers on ½ toasted rye, top each burger with cheese, spoon sauerkraut mixture over cheese, drizzle Thousand Island salad dressing over sauerkraut, top with remaining toasted bread slices, and serve immediately.

South-of-the-Border Burgers

Serves: 4
Prep time: 25 minutes
Cook time: 13 to 16 minutes
Serving size: 1 hamburger

2 TB. bacon grease or vegetable oil

¾ cup finely chopped onion

1 (15-oz.) can refried beans

1½ lb. ground chuck (or 80 percent lean ground beef)

¼ cup dry breadcrumbs

1 (4-oz.) can chopped green chilies, drained

1 egg, beaten

1 tsp. Worcestershire sauce

½ tsp. salt

½ tsp. ground cumin

½ tsp. chili powder

8 slices sourdough bread

1 large tomato, rinsed, cored, and thickly sliced

1 large ripe avocado, pitted, peeled, and sliced

1. Fire up the grill:

 For a charcoal grill: Open the bottom vents. Ignite 6 quarts or 2½ pounds charcoal briquettes or hardwood charcoal. When the coals are hot, set up for a two-level fire: one side high heat (so you can hold your hand 1 to 2 inches above the cooking rack only 1 to 2 seconds), and the other medium heat (so you can hold your hand 1 to 2 inches above cooking rack only 4 to 5 seconds).

 For a gas grill: Turn each burner to high and ignite. Cover the grill. When hot, leave half the burners on high heat, and set the other half on medium heat.

2. Place a large skillet over medium heat, and heat bacon grease. Add ¼ cup onion and cook, stirring occasionally, until softened, about 5 minutes. Add refried beans, and simmer until heated through. Keep warm.

3. Place ground chuck in a large mixing bowl along with remaining ½ cup chopped onion, breadcrumbs, green chilies, beaten egg, Worcestershire sauce, salt, cumin, and chili powder. With clean hands, lightly mix seasonings into meat. Gently shape into 4 (½- to ¾-inch-thick) patties, being careful not to press too hard.

4. Grill burgers, uncovered, over high heat for 1 to 2 minutes per side. *On a charcoal grill:* move burgers to medium heat, and grill for 10 to 12 minutes total, turning every 30 seconds to 1 minute, until medium-done (155°F). *On a gas grill:* move burgers to medium heat, and grill 6 to 7 minutes, covered. Turn and grill 6 to 7 minutes more, covered, until medium-done (155°F). Remove burgers from the grill, and let rest for 5 minutes.

5. While hamburgers rest, lightly toast sourdough bread slices on high heat, about 1 to 2 minutes. Place hamburgers on ½ toasted sourdough, top each with 1 scoop refried beans, add tomato slice and then avocado slice on top of beans. Top with remaining toasted bread slice, and serve immediately.

Barbecue Banter

You can easily find canned green chilies in the Mexican or Hispanic section of your supermarket.

BBQ Sauced Burgers

½ cup Charles Harrison's Favorite Barbecue Sauce (recipe in Chapter 7) or sweet and smoky–flavor bottled barbecue sauce plus more for serving

½ tsp. hot pepper sauce

1½ lb. ground chuck (or 80 percent lean ground beef)

½ tsp. salt

½ tsp. fresh-ground black pepper

4 whole-grain hamburger buns

4 (¾-oz.) American cheese slices

Lettuce leaves

Tomato slices

Onion slices

Pickle slices

Serves: 4	
Prep time: 10 to 12 minutes	
Cook time: 13 to 16 minutes	
Serving size: 1 hamburger	

1. Fire up the grill:

> *For a charcoal grill:* Open the bottom vents. Ignite 6 quarts or 2½ pounds charcoal briquettes or hardwood charcoal. When the coals are hot, set up for a two-level fire: one side high heat (so you can hold your hand 1 to 2 inches above the cooking rack only 1 to 2 seconds), and the other medium heat (so you can hold your hand 1 to 2 inches above cooking rack only 4 to 5 seconds).
>
> *For a gas grill:* Turn each burner to high and ignite. Cover the grill. When hot, leave half the burners on high heat, and set the other half on medium heat.

2. In a small bowl, whisk together barbecue sauce and hot pepper sauce until combined.

Barbecue Banter

If you can only find barely ripe—hardball—tomatoes, skip them and let the tomato in the barbecue sauce carry the flavor.

3. Place ground chuck in a large mixing bowl, add barbecue sauce mixture, salt, and black pepper. With clean hands, lightly mix sauce and seasonings into meat. Gently shape into 4 (½-inch-thick) patties, being careful not to press too hard.

4. Grill burgers, uncovered, over high heat for 1 to 2 minutes per side. *On a charcoal grill:* move burgers to medium heat, and grill for 10 to 12 minutes total, turning every 2 minutes, until medium-done (155°F). *On a gas grill:* move burgers to medium heat, and grill 5 to 6 minutes, covered. Turn and grill 5 to 6 minutes more, covered, until medium-done (155°F). Remove burgers from the grill, and let rest for 5 minutes.

5. While hamburgers rest, lightly toast cut sides of hamburger buns on high heat, about 1 to 2 minutes. Place hamburgers on bottom of toasted buns, top each with 1 slice cheese, and cover with remaining buns. Serve immediately, passing barbecue sauce, lettuce leaves, tomato slices, onion slices, and pickle slices.

Pizza Burgers

Serves: 6
Prep time: 18 to 20 minutes
Cook time: 13 to 16 minutes
Serving size: 1 hamburger

2¼ lb. fresh ground chuck (or 80 percent lean ground beef)

2 oz. (about 30) pepperoni slices, coarsely chopped

½ cup finely chopped onion

½ cup finely chopped green bell peppers

⅓ cup canned pizza sauce

1 tsp. dried basil, crumbled

1 tsp. fresh-ground black pepper

½ tsp. garlic powder

½ tsp. whole fennel seeds

½ tsp. salt

6 (¾-oz.) slices part-skim milk mozzarella cheese

6 whole-grain hamburger buns

1. Fire up the grill:

For a charcoal grill: Open the bottom vents. Ignite 6 quarts or 2½ pounds charcoal briquettes or hardwood charcoal. When the coals are hot, set up for a two-level fire: one side high heat (so you can hold your hand 1 to 2 inches above the cooking rack only 1 to 2 seconds), and the other medium heat (so you can hold your hand 1 to 2 inches above cooking rack only 4 to 5 seconds).

For a gas grill: Turn each burner to high and ignite. Cover the grill. When hot, leave half the burners on high heat, and set the other half on medium heat.

2. Place ground chuck, pepperoni, onion, green bell pepper, pizza sauce, basil, black pepper, garlic powder, fennel seeds, and salt in a large mixing bowl. With clean hands, lightly mix until combined. Gently shape into 6 (½- to ¾-inch-thick) patties, being careful not to press too hard.

3. Grill burgers, uncovered, over high heat for 1 to 2 minutes per side. *On a charcoal grill:* move burgers to medium heat, and grill for 10 to 12 minutes total, turning every 2 minutes, until medium-done (155°F). *On a gas grill:* move burgers to medium heat, and grill 5 to 6 minutes, covered. Turn and grill 5 to 6 minutes more, covered, until medium-done (155°F). Remove burgers from the grill, and let rest for 5 minutes.

4. While hamburgers rest, lightly toast cut sides of hamburger buns on high heat, about 1 to 2 minutes. Place hamburgers on bottom of toasted buns, top each with 1 slice cheese, and cover with remaining buns. Serve immediately.

Barbecue Banter

Canned and bottled pizza sauce works and tastes better than spaghetti sauce.

Black Jack Burgers

2¼ lb. fresh ground chuck (or 80 percent lean ground beef)

¼ cup Jack Daniel's Black Label whiskey or bourbon

4 oz. extra-sharp cheddar cheese, grated (about 1 cup)

1 tsp. salt

1 TB. coarse-ground black pepper (if you like some real heat, use 2 TB.)

6 hamburger buns, preferably whole grain

Sweet onion slices

A Honey of a Barbecue Sauce (recipe in Chapter 7) or sweet bottled barbecue sauce

Serves: 6		
Prep time: 5 to 7 minutes		
Cook time: 13 to 16 minutes		
Serving size: 1 hamburger		

1. Fire up the grill:

For a charcoal grill: Open the bottom vents. Ignite 6 quarts or 2½ pounds charcoal briquettes or hardwood charcoal. When the coals are hot, set up for a two-level fire: one side high heat (so you can hold your hand 1 to 2 inches above the cooking rack only 1 to 2 seconds), and the other medium heat (so you can hold your hand 1 to 2 inches above cooking rack only 4 to 5 seconds).

For a gas grill: Turn each burner to high and ignite. Cover the grill. When hot, leave half the burners on high heat, and set the other half on medium heat.

Flame Point

Do *not* baste the hamburgers with Jack Daniel's or any other high alcohol content hard liquor, as this could easily cause a big and dangerous flare-up.

2. Place ground chuck in a large mixing bowl. Add whiskey, cheddar cheese, salt, and black pepper. With clean hands, lightly mix whiskey and seasonings into meat until combined. Gently shape into 6 (½- to ¾-inch-thick) patties, being careful not to press too hard.

3. Grill burgers, uncovered, over high heat for 1 to 2 minutes per side. *On a charcoal grill:* move burgers to medium heat, and grill for 10 to 12 minutes total, turning every 2 minutes, until medium-done (155°F). *On a gas grill:* move burgers to medium heat, and grill 5 to 6 minutes, covered. Turn and grill 5 to 6 minutes more, covered, until medium-done (155°F). Remove burgers from the grill, and let rest for 5 minutes.

4. While hamburgers rest, lightly toast cut sides of hamburger buns on high heat, about 1 to 2 minutes. Place hamburgers on buns, and serve immediately, passing onion slices and barbecue sauce.

Sizzlin' Pepper-Bacon Burgers

Serves: 4
Prep time: 18 to 20 minutes
Cook time: 12 to 15 minutes
Serving size: 1 hamburger

1 TB. olive oil

1 small onion, peeled and thinly sliced

1 fresh Anaheim or mild green chili pepper, stem cut off, seeds and ribs discarded, and cut into rings

1 large egg, slightly beaten

¼ cup dry breadcrumbs

6 slices crisp-cooked bacon, crumbled

2 TB. whole milk

2 jalapeño peppers, seeds and ribs discarded, and finely chopped

1½ lb. fresh ground chuck (or 80 percent lean ground beef)

4 kaiser rolls, split, or hamburger buns

4 lettuce leaves

1. Fire up the grill:

For a charcoal grill: Open the bottom vents. Ignite 6 quarts or 2½ pounds charcoal briquettes or hardwood charcoal. When the coals are hot, set up for a two-level fire: one side high heat (so you can hold your hand 1 to 2 inches above the cooking rack only 1 to 2 seconds), and the other medium heat (so you can hold your hand 1 to 2 inches above cooking rack only 4 to 5 seconds).

For a gas grill: Turn each burner to high and ignite. Cover the grill. When hot, leave half the burners on high heat, and set the other half on medium heat.

2. Place a small saucepan over medium heat and heat olive oil. Add onion and Anaheim pepper, and cook about 8 minutes or until onion is tender. Cool.

3. In a large mixing bowl, stir together egg, breadcrumbs, bacon, milk, pepper, and cooled onion mixture until combined. Add ground chuck, and with clean hands, lightly mix together. Gently shape into 6 (½- to ¾-inch-thick) patties, being careful not to press too hard.

4. Grill burgers, uncovered, over high heat for 1 to 2 minutes per side. *On a charcoal grill:* move burgers to medium heat, and grill for 10 to 12 minutes total, turning every 2 minutes, until medium-done (155°F). *On a gas grill:* move burgers to medium heat, and grill 5 to 6 minutes, covered. Turn and grill 5 to 6 minutes more, covered, until medium-done (155°F). Remove burgers from the grill, and let rest for 5 minutes.

5. While hamburgers rest, toast the cut sides of Kaiser rolls on the grill, about 1 minute on high heat. Place hamburgers on rolls, top with lettuce leaves and onion mixture, and serve immediately, passing additional onion mixture.

Lean Note ___

Because bacon contributes some of its own fat, you can use leaner ground beef here, such as ground round.

Beer Burgers with Beer-Grilled Onions

1 large onion, peeled, ends trimmed, and cut into 4 thick slices

1 tsp. granulated sugar

1½ tsp. salt

1 cup full-flavored beer

8 bamboo skewers, soaked 20 minutes in warm water

1½ lb. ground chuck (or 80 percent lean ground beef)

½ tsp. fresh-ground black pepper

½ tsp. hot pepper sauce

¼ tsp. Worcestershire sauce

4 (¾-oz.) slices baby Swiss cheese

4 slices Pumpernickel bread

Ketchup

Mustard

Serves: 4
Prep time: 25 to 30 minutes
Cook time: 13 to 16 minutes
Serving size: 1 hamburger

1. Lay onion slices on a clean cutting board, and insert 2 bamboo skewers through each onion slice, edge to edge, about ½ inch apart. Dust both sides with sugar and ½ teaspoon salt, and set aside.

2. Fire up the grill:

For a charcoal grill: Open the bottom vents. Ignite 6 quarts or 2½ pounds charcoal briquettes or hardwood charcoal. When the coals are hot, set up for a two-level fire: one side high heat (so you can hold your hand 1 to 2 inches above the cooking rack only 1 to 2 seconds), and the other medium heat (so you can hold your hand 1 to 2 inches above cooking rack only 4 to 5 seconds).

For a gas grill: Turn each burner to high and ignite. Cover the grill. When hot, leave half the burners on high heat, and set the other half on medium heat.

Flame Point _____

Because bamboo is a type of wood, it will, if dry, burn easily over high-heat coals or flames. Soaking skewers slows this process down considerably, making it easy to use skewers.

3. Place ground chuck in a large mixing bowl. Add ¼ cup beer, 1 teaspoon salt, black pepper, hot pepper sauce, and Worcestershire sauce. With clean hands, lightly mix until combined. Gently shape into 4 (½-inch-thick) patties, being careful not to press too hard.

4. Grill burgers, uncovered, over high heat for 1 to 2 minutes per side. *On a charcoal grill:* move burgers to medium heat, and grill for 10 to 12 minutes total, turning every 2 minutes, until medium-done (155°F). *On a gas grill:* move burgers to medium heat, and grill 5 to 6 minutes, covered. Turn and grill 5 to 6 minutes more, covered, until medium-done (155°F). Remove burgers from the grill, and let rest for 5 minutes.

5. While burgers cook, place skewered onions over high heat and grill, basting with remaining ¾ cup beer, 5 minutes per side (discard what remains of beer after use). Remove from grill and remove skewers.

6. While hamburgers rest, lightly toast Pumpernickel bread on high heat, about 1 to 2 minutes. Place hamburgers between toasted pumpernickel slices, topping each with 1 slice grilled onion, and serve immediately, passing ketchup and mustard.

D'Best Not-All-Beef Burgers

In This Chapter

- ◆ Grind it up: selecting ground meats
- ◆ How hot is it?
- ◆ Cleanliness is next to … healthy!

In Chapter 8, I covered the many possibilities you have available when you're in the mood to grill all-beef hamburgers. However, if beef's not your thing, this chapter's for you.

Hamburgers don't have to be all-beef to be a hamburger or to be good. The fun with the burgers in this chapter is that you get to mix different ground meats and seasonings to come up with completely new hamburgers.

The Daily Grind

Not-all-beef hamburgers have one thing in common: ground meat. At one time in butcher shops and even grocery stores the butcher would grind meat for you while you waited. In most places, that's not the case any more. Ground meat, whether beef, pork, chicken, or turkey, is usually ground far from where you buy it.

To get the freshest ground meat possible, I suggest you do two things:

◆ If there's a butcher at your supermarket, talk to him and see if he'll share information on how you can get the freshest ground meat possible.

◆ Check the "pull date" on ground meat packages. This is the date stamped on the package which gives the store the last day it can sell the meat before it's "pulled" from the shelf. You might be surprised at the variety of "pull dates" you'll find in some meat sections. Always choose the "pull date" farthest from today.

Technical Stuff

As I've suggested before, an instant-read thermometer can make you the neighborhood "Grillmeister." An instant-read thermometer quickly tells the temperature of any meat it's stuck into. If you know 130°F equals rare or 170°F equals well-done, you'll never over- or undercook a piece of meat again on your grill. I don't know what I'd do without mine.

In few areas of food preparation is cleanliness as important as when your hands or your kitchen tools or your cutting board meets raw meat. You'll see the phrase "clean hands" or "a clean bowl" many times in this book. If you start with clean hands and the utensils you use are truly clean, you'll rarely, if ever, have any health issues caused by contamination in your kitchen.

Lamb and Feta Cheese Burgers

1½ lb. ground lamb

2 tsp. fresh-ground black pepper

4 lettuce leaves

¾ cup crumbled *feta cheese* (3 oz.)

4 tomato slices

1½ TB. snipped fresh mint leaves

4 kaiser rolls, split

Serves: 4
Prep time: 13 to 15 minutes
Cook time: 14 to 18 minutes
Serving size: 1 hamburger

1. Fire up the grill:

> *For a charcoal grill:* Open the bottom vents. Ignite 6 quarts or 2½ pounds charcoal briquettes or hardwood charcoal. When the coals are hot, set up for a one-level medium-heat fire (so you can hold your hand 5 inches above the cooking rack for only 4 to 5 seconds).
>
> *For a gas grill:* Turn each burner to high and ignite. Cover the grill. When hot, set the burners to medium heat.

2. With clean hands, gently shape ground lamb into 4 (½- to ¾-inch-thick) patties, being careful not to press too hard. Season with pepper, and lightly press pepper into patties.

3. *On a charcoal grill:* Grill lamb patties over medium-heat coals for 14 to 18 minutes total, turning every 2 minutes, until they reach medium doneness (155°F). *On a gas grill:* Grill burgers over medium heat, covered, for 7 to 9 minutes. Turn over burgers, and grill 7 to 9 minutes, covered, until medium-done (155°F). Remove burgers from the grill and let rest for 5 minutes.

4. While lamb patties rest, lightly toast cut sides of kaiser rolls on the grill for about 3 to 4 minutes. Place lettuce on bottom of rolls, and then add lamb burgers, cheese, tomato, and mint. Complete with roll tops and serve.

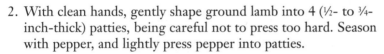

Grill Guide

Feta cheese is made from sheep's milk and has a deliciously bold flavor that works extremely well with lamb. It's produced mainly in Greece, but many believe Bulgarian-made feta cheese is the best.

Moist and Flavorful Turkey Burgers

Serves: 6
Prep time: 22 to 25 minutes
Cook time: 14 to 18 minutes
Serving size: 1 hamburger

2¼ lb. (80 to 85 percent lean) ground turkey (not all white meat)

1 tsp. salt

1 tsp. fresh-ground black pepper

1 cup whole-milk ricotta cheese

1 TB. plus 1 tsp. Dijon mustard

1 TB. plus 1 tsp. Worcestershire sauce

6 good-quality hamburger buns

Ketchup

Mustard

Sweet onion slices

1. Fire up the grill:

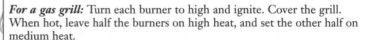

> *For a charcoal grill:* Open the bottom vents. Ignite 6 quarts or 2½ pounds charcoal briquettes or hardwood charcoal. When the coals are hot, set up for a two-level fire: one side high heat (so you can hold your hand 1 to 2 inches above the cooking rack for only 1 to 2 seconds) and the other medium heat (so you can hold your hand 1 to 2 inches above the cooking rack for only 4 to 5 seconds).
>
> *For a gas grill:* Turn each burner to high and ignite. Cover the grill. When hot, leave half the burners on high heat, and set the other half on medium heat.

2. Place ground turkey in a large, clean mixing bowl, and season with salt and black pepper. Add ricotta cheese, Dijon mustard, and Worcestershire sauce. With clean hands, lightly mix seasonings into meat. Gently shape turkey mixture into 6 (¾-inch-thick) patties, being careful not to press too hard.

3. Grill burgers, uncovered, over high heat for 2 minutes per side. *On a charcoal grill:* Move burgers to medium heat, and grill for 12 to 16 minutes total, uncovered, turning every 2 minutes until they reach medium doneness (165°F). *On a gas grill:* Move burgers to medium heat side, and grill 6 to 8 minutes, covered. Turn and grill 6 to 8 more minutes, covered, until they reach medium doneness (165°F). Remove burgers from the grill and let rest for 5 minutes.

4. While hamburgers rest, toast cut sides of buns on the grill for about 2 minutes on high heat. Place hamburgers on buns, and serve immediately, passing ketchup, mustard, and sweet onion slices.

Flame Point

Ricotta cheese burns easily over high heat, so watch the burgers closely to be sure they're just browning nicely.

Gyros Burgers

¾ lb. ground lamb

¾ lb. fresh ground chuck (or 80 percent lean ground beef)

1½ cups fresh breadcrumbs

¼ cup plus 1 TB. minced fresh parsley leaves

1 large egg, lightly beaten

2 small cloves garlic, peeled and minced, or pushed through a garlic press

¾ tsp. ground cumin

1½ tsp. salt

¾ tsp. fresh-ground black pepper or to taste

8 small (4-inch) pita breads

Gyros Sandwich Sauce (recipe follows)

12 Greek black olives (optional)

Serves: 4
Prep time: 15 to 18 minutes
Cook time: 14 to 18 minutes
Serving size: 1 hamburger

1. Fire up the grill:

   For a charcoal grill: Open the bottom vents. Ignite 6 quarts or 2½ pounds charcoal briquettes or hardwood charcoal. When the coals are hot, set up for a two-level fire: one side high heat (so you can hold your hand 1 to 2 inches above the cooking rack for only 1 to 2 seconds) and the other medium heat (so you can hold your hand 1 to 2 inches above the cooking rack for only 4 to 5 seconds).

   For a gas grill: Turn each burner to high and ignite. Cover the grill. When hot, leave half the burners on high heat, and set the other half on medium heat.

2. Place ground lamb and ground chuck in a large, clean mixing bowl. Using a dinner fork, break ground meat into chunks. Add breadcrumbs, parsley, egg, garlic, cumin, salt, and black pepper. Using the fork, mix together until well combined and seasonings are distributed evenly throughout. Gently shape into 4 (½- to ¾-inch-thick) patties.

3. Grill burgers, uncovered, over high heat for 2 minutes per side. *On a charcoal grill:* Move burgers to medium heat and grill 10 to 12 minutes total, turning every 2 minutes, until medium-done (155°F). *On a gas grill:* Move burgers to medium heat and grill, covered, 5 to 6 minutes. Turn burgers and grill, covered, 5 to 6 more minutes until medium-done (155°F). Remove burgers from the grill, and let rest for 5 minutes.

4. While burgers rest, warm pita breads for 2 to 3 minutes on medium heat. Place 1 burger on 1 pita bread, spoon a tablespoon or 2 Gyros Sandwich Sauce over burger, and top with second pita. Serve, garnished with Greek olives (if using).

Barbecue Banter

Pita breads or pita pockets can be split open from the side. You can fill them with sandwich fillings or thin strips of grilled steak. And to make your own fresh breadcrumbs, pulse 2 or 3 slices of white sandwich bread in a food processor until desired crumby-ness.

Gyros Sandwich Sauce

Serves: 8
Prep time: 10 to 12 minutes plus 30 minutes for chilling
Serving size: 1 to 2 tablespoons

¼ cup plus 2 TB. mayonnaise

¼ cup regular plain yogurt (low-fat yogurt may be substituted, nonfat yogurt is not recommended)

½ cup snipped fresh dill

4 green onions, chopped (green parts included)

1 TB. Dijon mustard

1 tsp. distilled white vinegar

½ tsp. granulated sugar

¼ tsp. hot pepper sauce

1. In a medium mixing bowl, whisk together mayonnaise, yogurt, dill, onions, Dijon mustard, vinegar, sugar, and hot pepper sauce until combined.

2. Cover and chill 30 minutes.

Bratwurst Sausage–Flavored "Brat" Burgers

Serves: 6
Prep time: 15 to 18 minutes
Cook time: 14 to 18 minutes
Serving size: 1 hamburger

1 lb. ground pork

1 lb. fresh ground chuck (or 80 percent lean ground beef)

½ cup good-quality cold beer

1¾ tsp. marjoram, crumbled

1½ tsp. dry mustard

1½ tsp. kosher salt

1½ tsp. paprika

¾ tsp. fresh-ground black pepper

¾ tsp. ground caraway seed

⅛ tsp. ground cayenne

6 hamburger buns

Coarse mustard, such as Dijon or German-style

6 sweet onion slices

1. Fire up the grill:

> *For a charcoal grill:* Open the bottom vents. Ignite 6 quarts or 2½ pounds charcoal briquettes or hardwood charcoal. When the coals are hot, set up for a two-level fire: one side high heat (so you can hold your hand 1 to 2 inches above the cooking rack for only 1 to 2 seconds) and the other medium heat (so you can hold your hand 1 to 2 inches above the cooking rack for only 4 to 5 seconds).
>
> *For a gas grill:* Turn each burner to high and ignite. Cover the grill. When hot, leave half the burners on high heat, and set the other half on medium heat.

2. Place ground pork and ground chuck in a large, clean mixing bowl. Using a dinner fork, break meat into chunks. Add beer, marjoram, dry mustard, kosher salt, paprika, black pepper, caraway seed, and cayenne. Using the fork, mix together until well combined and seasonings are distributed evenly throughout. Gently shape into 6 (½- to ¾-inch-thick) patties.

3. Grill burgers, uncovered, over high heat for 2 minutes per side. *On a charcoal grill:* Move burgers to medium heat and grill for 10 to 12 minutes total, turning every 2 minutes, until medium-done (160°F). *On a gas grill:* Move burgers to medium heat and grill, covered, 5 to 6 minutes. Turn burgers and grill, covered, 5 to 6 more minutes until medium-done (160°F). Remove burgers from the grill, and let rest for 5 minutes.

4. While burgers rest, toast cut sides of buns on the grill for about 1 or 2 minutes on high heat. Place each burger on a bun, smear on mustard and add onion slice, top with bun, and serve.

Barbecue Banter

Caraway seeds add a truly terrific flavor to these "brat" burgers. They're also what makes rye bread taste the way it does.

Spicy Chorizo Burgers

2¼ lb. ground pork

⅓ cup red wine vinegar

¼ cup ice water

3 TB. sweet paprika

1 TB. hot paprika

1 TB. hot red pepper flakes

1 TB. kosher salt

2 tsp. dried oregano, crumbled

2 tsp. ground cumin

2 tsp. ground coriander

5 cloves garlic, peeled and minced, or pushed through a garlic press

1 TB. granulated sugar

1 tsp. fresh-ground black pepper

6 good-quality hamburger buns

6 thin slices sweet onion

Serves: 6
Prep time: 24 to 28 minutes
Cook time: 15 to 18 minutes
Serving size: 1 hamburger

1. Fire up the grill:

For a charcoal grill: Open the bottom vents. Ignite 6 quarts or 2½ pounds charcoal briquettes or hardwood charcoal. When the coals are hot, set up for a two-level fire: one side high heat (so you can hold your hand 1 to 2 inches above the cooking rack for only 1 to 2 seconds) and the other medium heat (so you can hold your hand 1 to 2 inches above the cooking rack for only 4 to 5 seconds).

For a gas grill: Turn each burner to high and ignite. Cover the grill. When hot, leave half the burners on high heat, and set the other half on medium heat.

2. Place ground pork in a large, clean mixing bowl, and using a dinner fork, break pork into chunks. Add vinegar, water, sweet paprika, hot paprika, red pepper flakes, kosher salt, oregano, cumin, coriander, garlic, sugar, and black pepper. Using the fork, mix together until well combined and seasonings are distributed evenly throughout. Gently shape into 6 (½- to ¾-inch-thick) patties.

3. Grill burgers, uncovered, over high heat for 2 minutes per side. *On a charcoal grill:* Move burgers to medium heat and grill 12 to 14 minutes total, turning every 2 minutes, until they reach the high side of medium-done (160°F). *On a gas grill:* Move burgers to medium heat and grill, covered, 5 to 6 minutes. Turn and grill, covered, 5 to 6 more minutes until they reach the high side of medium-done (160°F). Remove burgers from the grill, and let rest for 5 minutes.

4. While burgers rest, toast cut sides of buns on the grill for about 1 to 2 minutes on high heat. Place burgers on buns, top with onion slices, and serve.

Barbecue Banter

If you live near a local bakery, stop by and see what variety they have in buns and rolls that could make a difference in your hamburgers.

Sweet Chinatown Pork Burgers

Serves: 6
Prep time: 20 minutes
Cook time: 13 to 16 minutes
Serving size: 1 hamburger

2¼ lb. ground pork

2 TB. firmly packed light brown sugar

2 TB. Scotch whisky

1½ TB. soy sauce plus additional for passing

1½ TB. water

2 tsp. dry sherry

1 TB. plus 1 tsp. kosher salt

¾ tsp. Chinese five-spice powder

6 good-quality hamburger buns

1 bunch green onions, roots trimmed, washed, and chopped

1. Fire up the grill:

For a charcoal grill: Open the bottom vents. Ignite 6 quarts or 2½ pounds charcoal briquettes or hardwood charcoal. When the coals are hot, set up for a two-level fire: one side high heat (so you can hold your hand 1 to 2 inches above the cooking rack for only 1 to 2 seconds) and the other medium heat (so you can hold your hand 1 to 2 inches above the cooking rack for only 4 to 5 seconds).

For a gas grill: Turn each burner to high and ignite. Cover the grill. When hot, leave half the burners on high heat, and set the other half on medium heat.

2. Place ground pork in a large, clean mixing bowl. Using a dinner fork, break pork into chunks. Add sugar, Scotch, soy sauce, water, sherry, kosher salt, and Chinese five-spice powder. Using the fork, mix together until well combined and seasonings are distributed evenly throughout. Gently shape into 6 (½- to ¾-inch-thick) patties.

3. Grill burgers, uncovered, over high heat for 2 minutes per side. *On a charcoal grill:* Move burgers to medium heat and grill 10 to 12 minutes total, turning every 2 minutes, until they reach the high side of medium-done (160°F). *On a gas grill:* Move burgers to medium heat and grill, covered, 5 to 6 minutes. Turn and grill, covered, 5 to 6 more minutes until they reach the high side of medium-done (160°F). Remove burgers from the grill, and let rest for 5 minutes.

4. While burgers rest, toast hamburger buns on grill for about 1 or 2 minutes on high heat. Place burgers on buns, top with chopped green onions, and serve, passing soy sauce.

Barbecue Banter

If you're watching your sodium intake, consider substituting reduced-sodium soy sauce for regular soy sauce.

West Indies–Flavored Pork Burgers

1½ lb. lean ground pork

1½ TB. grated lime zest

1½ tsp. dried thyme, crumbled

¾ tsp. ground allspice

¾ tsp. crushed red pepper

½ tsp. salt

8 slices French bread (4-inch diameter), ¾ inch thick

1 TB. olive oil

1 medium red onion, cut into ¼-inch slices

Serves: 4
Prep time: 20 minutes
Cook time: 13 to 16 minutes
Serving size: 1 hamburger

1. Fire up the grill:

For a charcoal grill: Open the bottom vents. Ignite 6 quarts or 2½ pounds charcoal briquettes or hardwood charcoal. When the coals are hot, set up for a two-level fire: one side high heat (so you can hold your hand 1 to 2 inches above the cooking rack for only 1 to 2 seconds) and the other medium heat (so you can hold your hand 1 to 2 inches above the cooking rack for only 4 to 5 seconds).

For a gas grill: Turn each burner to high and ignite. Cover the grill. When hot, leave half the burners on high heat, and set the other half on medium heat.

2. Place ground pork in a large, clean mixing bowl. Using a dinner fork, break pork into chunks. Add lime zest, thyme, allspice, crushed red pepper, and salt. Using the fork, mix ingredients until well combined and seasonings are distributed evenly throughout. Gently shape into 6 (½- to ¾-inch-thick) patties.

3. Grill burgers, uncovered, over high heat for 2 minutes per side. *On a charcoal grill:* Move burgers to medium heat and grill 10 to 12 minutes total, turning every 2 minutes, until they reach the high side of medium-done (160°F). *On a gas grill:* Move burgers to medium heat and grill, covered, 5 to 6 minutes. Turn and grill 5 to 6 minutes, covered, until they reach the high side of medium-done (160°F). Remove burgers from the grill, and let rest for 5 minutes.

4. While burgers rest, toast bread slices on the grill for about 1 or 2 minutes per side on high heat. Brush one cut side of bread only with olive oil. Place burgers on brushed side of bread, top each burger with sliced onion, top with brushed side of bread, and serve.

Barbecue Banter

Be sure the dried herbs and spices you use are as fresh as possible.

Jamaican Jerk Chicken Burgers

Serves: 6
Prep time: 20 minutes
Cook time: 13 to 16 minutes
Serving size: 1 hamburger

2 tsp. granulated sugar

1½ tsp. dried thyme, crumbled

1½ tsp. onion powder

1 tsp. fresh-ground black pepper

1 tsp. ground allspice

1 tsp. cayenne

½ tsp. salt

¼ tsp. ground nutmeg

Pinch of ground cloves

2¼ lb. (80 to 85 percent lean) ground chicken

12 slices sourdough bread

2 TB. olive oil

¼ cup fresh-squeezed lemon juice (from about 2 lemons)

1. Fire up the grill:

For a charcoal grill: Open the bottom vents. Ignite 6 quarts or 2½ pounds charcoal briquettes or hardwood charcoal. When the coals are hot, set up for a two-level fire: one side high heat (so you can hold your hand 1 to 2 inches above the cooking rack for only 1 to 2 seconds) and the other medium heat (so you can hold your hand 1 to 2 inches above the cooking rack for only 4 to 5 seconds).

For a gas grill: Turn each burner to high and ignite. Cover the grill. When hot, leave half the burners on high heat, and set the other half on medium heat.

2. In a medium mixing bowl, stir together sugar, thyme, onion powder, black pepper, allspice, cayenne, salt, nutmeg, and cloves until combined.

3. With clean hands, gently shape ground chicken into 6 (¾-inch-thick) patties, being careful not to press too hard. Coat the top and bottom of patties with spice mixture. As each is completed, set burgers on a clean plate or tray.

4. Grill burgers, uncovered, over high heat for 2 minutes per side. *On a charcoal grill:* Move burgers to medium heat and grill 10 to 12 minutes total, turning every 2 minutes, until they reach the high side of medium-done (165°F). *On a gas grill:* Move burgers to medium heat and grill, covered, 5 to 6 minutes. Turn and grill, covered, 5 to 6 more minutes until they reach the high side of medium-done (165°F). Remove burgers from the grill, and let rest for 5 minutes.

5. While burgers rest, toast sourdough bread slices on the grill for about 1 or 2 minutes per side on high heat. Brush one side of 6 toasted bread slices with olive oil, place chicken burger on bread, drizzle 1 teaspoon lemon juice on each burger, brush remaining bread slices with olive oil, and top with second bread slice, oil side down. Serve.

Barbecue Banter

You can now find good-quality olive oils at your local supermarket. Some of the good but less-expensive olive oils come from Spain and Greece, so give them some consideration, too. California produces some excellent olive oils, but they're mostly short-run, "boutique" oils with higher price tags.

Homemade Veggie Burger

Serves: 6
Prep time: 20 minutes
Cook time: 11 to 12 minutes
Serving size: 1 hamburger

1 TB. vegetable oil, plus additional for brushing on burgers and grill

½ cup diced yellow (not sweet) onion

2 cups (or 1 15-oz.] can) cooked black beans, drained and rinsed

2 cups shredded Monterey Jack cheese

1 cup cooked brown rice

1½ cups fresh breadcrumbs

½ cup chopped green onion, white and green parts

1½ tsp. tomato paste

1 tsp. soy sauce

1½ tsp. garlic powder

1½ tsp. dried oregano, crumbled or 1 TB. fresh oregano leaves, chopped fine

¼ to ½ tsp. ground cayenne

1 tsp. ground cumin

½ tsp. fresh-ground black pepper

6 whole grain, whole-wheat hamburger buns

Ketchup

Yellow mustard

Sweet relish

Bottled horseradish

Lettuce

Ripe tomato slices

1. Heat oil in a skillet over medium-high heat. Add onion and cook 5 to 6 minutes, stirring occasionally, until lightly browned. Transfer onion to a large mixing bowl.

2. To onion, add black beans, Monterey Jack cheese, rice, breadcrumbs, green onion, tomato paste, soy sauce, garlic powder, oregano, cayenne, cumin, and pepper. Mix well, mashing beans with a fork (or a potato masher, if you have one).

3. Working with clean hands or a burger press, mold burgers into 6 patties. Cover and chill.

4. Fire up the grill:

> *For a charcoal grill:* Open the bottom vents. Ignite 6 quarts or 2½ pounds charcoal briquettes or hardwood charcoal. When the coals are hot, set up for a one-level medium-heat fire (so you can hold your hand 5 inches above the cooking rack for only 4 to 5 seconds).
>
> *For a gas grill:* Turn each burner to high and ignite. Cover the grill. When hot, set the burners to medium heat.

5. Brush tops of burgers with oil. *On a charcoal grill:* Brush the grill rack with oil. Grill burgers, oiled side down, uncovered, 4 minutes. Brush tops of burgers with oil, turn burgers, and grill 4 more minutes or until golden. *On a gas grill:* Brush the grill rack with oil. Grill burgers, oiled side down, uncovered, 4 or 5 minutes. Brush tops of burgers with oil, turn burgers, and grill 4 or 5 more minutes or until golden.

6. While burgers grill, toast cut sides of buns on grill for about 3 or 4 minutes. Place burgers on bottom of buns and serve, passing ketchup, mustard, relish, horseradish, lettuce and tomato slices.

Variation: For an extra flavor kick, substitute an equal amount of shredded processed cheddar or processed Swiss cheese for the Monterey Jack cheese.

Barbecue Banter

If your veggie burgers don't stick together well, mix in 2 tablespoons water and try to form another patty. These burgers stay formed better if they're refrigerated, covered, for at least 30 minutes before they head to the grill.

Barbecue Banter

A burger press easily and quickly forms ground beef into the same size and weight hamburgers. I usually don't recommend them because they "press" (read "squeeze") the meat to force it into the mold, which compresses the meat, producing less than desirable end results. However, compressing these all-vegetable burgers is not bad, because you want them to hang together well from forming to serving. The size of your hamburger press may produce more than 6 burgers; adjust grill time.

Teriyaki Turkey Burgers

1 large egg, beaten

½ cup soft breadcrumbs

½ cup (from about ½ (8-oz.) can) chopped water chestnuts

2 TB. chopped onions

2 TB. bottled teriyaki sauce

1½ lb. (80 to 85 percent lean) ground turkey

¼ cup apricot preserves

1 tsp. sesame seeds

4 good-quality round sandwich or hamburger buns

Serves: 4
Prep time: 18 to 20 minutes
Cook time: 14 to 18 minutes
Serving size: 1 hamburger

1. Fire up the grill:

> *For a charcoal grill:* Open the bottom vents. Ignite 6 quarts or 2½ pounds charcoal briquettes or hardwood charcoal. When the coals are hot, set up for a two-level fire: one side high heat (so you can hold your hand 1 to 2 inches above the cooking rack for only 1 to 2 seconds) and the other medium heat (so you can hold your hand 1 to 2 inches above the cooking rack for only 4 to 5 seconds).
>
> *For a gas grill:* Turn each burner to high and ignite. Cover the grill. When hot, leave half the burners on high heat, and set the other half on medium heat.

Barbecue Banter

Can't find apricot preserves? Peach preserves or peach jam works just as well and so will plum and even orange marmalade.

2. In a medium, clean mixing bowl, stir together egg, breadcrumbs, water chestnuts, onions, and 1 tablespoon teriyaki sauce. Add ground turkey, and with clean hands, lightly mix seasonings into meat. Gently shape into 4 (¾-inch-thick) patties. (Mixture will be soft.)

3. Place a small saucepan over medium-low heat, and stir together apricot preserves, remaining 1 tablespoon teriyaki sauce, and sesame seeds. Stir occasionally until preserves melt. Remove from heat, and take sauce to the grill along with a spoon, turkey burgers, and buns.

4. Grill burgers, uncovered, over high heat for 2 minutes per side. *On a charcoal grill:* Move burgers to medium heat and grill 12 to 16 minutes total, turning every 2 minutes, until medium-done (165°F.). *On a gas grill:* Move burgers to medium heat and grill, covered, 7 to 9 minutes. Turn burgers and grill 7 to 9 more minutes, covered, until medium-done (165°F.). Remove burgers from the grill and let rest for 5 minutes.

5. While turkey burgers rest, toast cut sides of buns on the grill for about 1 to 2 minutes on high heat. Place turkey burgers on buns, spoon apricot sauce over burgers, and serve.

Chapter

10

Hot Diggity Dogs and Other Sausages

In This Chapter

- ◆ A closer look at hot dogs
- ◆ Sausage: tips on finding the best (or making your own!)
- ◆ Food safety

For years now, hot dogs and hamburgers have fought a popularity contest. Who's winning is not quite certain, but the numbers are astounding: on the Fourth of July alone, Americans eat 150 million hot dogs. But that's a mere fraction of the 20 billion hot dogs Americans are expected to eat this year.

More than half of the folks who eat hot dogs prefer them grilled. Sure, you can cook hot dogs in boiling water, but what's the sense in that when the water doesn't add anything except heat? Grilling a hot dog doesn't just heat a hot dog; it adds the flavor of the grill and crisps the outside. No wonder it's the preferred cooking method!

And that's why you're here. In this chapter, you'll find out how to grill and dress some of the best hot dogs in the world.

America's Favorite: The Hot Dog

Ever wonder what actually makes a hot dog a hot dog? I did, so I searched for a recipe so I could make one at home. Let me tell you, finding a recipe for making a homemade hot dog is almost impossible. Even though a hot dog is classified as a sausage, its texture is quite different from most sausages (except bologna and a couple others). It's very smooth, not rough like, say, an Italian sausage, so just getting that texture right at home would be hard. (I mean, who makes homemade bologna?) But handling that smooth filling requires careful temperature control. It's too much hassle for the home chef.

Hot dogs are made by first grinding together pork butt and beef chuck. Then it's seasoned with salt, sweet paprika, dry mustard, garlic, black pepper, coriander, mace (nutmeglike flavor), cardamom, and cumin. Ta-da, you have that hot dog flavor!

Barbecue Banter _____

Standard ball park dogs aren't the only dogs available. Next to regular hot dogs, the most popular has to be the all-beef or kosher hot dog. All-beef hot dogs taste meatier, and some folks won't eat any other kind than all-beef (fretting over the old phrase about pork hot dogs containing: "Everything but the oink"). Plus you can find chicken and turkey franks for those who prefer a lighter, lower-fat hot dog. Natural hot dogs don't contain any artificial color or flavor and don't use sodium nitrate or nitrite in the curing process. Finally, fat-free hot dogs are made from a combination of pork and turkey and are okay for a restricted food plan, but end up being a pale relation of the all-mighty hot dog.

What defines a great hot dog varies from person to person. Some like hot dogs in a crisp casing that snaps when they bite into it; others prefer skinless hot dogs that don't snap when bitten. Some like their spices cranked up a notch; others prefer a nice, mild hot dog.

Your local supermarket can be a good source for mainstream hot dogs. They come in a wide variety of sizes, lengths, flavors, meats, etc. so you'll probably be able to find something that satisfies everybody at home. If you like a more authentic hot dog, head to your closest butcher shop. Usually a butcher shop carries hot dogs you'll never see in a supermarket. Also check your local natural or health food store. Although you'll find soy dogs—ugh—you'll also find butcher shop–like hot dogs.

You can also find meat companies and butcher shops on the web who'll ship superior hot dogs right to your front door. Just search for "hot dogs" and see what happens.

Barbecue Banter

Grilling a great hot dog is one thing, but the toppings are, as they say, the icing on the cake. Universally, ketchup is for hamburgers and mustard is for hot dogs. You can also try sweet pickle relish, dill pickle relish, mustard relish (a combination), dill pickle slices, dill pickle spears, chopped onions, sport peppers (hot), pepperoncini (hot but not as hot as sport peppers), sauerkraut, halved thin tomato slices, and celery salt. With the right kind and the right proportions, your condiments will put the shine on your hot dog's shoes.

The Hot Dog's Cousin: Sausage

Next to the hot dog, sausage is also a popular grill item. Whether you're having a backyard picnic or cooking for a get-together, grilled sausages are always a winner.

Making your own homemade sausage allows you to control the ingredients—and put in any special seasonings you prefer. And it's not as hard as you might think.

When folks used to make homemade sausage, they first clamped their hand-cranked meat grinder to the kitchen counter, dropped in cubes of meat, and turned the crank to produce ground meat. Today, you can buy a variety of already-ground meats such as beef, pork, lamb, bison, ostrich, chicken, and turkey that will get homemade sausages on your grill in no time at all.

You can use your hands to mix together the meat and seasoning, but I prefer using a fork. You'll be amazed at how quickly a fork breaks up ground meat and mixes in all the seasonings. However, you will use your hands to form the newly seasoned and mixed sausage into patties. But handle the meat gingerly because overhandling while making patties will create tough, compressed, probably dry grilled sausage.

Flame Point

When making your own sausage, because you're going to be handling raw meat, wash your hands well with warm soapy water, rinse them even better, and dry them with a clean paper towel. If you're also handling hot peppers when making sausage, follow the same procedure after working with the peppers, especially before touching your eyes or face. When working with hot peppers, it's also highly recommended that you wear rubber gloves.

If you're not up to making your own sausage, you can, of course, purchase some. Depending on where it comes from and how it's made, commercially prepared sausage can save you time and aggravation. There's been sort of a renaissance in sausage, brought about mainly by Bruce Aidells, whose wonderful Aidells Sausage you can likely find in your supermarket. This sausage beats almost all commercially available sausage by a mile.

You can also find decent commercial sausage at some health food or natural food stores. It'll probably have more fat and calories than homemade sausage, though. A butcher shop is also a great place to find sausage. I once lived down the street from a butcher shop in Chicago where they made several different kinds of sausage right there in the shop.

Sausage Safety

Once you've made up a bunch of sausage patties, how are going to keep them, especially during those warm summer months? It's easy: freeze them. After you've formed your sausage patties, wrap each of 2 to 4 (some patties may be larger than others) sausage patties in plastic wrap and then seal them all in a 1-quart reclosable freezer bag, and freeze. They should keep, well frozen, for at least 90 days. Oh, and don't forget to use a permanent marker to clearly mark the sausage's name and the day's date.

Doggoned-Good Classic Dog

8 to 10 high-quality hot dogs

8 to 10 bakery-quality hot dog buns

Yellow ballpark mustard

Sweet pickle relish (optional)

Sliced dill pickles (optional)

Chopped onions (optional)

Ketchup (optional)

Serves: 4 or 5
Prep time: 3 to 5 minutes
Cook time: 4 to 7 minutes
Serving size: 2 hot dogs

1. Fire up the grill:

> *For a charcoal grill:* Open the bottom vents. Ignite 6 quarts or 2½ pounds charcoal briquettes or hardwood charcoal. When the coals are hot, set up for a one-level high-heat fire (so you can hold your hand 5 inches above cooking rack for only 1 to 2 seconds).
>
> *For a gas grill:* Turn each burner to high and ignite. Cover the grill. When hot, leave the burners on high heat.

2. *On a charcoal or gas grill:* Place hot dogs on the grill rack over hot coals or heat and grill, uncovered, 3 to 5 minutes, rolling over to cook evenly until a deep brown. While hot dogs cook, place buns, cut side down, on the grill and toast for 1 or 2 minutes until lightly browned.

3. Arrange buns on a large plate or platter, and place cooked hot dogs in toasted buns. Serve, passing sweet pickle relish, sliced dill pickles, chopped onions, and ketchup (if using).

Barbecue Banter

Condiments really do make the hot dog. Ever have just a plain hot dog in a bun? Sure, it's possible, but it's more fun with the relish, ketchup, onions—or whatever you want to add.

"Chicawgo" Hot Dogs

8 (2-oz.) all-beef hot dogs

8 poppyseed hot dog buns or other bakery-style hot dog buns

Dill pickle spears

Yellow ballpark mustard

Chopped onions

Thin slices, red-ripe tomato cut in half

Celery salt

Sport peppers or pepperoncini (optional)

Serves: 4
Prep time: 5 minutes
Cook time: 4 to 7 minutes
Serving size: 2 hot dogs

1. Fire up the grill:

For a charcoal grill: Open the bottom vents. Ignite 6 quarts or 2½ pounds charcoal briquettes or hardwood charcoal. When the coals are hot, set up for a one-level high-heat fire (so you can hold your hand 5 inches above cooking rack for only 1 to 2 seconds).

For a gas grill: Turn each burner to high and ignite. Cover the grill. When hot, leave the burners on high heat.

2. *On a charcoal or gas grill:* Place hot dogs on the grill rack over hot coals or heat and grill, uncovered, 3 to 5 minutes, rolling over to cook evenly until a deep brown. While hot dogs cook, place buns, cut side down, on the grill and toast for 1 or 2 minutes until lightly browned.

3. Place grilled hot dogs in toasted buns, slide a dill pickle spear next to hot dog, squirt on mustard, distribute onions evenly over hot dog, lay 3 half-round tomato slices on top of onions, dust with celery salt, serve, passing sport peppers or pepperoncini (if using).

Barbecue Banter _____

If you have a local butcher shop, see if it carries its own old-fashioned hot dogs. These usually have a spicier flavor profile and crisp skins you'll enjoy as a change of pace from soft, mild-flavored supermarket hot dogs.

Old-Fashioned Cheese and Bacon Dogs with BBQ Sauce

Serves: 8
Prep time: 30 to 35 minutes
Cook time: 10 to 13 minutes
Serving size: 1 hot dog

1 (8-oz.) can tomato sauce

¼ cup chopped onion

1 TB. Dijon mustard

1 tsp. granulated sugar

1 tsp. fresh lemon juice

¼ tsp. garlic powder

8 good-quality hot dogs

8 slices lean bacon

8 good-quality hot dog buns

8 (¾-oz.) slices American processed or sharp processed cheese

1. In a medium saucepan over medium heat, stir together tomato sauce, onion, Dijon mustard, sugar, lemon juice, and garlic powder. Bring to a boil, reduce heat, and cook at a low simmer, covered, about 15 minutes or until onion is tender. Remove from heat and set aside.

Barbecue Banter
The better the quality of bacon and cheese, the better this hot dog becomes.

2. Fire up the grill:

   For a charcoal grill: Open the bottom vents. Ignite 6 quarts or 2½ pounds charcoal briquettes or hardwood charcoal. When the coals are hot, set up for a one-level medium-heat fire (so you can hold your hand 5 inches above cooking rack for only 1 to 2 seconds).

   For a gas grill: Turn each burner to high and ignite. Cover the grill. When hot, leave half the burners on high heat, and set the other burners to medium heat.

3. While grill starts: starting at the top of each hot dog, secure 1 bacon slice to each hot dog with a toothpick and then roll bacon, in a spiral, around hot dog to the bottom, securing with another toothpick.

4. *On a charcoal grill:* Place hot dogs on the grill rack over medium coals, and grill, uncovered, 8 to 10 minutes, rolling hot dogs over to cook evenly until bacon is light brown and crisp and hot dogs are heated through. *On a gas grill:* Place hot dogs on the medium-heat rack and grill, covered, 10 to 12 minutes or until bacon is light brown and crisp and hot dogs are heated through. *On a charcoal or gas grill:* While hot dogs cook, place buns, cut side down, on the grill and toast for 2 or 3 minutes until lightly browned. Place a cheese slice in each toasted bun on a tray, cut-side up.

5. As each hot dog finishes cooking, remove and discard toothpicks, and place cooked hot dog on cheese in bun. Spoon a tablespoon or more sauce over each hot dog, and serve, passing more sauce.

New York–Style Red Hots

Serves: 8
Prep time: 5 to 7 minutes
Cook time: 4 to 7 minutes
Serving size: 1 hot dog

8 hot dogs (look for Coney Island–style hot dogs)

8 good-quality hot dog buns

Yellow ballpark mustard

Chopped onions

1 cup sauerkraut, rinsed under cold water and well drained (preferably packaged in plastic pouch, not canned)

1. Fire up the grill:

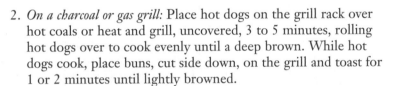

For a charcoal grill: Open the bottom vents. Ignite 6 quarts or 2½ pounds charcoal briquettes or hardwood charcoal. When the coals are hot, set up for a one-level high-heat fire (so you can hold your hand 5 inches above cooking rack for only 1 to 2 seconds).

For a gas grill: Turn each burner to high and ignite. Cover the grill. When hot, leave the burners on high heat.

 Flame Point ___

Don't become the neighborhood "weenie." When grilling over high heat, it's easy to overcook a hot dog and end up with a "char" dog. Keep a tenacious eye on your hot dogs as they cook, and continue moving them over the coals until they're just done.

2. *On a charcoal or gas grill:* Place hot dogs on the grill rack over hot coals or heat and grill, uncovered, 3 to 5 minutes, rolling hot dogs over to cook evenly until a deep brown. While hot dogs cook, place buns, cut side down, on the grill and toast for 1 or 2 minutes until lightly browned.

3. Place grilled hot dogs in toasted buns, squirt on mustard, distribute onions evenly over hot dogs, top each with about 2 tablespoons sauerkraut, and serve.

Brewed Brats with Kraut for a Crowd

6 (12-oz.) cans full-flavored beer

1 large sweet onion, peeled and sliced

2 medium bay leaves

12 whole black peppercorns

12 (4- to 5-oz.) fresh uncooked bratwursts

12 bakery-quality, whole-wheat hot dog–style buns

Coarse Dijon mustard

Chopped onion

6 cups (about 2 lb.) sauerkraut, rinsed and drained (preferably packaged in plastic pouch, not canned)

Serves: 12
Prep time: 15 to 20 minutes
Cook time: 8 to 10 minutes
Serving size: 1 brat

1. Fire up the grill:

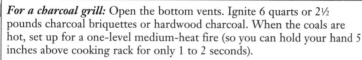

> *For a charcoal grill:* Open the bottom vents. Ignite 6 quarts or 2½ pounds charcoal briquettes or hardwood charcoal. When the coals are hot, set up for a one-level medium-heat fire (so you can hold your hand 5 inches above cooking rack for only 1 to 2 seconds).
>
> *For a gas grill:* Turn each burner to high and ignite. Cover the grill. When hot, leave half the burners on high heat, and set the other burners to medium heat.

2. Open and add beer to a large saucepan, and place over high heat. Stir in onion, bay leaves, and black peppercorns. With the tines of a dinner fork, poke several holes all around each bratwurst, and add to the saucepan. Bring to a boil, reduce heat to low, and simmer, gently stirring occasionally, for 10 minutes. Remove brats from cooking liquid, and lay out on a plate or tray for grilling. Reserve 2 cups warm beer liquid, and discard the rest.

3. *On a charcoal or gas grill:* Place bratwursts on the grill rack over hot coals and grill, uncovered, basting frequently with the reserved beer, 8 to 10 minutes, rolling sausages over to cook evenly, until a golden brown. While brats cook, place buns, cut side down, on the grill and toast for 2 or 3 minutes until lightly browned.

4. Place cooked bratwursts in toasted buns, squirt on mustard, add chopped onions and sauerkraut, and serve, passing more mustard.

Barbecue Banter

Bratwurst comes in two varieties: uncooked bratwursts, which are pink and look like overgrown breakfast sausage links, and cooked bratwursts, which are white. It's best to use uncooked brats in this recipe because once they're cooked, they won't absorb any of the beer and only a little beer flavor.

Spicy South Texas Sausage Sandwich

Serves: 10
Prep time: 28 to 30 minutes plus 1 hour for chilling
Cook time: 13 to 17 minutes
Serving size: 1 sausage sandwich

1¼ lb. fresh ground beef chuck (or 85-percent lean ground beef)

1¼ lb. ground pork

¾ cup good-quality dark beer, imported or domestic

4 cloves garlic, peeled and minced, or pushed through a garlic press

1 TB. kosher salt

1 TB. ground chili powder

1 TB. sweet paprika

1 TB. ground cumin

2 tsp. granulated sugar

1 tsp. coarse-ground black pepper

1 tsp. crushed red pepper flakes

⅛ tsp. ground cinnamon

⅛ tsp. ground cloves

6 good-quality hamburger buns

Thinly sliced sweet onion

1. Place ground beef chuck and ground pork in a large, clean mixing bowl. Using a dinner fork, break meat into chunks. Add beer, garlic, salt, chili powder, paprika, cumin, sugar, black pepper, red pepper flakes, cinnamon, and cloves. Using the fork, mix together until well combined and seasonings are distributed evenly throughout. For the best flavor, cover and chill sausage mixture for 1 hour.

2. Fire up the grill:

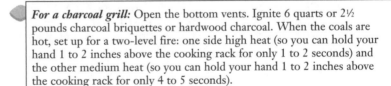

For a charcoal grill: Open the bottom vents. Ignite 6 quarts or 2½ pounds charcoal briquettes or hardwood charcoal. When the coals are hot, set up for a two-level fire: one side high heat (so you can hold your hand 1 to 2 inches above the cooking rack for only 1 to 2 seconds) and the other medium heat (so you can hold your hand 1 to 2 inches above the cooking rack for only 4 to 5 seconds).

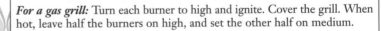

For a gas grill: Turn each burner to high and ignite. Cover the grill. When hot, leave half the burners on high, and set the other half on medium.

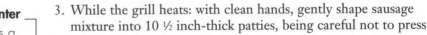

Barbecue Banter

Dark beer has a robust flavor, with molasses undertones that add complexity to this sausage mixture. I like Newcastle Brown Ale, but feel free to use whatever dark beer you like.

3. While the grill heats: with clean hands, gently shape sausage mixture into 10 ½ inch-thick patties, being careful not to press too hard.

4. Grill sausage patties, uncovered, over high heat for 2 to 3 minutes per side. *On a charcoal grill:* Move sausage patties to medium heat, and grill 10 to 12 minutes total, turning every 2 minutes or until instant-read thermometer inserted horizontally into patty's center registers 160°F for medium. *On a gas grill:* Move sausage patties to medium heat, and grill, covered, 10 to 12 minutes, turning once halfway through, until instant-read thermometer inserted

horizontally into patty's center registers 160°F for medium. Remove sausages from the grill, and let rest for 5 minutes.

5. Lightly toast cut sides of buns on the grill's high heat side about 1 to 2 minutes. Place cooked patties on buns, and serve immediately, passing sliced sweet onions.

Jalapeño Sausage Roll-Ups

1 lb. ground pork

1 (4-oz.) can jalapeño peppers, drained and chopped

2 TB. chopped fresh cilantro

2 TB. good-quality beer

1 tsp. ground cumin

1 clove garlic, peeled and minced, or pushed through a garlic press

½ tsp. salt

¼ tsp. fresh-ground black pepper

¼ tsp. ground cayenne

4 (8-inch) whole-wheat flour tortillas

Sour cream

Shredded lettuce

Serves: 4
Prep time: 18 to 20 minutes plus 1 hour for chilling
Cook time: 18 to 22 minutes
Serving size: 1 roll-up

1. Place ground pork in a large, clean mixing bowl. Using a dinner fork, break pork into chunks. Add jalapeño peppers, cilantro, beer, cumin, garlic, salt, pepper, and cayenne. Using the fork, mix together until well combined and seasonings are distributed evenly throughout. Cover and chill sausage mixture for 1 hour.

2. Fire up the grill:

> **For a charcoal grill:** Open the bottom vents. Ignite 6 quarts or 2½ pounds charcoal briquettes or hardwood charcoal. When the coals are hot, set up for a two-level fire: one side high heat (so you can hold your hand 1 to 2 inches above cooking rack for only 1 to 2 seconds) and the other medium heat (so you can hold your hand 1 to 2 inches above cooking rack for only 4 to 5 seconds).
>
> **For a gas grill:** Turn each burner to high and ignite. Cover the grill. When hot, leave half the burners on high heat, and set the other half on medium heat.

3. With clean hands, gently shape sausage mixture into 4 (6-inch-long) logs and place on small plate. Stack tortillas, wrap them in foil, and set aside.

4. Grill sausages, uncovered, over high heat for 8 to 10 minutes, turning over every 1 or 2 minutes. *On a charcoal grill:* Move sausages to medium heat, and grill 10 to 12 minutes total, turning every 2 minutes or until an instant-read thermometer inserted horizontally into sausage's center registers 160°F for medium. *On a gas grill:* Move sausage patties to medium heat, and grill, covered, 10 to 12 minutes, turning every 2 minutes, until an instant-read thermometer inserted horizontally into sausage's center registers 160°F for medium. *On a charcoal or gas grill:* Move sausages to the coolest part of the grill, place tortilla packet over medium coals or heat, cover, and grill 5 to 10 minutes until warm. Remove sausages from the grill, and let rest for 5 minutes.

5. When tortillas are ready, place 1 sausage at the end of 1 tortilla, spoon on sour cream, sprinkle with shredded lettuce, roll up, and serve.

Barbecue Banter

When purchasing a package of tortillas, you will usually get more than you immediately need. But many recipes call for roll-ups, and most use 8-inch flour tortillas, so it won't take much looking to find another recipe to use up your remaining tortillas.

One Great Sausage Sandwich

Serves: 6
Prep time: 5 minutes
Cook time: 20 to 25 minutes
Serving size: 1 sandwich

6 (4 oz.) fresh uncooked sweet or hot Italian sausages

6 Italian rolls or pieces of Italian bread cut into 6-inch lengths

6 thin slices provolone cheese, at room temperature

2 pt. prepared creamy cabbage slaw

1. Fire up the grill:

> *For a charcoal grill:* Open the bottom vents. Ignite 6 quarts or 2½ pounds charcoal briquettes or hardwood charcoal. When the coals are hot, set up for a two-level fire: one side high heat (so you can hold your hand 1 to 2 inches above cooking rack for only 1 to 2 seconds) and the other medium heat (so you can hold your hand 1 to 2 inches above cooking rack for only 4 to 5 seconds).
>
> *For a gas grill:* Turn each burner to high and ignite. Cover the grill. When hot, leave half the burners on high heat, and set the other half on medium heat.

Barbecue Banter

Fresh, uncooked sausages take longer to cook than hot dog–like sausages. You basically just have to warm up a hot dog; you have to cook a sausage all the way to the center.

2. Grill sausages, uncovered, over high heat 6 to 8 minutes, turning over every 1 or 2 minutes. *On a charcoal grill:* Move sausages to medium heat, and grill 14 to 17 minutes total, turning every 2 minutes or until an instant-read thermometer inserted horizontally into center registers 160°F for medium.

On a gas grill: Move sausages to medium heat, and grill, covered, 14 to 17 minutes, turning every 3 minutes, until an instant-read thermometer inserted horizontally into center registers 160°F for medium. Remove sausages from the grill, and let rest for 5 minutes.

3. Place rolls or bread cut side down over the grill's high heat, and toast 2 or 3 minutes. Lay cheese slices on toasted rolls or bread, arrange sausages on top of cheese and top with slaw. Serve immediately.

New York "Street Food" Sausage Sandwiches

4 (about 1 lb.) uncooked sweet Italian sausage links

4 TB. coarse-grain Dijon mustard

1 TB. water

2 green, yellow, and/or red sweet bell peppers, seeds and ribs discarded, and quartered lengthwise

¼ cup mayonnaise or salad dressing

4 (6-inch) French-style rolls, split

Serves: 4	
Prep time: 17 to 19 minutes	
Cook time: 12 to 15 minutes	
Serving size: 1 sandwich	

1. With a fork, prick several holes in each sausage link. In a large saucepan, combine sausage and enough water to cover. Bring to a boil, reduce heat to low and simmer, covered, for 5 minutes and drain.

2. Fire up the grill:

For a charcoal grill: Open the bottom vents. Ignite 6 quarts or 2½ pounds charcoal briquettes or hardwood charcoal. When the coals are hot, set up for a one-level medium-heat fire (so you can hold your hand 5 inches above coals for only 4 to 5 seconds).

For a gas grill: Turn each burner to high and ignite. Cover the grill. When hot, set all burners to medium heat.

3. In a small bowl, combine 2 tablespoons mustard and water; set aside.

Lean Note

One tablespoon mayonnaise delivers a whopping 100 calories and 11 fat grams. One tablespoon reduced-fat mayonnaise delivers just 25 calories and 2 fat grams—and most people can't tell the difference!

4. *On a charcoal or gas grill:* Grill sausage and sweet peppers on the rack of an uncovered grill directly over medium coals or heat for 10 to 12 minutes or until sausage is evenly browned and juices run clear, turning and brushing sausage and peppers once with mustard mixture halfway through grilling. Remove sausage and peppers from grill.

5. Lightly toast cut sides of rolls over coals about 2 to 3 minutes.

6. In a small bowl, combine remaining 2 tablespoons mustard and mayonnaise. Spread mustard mixture on cut sides of toasted rolls. Divide sausage and peppers evenly among rolls, cut sandwiches in half, and serve.

Apple-Flavored Chicken Sausage

Serves: 4
Prep time: 20 minutes
Cook time: 12 to 15 minutes
Serving size: 1 sausage patty

1½ lb. regular ground chicken

¼ cup plus 2 TB. apple juice

1 small apple, rinsed, cut in quarters, cored, and chopped

2 tsp. kosher salt

1 tsp. fresh-ground black pepper

1 tsp. dried sage, crumbled

⅛ tsp. ground ginger

Pinch ground cinnamon

Pinch ground nutmeg

1 chicken bouillon cube dissolved in 2 TB. boiling apple juice

1. Place ground chicken in a large clean bowl, and using a dinner fork, break into chunks. Add apple juice, apple, kosher salt, pepper, sage, ginger, cinnamon, nutmeg, and bouillon broth. Mix until well combined and seasonings are distributed evenly throughout.

2. Fire up the grill:

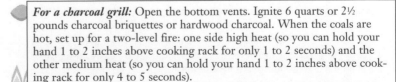

For a charcoal grill: Open the bottom vents. Ignite 6 quarts or 2½ pounds charcoal briquettes or hardwood charcoal. When the coals are hot, set up for a two-level fire: one side high heat (so you can hold your hand 1 to 2 inches above cooking rack for only 1 to 2 seconds) and the other medium heat (so you can hold your hand 1 to 2 inches above cooking rack for only 4 to 5 seconds).

For a gas grill: Turn each burner to high and ignite. Cover the grill. When hot, leave half the burners on high heat, and set the other half on medium heat.

3. With clean hands, gently shape sausage mixture into 4 (½- to ¾-inch-thick) patties, being careful not to press too hard.

4. Grill sausage patties, uncovered, over high heat for 2 to 3 minutes per side. *On a charcoal grill:* Move sausage patties to medium heat, and grill 10 to 12 minutes total, turning every 2 minutes or until an instant-read thermometer inserted horizontally into patty's center registers 165°F for medium. *On a gas grill:* Move sausage patties to medium heat, and grill, covered, 10 to 12 minutes, turning once halfway through, until an instant-read thermometer inserted horizontally into patty's center registers 165°F for medium. Remove sausages from the grill, and let rest for 5 minutes. Cut cooked patties into 6 equal pieces, lay over chilled Romaine, and dress with Caesar dressing or your favorite dressing.

Barbecue Banter

Nutmeg has a great flavor and terrific aroma, and it's at its best when freshly grated. If you like eggnog during the holidays, grate fresh nutmeg over eggnog just before serving it.

Homemade Fennel-Scented Italian Sausage Sandwiches

2 lb. regular ground pork

¼ cup dry red wine

2 cloves garlic, peeled and minced

1 rounded TB. whole fennel seeds

2 tsp. kosher salt

1½ tsp. fresh-ground black pepper

1 tsp. dried oregano, crumbled

1 tsp. dried basil, crumbled

1 large sweet onion, peeled and sliced into 6 rounds

1 large green bell pepper, top cut off, seeds and ribs discarded, and sliced crosswise into paper-thin slices

6 sandwich buns

Serves: 6
Prep time: 20 minutes
Cook time: 14 to 18 minutes
Serving size: 1 patty

1. In a large bowl, combine ground pork, red wine, garlic, fennel seeds, kosher salt, black pepper, oregano, and basil. Mix well.

2. Fire up the grill:

> ***For a charcoal grill:*** Open the bottom vents. Ignite 6 quarts or 2½ pounds charcoal briquettes or hardwood charcoal. When the coals are hot, set up for a two-level fire: one side high heat (so you can hold your hand 1 to 2 inches above cooking rack for only 1 to 2 seconds) and the other medium heat (so you can hold your hand 1 to 2 inches above cooking rack for only 4 to 5 seconds).
>
> ***For a gas grill:*** Turn each burner to high and ignite. Cover the grill. When hot, leave half the burners on high heat, and set the other half on medium heat.

3. With clean hands, gently shape sausage mixture into 6 ½-inch-thick patties, being careful not to press too hard.

4. Grill sausage patties, uncovered, over high heat for 2 to 3 minutes per side. *On a charcoal grill:* Move sausage patties to medium heat, and grill 10 to 12 minutes total, turning every 2 minutes or until an instant-read thermometer inserted horizontally into patty's center registers 160°F for medium. *On a gas grill:* Move sausage patties to medium heat, and grill, covered, 10 to 12 minutes, turning once halfway through, until an instant-read thermometer inserted horizontally into patty's center registers 160°F for medium. Remove sausages from the grill, and let rest for 5 minutes.

5. Lightly toast cut sides of buns over coals about 2 to 3 minutes. Place sausages on buns, divide onion and green peppers evenly among sandwiches, and top with bun. Serve.

Barbecue Banter

When purchasing green or any other color sweet pepper, look for firm, shiny skins with no bruises or damage of any kind, and stem ends that look bright green and freshly cut (not brown and shriveled). If a pepper feels heavy for its size, it usually means the pepper has thicker walls and you'll be getting more of your money's worth.

Part 4

Beef, Bison, and Lamb

A nice, thick, juicy steak, sizzlin' on the grill—can't you just hear it and catch that great aroma drifting on a late afternoon summer breeze? Steaks are popular grill food because they seem made just for grilling. Steaks are already tender, or should be, and as long as they're not cooked to the gray, tight, well-done stage, they'll remain juicy until you spear them with your fork. But there's more to beef than steak; beef back ribs or brisket, for example, take a little more time and expertise to produce tender, flavorful results—but they're worth it!

In Part 4, you'll also find recipes for grilling bison (a.k.a. buffalo), a nineteenth-century animal with twenty-first-century lean characteristics and great flavor.

And unless it's lamb stew, there's no other way to prepare lamb than on the grill. Grilling builds up flavors that complement lamb's already-excellent flavors.

Beef: Steaks

In This Chapter

- ◆ Tips on picking the perfect cut of steak
- ◆ Your grill: Steak Cooker Extraordinaire
- ◆ Hints for checking doneness

I'd be willing to bet that the man who designed the first grill dreamed about the steaks he'd cook on that grill. For some reason, a good-quality steak, properly grilled—with a nice, flavorful crust on the exterior and a juicy pink interior, seasoned just right—seems invented for just that purpose.

Today, it's almost impossible to get your hands on a true prime-graded steak without breaking into your kid's college fund. Even if you can afford it, you'll probably have to wait a day or two for it to arrive—frozen solid— at your front door. The best grade of graded steak I get is choice. It would be great to have a source for choice, dry-aged steaks, but where I live, dry-aged steaks are almost impossible to find. If dry-aged steaks are available in your area, by all means, spend the extra money for one, just to taste the difference.

Dry-aged steaks come from beef hung in a cooler kept at less than 36 degrees but above freezing for several weeks. During that time, the natural enzymes begin to work on the beef and tenderize it. Also it loses about

20 percent of its weight in water, concentrating the flavor of the meat. A dry-aged steak is usually either prime or choice in grade.

Wet-aged steaks are similar to but different from dry-aged steaks. This beef has also spent a week or 2 in the cooler, but it's still in its original vacuum pack. During that cooler time, enzymes work their tenderizing magic on the beef, but because it can't lose any moisture through the plastic, the flavor doesn't intensify.

Because choice and lower grades don't have the flavor of prime or dry-aged or the tenderness of wet-aged steaks, I've come up with ways to season steaks—some simple, some complex—that enhance the steak's flavor.

And I don't suggest grilling a steak past medium-rare. Even good seasonings can't save a dry, tough, well-done steak.

A Few Notes on Steak

According to the National Cattleman's Beef Association, the top 10 most tender cuts of steak, in descending order, are as follows:

- Tenderloin comes from the short loin area; up near the back midway to the steer's rear.
- Chuck top blade or flat iron comes from the chuck, the front shoulder area of the steer.
- Top loin or New York strip comes from the same area of the steer as the tenderloin.
- Porterhouse/T-bone comes from the same area of the steer as the tenderloin.
- Rib eye comes from—where else?—the rib area near the front half of a steer.
- Rib comes from the same area as rib eyes.
- Chuck eye comes from a similar area on the steer as chuck top blade steak.
- Top sirloin comes from the sirloin section located at the hind end of the steer.
- Round tip comes from the round section, located in the rear hind quarter of the steer.
- Chopped (a.k.a. ground beef) could come from the round, sirloin, or chuck areas of the steer, or could be made from scrap cuttings from anywhere on the steer.

Surprised? In some ways I was. The second-most tender cut of beef is a piece of chuck—amazing! So use this list when you go shopping to select tender steaks that will most likely come off your grill tasting great and still be tender.

Before you head out to buy any steak, though, keep in mind that unless your supermarket carries USDA (United States Department of Agriculture)-graded beef—it should clearly state the grade, such as USDA-graded choice or select—it's ungraded beef. Ungraded beef costs supermarkets less, and it's generally leaner (good) and tougher (not so good). Labels declaring "Butcher's Prime" or "Rancher's Choice" mean nothing, legally. They just create the illusion of grading. So if the first steak you buy for grilling tastes less than wonderful, it's probably ungraded.

> **Barbecue Banter**
>
> Always have your instant-read meat thermometer available so you can turn out perfect steaks every time, whether you start with ice-cold steaks from the fridge or room-temperature steaks.

Rare? Medium? Well-Done?

My brother, Chef Tom Mauer, taught me this easy method for telling when and how well a steak is done: using your fingertip, quickly press the center of a steak and use the following table to gauge the doneness.

If the Steak ...	It's ...
Feels very soft	Very-rare (115°F to 120°F)
Feels fairly soft—and gives with little resistance	Rare (120°F to 130°F)
Feels more firm than rare	Medium-rare (130°F to 135°F)
Feels quite firm, offers resistance	Medium (135°F to 165°F)
Feels hard and doesn't give at all	Well-done (165°F to 170°F)

If your finger can't take the heat, use the rounded, underside of your tongs, and watch how the meat responds when pressed.

Simply Grilled T-Bone Steaks

Serves: 4
Prep time: 7 to 8 minutes
Cook time: 12 to 14 minutes
Serving size: ½ steak

2 (1½-inch-thick) T-bone steaks (about 1½ lb. each)

1½ to 2 tsp. kosher salt

1 tsp. coarse-ground black pepper

1. Fire up the grill:

 For a charcoal grill: Open the bottom vents. Ignite 6 quarts or 2½ pounds charcoal briquettes or hardwood charcoal. When the coals are hot, set up for a one-level medium-heat fire (so you can hold your hand 5 inches above the cooking rack for only 4 to 5 seconds).

For a gas grill: Turn each burner to high and ignite. Cover the grill. When hot, leave half the burners on high heat, and set the other half on medium heat.

2. With a paper towel, pat steaks dry. Season generously with salt and pepper. *On a charcoal grill:* Place steaks directly above the coals, and grill 12 to 14 minutes, turning over once halfway through, or until an instant-read thermometer inserted horizontally 2 inches into meat (do not touch bone) registers about 135°F for medium-rare. *On a gas grill:* Grill both sides of steaks on high heat, uncovered, for 2½ to 3 minutes. Finish cooking, covered, over medium heat for 9 to 11 minutes, turning steaks once midway until an instant-read thermometer inserted horizontally 2 inches into meat (do not touch bone) registers about 135°F for medium-rare.

3. Transfer steaks to a serving platter and let rest, uncovered, 5 minutes before serving.

Barbecue Banter

Resting a steak allows the internal temperature of the steak to naturally rise 5°F and hit the bull's-eye in terms of being truly rare, medium, or well-done.

It's a Classic—the Porterhouse

Serves: 4
Prep time: 30 minutes
Cook time: 12 to 14 minutes
Serving size: ½ steak

2 (1½-inch-thick) porterhouse steaks (about 2 lb. each)

Kosher salt

Fresh-ground black pepper

4 TB. unsalted butter, at room temperature

1. Cover steaks and let sit at room temperature for 30 minutes. Season steaks with kosher salt and pepper.

2. Fire up the grill:

> *For a charcoal grill:* Open the bottom vents. Ignite 6 quarts or 2½ pounds charcoal briquettes or hardwood charcoal. When the coals are hot, set up for a two-level fire: one side high heat (so you can hold your hand 5 inches above the cooking rack for only 1 to 2 seconds) and the other medium heat (so you can hold your hand 5 inches above the cooking rack for only 4 to 5 seconds).
>
> *For a gas grill:* Turn each burner to high and ignite. Cover the grill. When hot, leave half the burners on high heat, and set the other half on medium heat.

3. *On a charcoal grill:* Grill steaks uncovered over high-heat coals for 2½ to 3 minutes per side. Move steaks to medium-heat coals, turning them again, and continue grilling 5 to 6 minutes per side or until an instant-read thermometer inserted horizontally 2 inches into meat (do not touch bone) registers about 135°F for medium-rare. Turn steaks every 2 minutes until done. *On a gas grill:* Grill both sides of steaks on high heat, uncovered, 2½ to 3 minutes. Finish cooking, covered, over medium heat 8 to 10 minutes, turning steaks once midway until an instant-read thermometer inserted horizontally 2 inches into meat (do not touch bone) registers about 135°F for medium-rare.

4. Transfer steaks to a cutting board, spread butter over each steak and let rest, uncovered, 5 minutes. Divide steaks among dinner plates and serve.

Barbecue Banter

There's no need to oil a clean grill rack for grilling steaks. The steak will stick a little to the rack when it's first placed there, but it will naturally release when it's ready.

Herb and Black Pepper–Rubbed T-Bone Steak

3 TB. dried basil, crumbled

1 TB. dried sage, crumbled

1 TB. kosher salt

1 tsp. fresh-ground black pepper

4 (1- to 1¼-lb.) T-bone steaks, about 1 to 1¼ inches thick

Serves: 4
Prep time: 35 minutes plus 4 hours refrigerator time
Cook time: 11 to 13 minutes
Serving size: 1 steak

1. In a small bowl stir together basil, sage, kosher salt, and pepper until combined.

2. Four hours before you plan to grill, coat steaks thoroughly with herb mixture, wrap in plastic wrap, and refrigerate.

3. Fire up the grill:

For a charcoal grill: Open the bottom vents. Ignite 6 quarts or 2½ pounds charcoal briquettes or hardwood charcoal. When the coals are hot, set up for a two-level fire: one side high heat (so you can hold your hand 5 inches above the cooking rack for only 1 to 2 seconds) and the other medium heat (so you can hold your hand 5 inches above the cooking rack for only 4 to 5 seconds).

For a gas grill: Turn each burner to high and ignite. Cover the grill. When hot, leave half the burners on high heat, and set the other half on medium heat.

4. Remove steaks from the refrigerator, unwrap them, and let them sit at room temperature for about 30 minutes.

5. *On a charcoal grill:* Grill steaks uncovered over high-heat coals 2½ to 3 minutes per side. Move steaks to medium-heat coals, turning again, and continue grilling 4 to 5 minutes per side or until an instant-read thermometer inserted horizontally 2 inches into meat (do not touch bone) registers about 135°F for medium-rare. Turn steaks every 2 minutes until done. *On a gas grill:* Grill both sides of steaks on high heat, uncovered, for 2½ to 3 minutes; finish cooking, covered, over medium heat for 8 to 10 minutes, turning steaks once halfway through until an instant-read thermometer inserted horizontally 2 inches into meat (do not touch bone) registers about 135°F for medium-rare.

6. Transfer steaks to dinner plates and let rest, uncovered, 5 minutes. Serve.

Barbecue Banter

When using dried herbs to season a steak, it's a nice touch to garnish each serving plate with a sprig of the same herb in its fresh form.

Easy Grilled Filet Mignon

Serves: 4
Prep time: 40 minutes
Cook time: 11 to 13 minutes
Serving size: 1 steak

4 (1½- to 2-inch-thick) center-cut filets mignon, patted dry with paper towels

4 tsp. olive oil

Salt

Fresh-ground black pepper

1. Fire up the grill:

> *For a charcoal grill:* Open the bottom vents. Ignite 6 quarts or 2½ pounds charcoal briquettes or hardwood charcoal. When the coals are hot, set up for a two-level fire: one side high heat (so you can hold your hand 5 inches above the cooking rack for only 1 to 2 seconds) and the other medium heat (so you can hold your hand 5 inches above the cooking rack for only 4 to 5 seconds).
>
> *For a gas grill:* Turn each burner to high and ignite. Cover the grill. When hot, leave half the burners on high heat, and set the other half on medium heat.

2. Remove steaks from the refrigerator, unwrap them, and let them sit at room temperature for about 30 minutes. After 30 minutes, rub each side of steaks with ½ teaspoon olive oil, and season generously with salt and pepper.

3. *On a charcoal grill:* Grill steaks uncovered over high-heat coals 2½ to 3 minutes per side. Move steaks to medium-heat coals, turning them again, and continue grilling 3 to 4 minutes per side or until an instant-read thermometer inserted horizontally 2 inches into meat registers about 135°F for medium-rare. Turn steaks every 2 minutes until done. *On a gas grill:* Grill both sides of steaks on high heat, uncovered, 2½ to 3 minutes. Finish cooking, covered, over medium heat for 6 to 8 minutes, turning steaks once halfway through until an instant-read thermometer inserted horizontally 2 inches into meat registers about 135°F for medium-rare.

Barbecue Banter

Beef tenderloins are tender, but they're also very lean, which means they don't have the big flavor of other beef steaks that carry more fat.

4. Remove steaks from the grill, and let rest 5 minutes. Serve.

Chili-Rubbed and Grilled Flank Steak

1 TB. chili powder

1 large clove garlic, chopped and mashed to a paste with ½ tsp. salt

½ tsp. ground cumin

½ tsp. sugar

1 TB. plus 2 tsp. Worcestershire sauce

1 (1½- to 2-lb.) beef flank steak, trimmed of visible fat and scored on both sides

Serves: 4
Prep time: 10 minutes plus 4 hours to 2 days to marinate
Cook time: 10 to 12 minutes
Serving size: ¼ steak

1. In a small bowl, mix together chili powder, garlic paste, cumin, and sugar. Stir in Worcestershire sauce to make a paste.

2. Place flank steak on a plate large enough to hold it, and rub both sides with chili paste. Transfer steak to a large resealable plastic bag, remove as much air as possible, seal, and chill for at least 4 hours and up to 2 days.

3. Fire up the grill:

> *For a charcoal grill:* Open the bottom vents. Ignite 6 quarts or 2½ pounds charcoal briquettes or hardwood charcoal. When the coals are hot, set up for a one-level high-heat fire (so you can hold your hand 5 inches above the cooking rack for only 1 to 2 seconds).
>
> *For a gas grill:* Turn each burner to high and ignite. Cover the grill. When hot, leave burners on high heat.

4. Bring steak to room temperature. *On a charcoal grill:* Grill steak directly over coals for 5 to 6 minutes on each side for medium-rare (135°F). *On a gas grill:* Grill steaks, covered, 5 to 6 minutes on each side for medium-rare (135°F).

5. Transfer steak to a cutting board, and let stand 5 minutes. Holding a knife at a 45-degree angle, cut steak across the grain into thin slices. Serve.

Barbecue Banter

Turning garlic into garlic paste is easy: on a clean wooden cutting board, remove the garlic's outer papery skin (smash with the side of the knife, trim off the end, remove the skin, and discard). Mince garlic, spread minced garlic out flat with the flat side of the knife, sprinkle with salt, and, with strong downward pressure, drag the flat side of the knife over the garlic several times to form the paste.

Peppery Flank Steak

½ cup dry red wine

¼ cup olive oil

2 TB. fresh lime juice

2 TB. soy sauce

1 TB. granulated sugar

2 cloves garlic, peeled and minced or pushed through a garlic press

Grated zest of 1 lime

1 tsp. red pepper flakes

⅛ tsp. ground cayenne

1½ lb. flank steak, trimmed of all visible fat and scored on both sides

Serves: 4
Prep time: 13 to 15 minutes plus 2 to 8 hours to marinate
Cook time: 10 to 12 minutes
Serving size: ¼ steak

1. In a small stainless-steel or glass bowl, stir together red wine, olive oil, lime juice, soy sauce, sugar, garlic, lime zest, red pepper flakes, and cayenne until combined. Reserve and refrigerate ¼ cup marinade.

2. Place steak in a 1-gallon reclosable plastic bag, pour remaining marinade over steak, press out as much air as possible, seal, and refrigerate for 2 to 8 hours. To marinate evenly, turn bag occasionally.

3. Fire up the grill:

> *For a charcoal grill:* Open the bottom vents. Ignite 6 quarts or 2½ pounds charcoal briquettes or hardwood charcoal. When the coals are hot, set up for a two-level fire: one side high heat (so you can hold your hand 5 inches above the cooking rack for only 1 to 2 seconds) and the other medium heat (so you can hold your hand 5 inches above the cooking rack for only 4 to 5 seconds).
>
> *For a gas grill:* Turn each burner to high and ignite. Cover the grill. When hot, leave half the burners on high heat, and set the other half on medium heat.

4. Remove steak from bag, discarding bag and marinade, and bring steak to room temperature. *On a charcoal grill:* Grill steak directly over coals for 5 to 6 minutes on each side for medium-rare (130-135°F), brushing each side once with reserved marinade. *On a gas grill:* Grill steaks, covered, 5 to 6 minutes on each side for medium-rare (135°F), brushing each side once with reserved marinade.

5. Transfer steak to a cutting board, and let stand 5 minutes. Holding knife at a 45-degree angle, cut steak across the grain into thin slices. Serve.

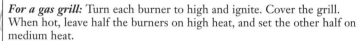

Barbecue Banter

Scoring aids in heating meat slightly faster and allows flavorings to enhance the meat below the surface.

Mustard and Rosemary–Seasoned Strip Steaks

Serves: 4
Prep time: 10 minutes plus 1 hour to marinate
Cook time: 10 to 13 minutes
Serving size: 1 steak

4 (14- to 16-oz.) boneless beef strip (top loin) steaks about 1 to 1¼ inches thick

4 TB. Dijon mustard

2 TB. dried rosemary, ground in an electric spice grinder

Kosher salt

Fresh-ground black pepper

1. One hour before you plan to grill, rub steaks with mustard and sprinkle with rosemary, kosher salt, and pepper. Place steaks on a dinner plate, cover with plastic wrap and let rest at room temperature for one hour.

2. Fire up the grill:

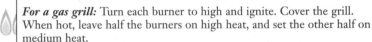

> *For a charcoal grill:* Open the bottom vents. Ignite 6 quarts or 2½ pounds charcoal briquettes or hardwood charcoal. When the coals are hot, set up for a two-level fire: one side high heat (so you can hold your hand 5 inches above the cooking rack for only 1 to 2 seconds) and the other medium heat (so you can hold your hand 5 inches above cooking rack for only 4 to 5 seconds).
>
> *For a gas grill:* Turn each burner to high and ignite. Cover the grill. When hot, leave half the burners on high heat, and set the other half on medium heat.

3. Uncover steaks, discard plastic wrap, and take to the grill.

4. *On a charcoal grill:* Grill steaks uncovered over high-heat coals for 2½ to 3 minutes per side. Move steaks to medium-heat coals, turning them again, and continue grilling for 4 to 5 minutes per side or until an instant-read thermometer inserted horizontally 2 inches into meat registers about 135°F for medium-rare. Turn steaks every 2 minutes until done. *On a gas grill:* Grill both sides of steaks on high heat, uncovered, for 2½ to 3 minutes. Finish cooking, covered, over medium heat for 8 to 10 minutes, turning steaks once halfway through until an instant-read thermometer inserted horizontally 2 inches into meat registers about 135°F for medium-rare. Let rest 5 minutes. Serve.

Balsamic Vinegar and Garlic–Glazed Strip Steak

¾ cup *balsamic vinegar*

½ cup olive oil

3 large cloves garlic, peeled and minced, or pushed through a garlic press

4 (14- to 16-oz.) strip steaks

Kosher salt or other coarse salt

Fresh-ground black pepper

Serves: 4
Prep time: 10 minutes plus 4 hours to marinate
Cook time: 10 to 13 minutes
Serving size: 1 steak

1. In a small bowl, whisk together balsamic vinegar, olive oil, and garlic. Reserve ⅓ cup marinade, cover, and refrigerate.

2. Four hours before you plan to grill, place steaks in a reclosable plastic bag, pour marinade over them, push out air, seal the bag, and refrigerate. To marinate evenly, turn bag occasionally.

3. Fire up the grill:

> *For a charcoal grill:* Open the bottom vents. Ignite 6 quarts or 2½ pounds charcoal briquettes or hardwood charcoal. When the coals are hot, set up for a two-level fire: one side high heat (so you can hold your hand 5 inches above the cooking rack for only 1 to 2 seconds) and the other medium heat (so you can hold your hand 5 inches above the cooking rack for only 4 to 5 seconds).
>
> *For a gas grill:* Turn each burner to high and ignite. Cover the grill. When hot, leave half the burners on high heat, and set the other half on medium heat.

4. Remove steaks from the refrigerator, and drain, discarding the bag and marinade. Let steaks sit, covered, at room temperature for 30 minutes. Blot steaks of any moisture on the surface with paper towels, and sprinkle both sides of steaks with kosher salt and pepper to taste.

5. *On charcoal grill*: Grill steaks uncovered over high-heat coals for 2½ to 3 minutes per side. Move steaks to medium-heat coals, turning them again, and continue grilling for 4 to 5 minutes per side or until an instant-read thermometer inserted horizontally 2 inches into meat registers about 135°F for medium-rare. Turn steaks every 2 minutes until done. Brush steaks with reserved marinade in the last few minutes of cooking on each side. *On a gas grill:* Grill both sides of steaks on high heat, uncovered, for 2½ to 3 minutes. Finish cooking, covered, over medium heat for 8 to 10 minutes, turning steaks once halfway through until an

instant-read thermometer inserted horizontally 2 inches into meat registers about 135°F for medium-rare. Brush steaks with reserved marinade in the last few minutes of cooking on each side. Let rest 5 minutes. Serve.

Grill Guide

Balsamic vinegar tastes like no other vinegar. It's darker in color and thicker than regular vinegar, and it has sweet notes hidden in its tanginess. Authentic balsamic vinegar is aged for years in oak casks and, where available, commands a steep price.

Herb and Garlic–Scented Strip Steak

Serves: 4
Prep time: 15 minutes plus 1 hour to marinate
Cook time: 12 to 14 minutes
Serving size: 1 steak

1 TB. sweet paprika

2 tsp. fresh-ground black pepper

1 tsp. garlic powder

1 tsp. fennel seed, ground through a pepper mill or in an electric spice grinder

1 tsp. kosher salt

½ tsp. dried thyme, crumbled

½ tsp. ground cayenne

½ tsp. dried oregano, crumbled

4 (10- to 12-oz.) New York–cut strip steaks

2 to 3 TB. olive oil

1. In a small bowl, stir together paprika, pepper, garlic powder, fennel seed, salt, thyme, cayenne, and oregano. Set aside.

2. Lightly brush steaks with olive oil, and then rub steaks with spice mixture until well coated. Cover and let rest for 1 hour at room temperature.

3. Fire up the grill:

For a charcoal grill: Open the bottom vents. Ignite 6 quarts or 2½ pounds charcoal briquettes or hardwood charcoal. When the coals are hot, set up for a one-level high-heat fire (so you can hold your hand 5 inches above the cooking rack for only 1 to 2 seconds).

For a gas grill: Turn each burner to high and ignite. Cover the grill. When hot, leave burners on high heat.

4. *On a charcoal grill:* Grill steaks uncovered over high-heat coals 4 to 5 minutes per side until rare (125°F) to medium-rare (135°F). Turn steaks every 2 minutes until done. *On a gas grill:* Grill both sides of steaks on high heat, covered, for 8 to 10 minutes, turning once halfway through until rare (125°F) to medium-rare (130°F to 135°F). Let rest 5 minutes. Serve.

Barbecue Banter

Letting a beef steak sit briefly before cutting it allows the heat from the grill to spread from the surface of the steak inward, cooking the meat a bit more. Slicing the steak immediately helps stop the cooking.

Southwest-Flavored Grilled Sirloin Steak

1 (1½-lb.) boneless beef sirloin steak

1 medium onion, chopped

⅓ cup fresh lime juice

¼ cup plus 2 TB. chopped fresh cilantro

3 fresh jalapeño peppers, stem end trimmed, cut in half, seeds removed, and finely chopped

3 TB. water

2 TB. olive oil

1 tsp. ground cumin

2 cloves garlic, peeled and minced, or pushed through a garlic press

½ tsp. ground cayenne

¼ tsp. kosher salt

Serves: 4
Prep time: 17 to 20 minutes
Cook time: 14 to 22 minutes
Serving size: ¼ steak

1. Trim any visible fat from steak.

2. In a small bowl, stir together onion, lime juice, cilantro, jalapeño peppers, water, olive oil, cumin, garlic, cayenne, and kosher salt. Reserve and refrigerate ¼ cup marinade. Place steak in a reclosable plastic bag, pour remaining marinade over steak, press as much air out of the bag as possible, and seal the bag. Marinate in refrigerator for 4 hours, turning bag occasionally.

3. Fire up the grill:

> *For a charcoal grill:* Open the bottom vents. Ignite 6 quarts or 2½ pounds charcoal briquettes or hardwood charcoal. When the coals are hot, set up for a one-level, medium-heat fire (so you can hold your hand 5 inches above the cooking rack for only 4 to 5 seconds).
>
> *For a gas grill:* Turn each burner to high and ignite. Cover the grill. When hot, turn the burners to medium heat.

Barbecue Banter

To keep any fresh herb really fresh, rinse it under cool, fresh water, trim ¼ inch off the stem end, and place it in a glass with enough water to only reach where the leaves begin on the stem.

4. Drain steak, discarding the bag and marinade. *On a charcoal grill:* Grill steak directly over medium coals 14 to 18 minutes for medium-rare (135°F) and 18 to 22 minutes for medium (145°F), turning every 2 minutes and brushing occasionally with reserved marinade. *On a gas grill:* Place steak on the grill rack over heat, turning only once. Cover and grill over medium heat 14 to 18 minutes for medium-rare (135°F) and 18 to 22 minutes for medium (145°F), turning once and brushing occasionally with reserved marinade.

5. Season steak with remaining 2 tablespoons cilantro and serve.

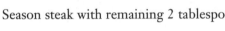

Three-Pepper Rubbed and Grilled Round Steak

Serves: 6
Prep time: 8 to 10 minutes plus 1 hour to marinate
Cook time: 12 to 14 minutes
Serving size: ⅙ steak

1 TB. fresh-ground black pepper

1½ tsp. kosher salt

1½ tsp. onion powder

1 tsp. ground white pepper

½ tsp. ground cayenne

Scant ½ tsp. dry mustard

1 (1¾- to 2-lb.) top round steak

1. In a small bowl, stir together black pepper, kosher salt, onion powder, white pepper, cayenne, and dry mustard. One hour before you plan to grill, coat steak with pepper rub, place on a dinner plate, cover with plastic wrap and rest for one hour.

2. Uncover steak and discard plastic wrap.

3. Fire up the grill:

> *For a charcoal grill:* Open the bottom vents. Ignite 6 quarts or 2½ pounds charcoal briquettes or hardwood charcoal. When the coals are hot, set up for a one-level high-heat fire (so you can hold your hand 5 inches above the cooking rack for only 1 to 2 seconds).
>
> *For a gas grill:* Turn each burner to high and ignite. Cover the grill. When hot, leave the burners on high heat.

4. *On a charcoal grill:* Grill steak, uncovered, over high-heat coals 4 to 6 minutes per side, until rare (125°F) to medium-rare (135°F). Turn steak every 2 minutes until done. *On a gas grill:* Grill both sides of steak over high heat, covered, for 8 to 12 minutes, turning once halfway through until rare (125°F) to medium-rare (135°F). Let rest 5 minutes.

5. Slice steak as thinly as possible across the grain and serve.

Barbecue Banter

Round steak is a less-expensive steak than a rib-eye or T-bone and for good reason. It's tougher and leaner, so it's important to slice a round steak across the grain for more tender results.

Fiery Texas Rib Eyes

1½ tsp. chili powder

¾ tsp. sweet paprika

¾ tsp. firmly packed dark brown sugar

½ tsp. dry mustard

Scant ½ tsp. ground cumin

¼ tsp. fresh-ground black pepper

⅛ tsp. dried oregano, crumbled

⅛ tsp. ground cayenne

4 (1- to 1¼-lb.) bone-in rib-eye steaks, at least choice grade

Serves: 4
Prep time: 10 minutes plus 4 hours to marinate
Cook time: 11 to 14 minutes
Serving size: 1 steak

1. In a small bowl, stir together chili powder, paprika, brown sugar, dry mustard, cumin, pepper, oregano, and cayenne until combined.

2. Four hours before you plan to grill, coat steaks thoroughly with spice mixture, wrap each steak in plastic wrap, and refrigerate.

3. Remove steaks from the refrigerator and let them sit at room temperature for about 30 minutes. Remove and discard plastic wrap before grilling.

4. Fire up the grill:

> *For a charcoal grill:* Open the bottom vents. Ignite 6 quarts or 2½ pounds charcoal briquettes or hardwood charcoal. When the coals are hot, set up for a two-level fire: one side high heat (so you can hold your hand 5 inches above cooking rack for only 1 to 2 seconds) and the other medium heat (so you can hold your hand 5 inches above cooking rack for only 4 to 5 seconds).
>
> *For a gas grill:* Turn each burner to high and ignite. Cover the grill. When hot, leave half the burners on high heat, and set the other half on medium heat.

Barbecue Banter

Rib-eye steaks are a favorite of mine, so I always trim as much fat from the edge of my steaks as possible to keep flare-ups, which can burn my steaks and give them an "off" flavor, to a minimum.

5. *On a charcoal grill:* Grill steaks uncovered over high-heat coals for 2½ to 3 minutes per side. Move steaks to medium-heat coals, turning again, and continue grilling for 3 to 4 minutes per side or until an instant-read thermometer inserted horizontally 2 inches into meat registers about 135°F for medium-rare. Turn steaks every 2 minutes until done. *On a gas grill:* Grill both sides of steaks over high heat, uncovered, for 2½ to 3 minutes. Finish cooking, covered, over medium heat for 6 to 8 minutes, turning steaks once halfway through, until an instant-read thermometer inserted horizontally 2 inches into meat registers about 135°F for medium-rare. Remove steaks from the grill, and place on serving plates. Serve.

12

Beef: Beyond Steaks

In This Chapter

- ◆ Grilling more than steaks: ribs, chops, and brisket
- ◆ Cooking techniques to produce tender results
- ◆ Grilling beef on a stick: satay and kabobs

Steaks are juicy and tender and just meant for the grill. Once you get past the 10 most tender cuts (see Chapter 11), though, things get a little more difficult.

The recipes in this chapter use all sorts of cooking techniques—marinating, rubbing, and slow cooking—to produce tender tasty results, even if the beef you start with isn't the most tender cut. You'll find out how to grill veal—tender, but very lean—so it doesn't dry out and get tough. You'll discover how to cook a brisket, slowly, for great flavor and tender results, as well as how to slow cook tough beef back and short ribs flavored with great spice rubs that turn into tender, fall-off-the-bone ribs grilled to perfection.

You'll also learn how to do shish-kabobs the right way and what to serve with them. By the end of this chapter, you'll be making Thai Satay (essentially, beef on a stick) like a pro.

Beef Satay

Serves: 5
Prep time: 25 to 30 minutes, plus 30 minutes to marinate
Cook time: 3 to 4 minutes
Serving size: 1 skewer

⅓ cup plus 2 TB. Homemade Teriyaki Sauce (recipe in Chapter 7)

½ tsp. hot pepper sauce

1 (1- to 1¼-lb.) beef flank steak

3 TB. smooth peanut butter

3 TB. water

4 green onions, trimmed and cut into 1-inch pieces

1 large green sweet bell pepper, stem end trimmed, seeds and ribs discarded, and cut into ¾-inch chunks

1. In a medium bowl, whisk together ⅓ cup teriyaki sauce and ¼ teaspoon hot pepper sauce.

2. Trim any visible fat from steak. With a knife tilted at a 45-degree angle, slice steak thinly across the grain into 15 pieces. Place sliced steak in marinade, and toss to coat. Cover and refrigerate, marinating for 30 minutes, stirring once. If you're using bamboo skewers, soak 5 of them in warm water for 20 minutes to prevent their catching fire on the grill, and drain.

3. In a small saucepan over medium heat, stir together peanut butter, water, remaining 2 tablespoons teriyaki sauce, and remaining ¼ teaspoon hot pepper sauce. Cook and stir just until smooth and heated through. Keep warm.

4. Fire up the grill:

For a charcoal grill: Open the bottom vents. Ignite 6 quarts or 2½ pounds charcoal briquettes or hardwood charcoal. When the coals are hot, set up for a single-level, medium heat fire (so you can hold your hand 5 inches above the cooking rack for only 4 to 5 seconds).

For a gas grill: Turn each burner to high and ignite. Cover the grill. When hot, set all burners on medium heat.

5. Drain steak, reserving marinade. On 10- to 12-inch bamboo or metal skewers, alternately thread steak slices, accordion style, with green onion and sweet pepper pieces. Brush with marinade, and discard any remaining marinade. Set aside.

6. *On a charcoal or gas grill:* Grill satay, uncovered, directly over medium coals or heat for 3 to 4 minutes or until steak is slightly pink in center, turning once halfway through grilling. Remove skewers from the grill and place on a platter, and serve immediately, passing peanut sauce.

 Lean Note

Using reduced-fat smooth peanut butter instead of regular trims both fat and calories without sacrificing flavor.

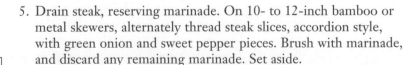

Brined and Beer-Simmered BBQ Beef Short Ribs

4 to 6 lb. beef short ribs (with bone)

1 cup kosher salt

1 cup granulated sugar

2 qt. water

6 (12-oz.) cans or bottles lager beer

Barbecue sauce (your favorite homemade or store-bought)

Serves: 4
Prep time: 20 minutes, plus 6 to 8 hours to brine
Cook time: 12 to 14 minutes
Serving size: 2 to 3, depending on size

1. Rinse beef short ribs under cold water, and set aside.

2. Add kosher salt, sugar, and water to a 2-gallon reclosable plastic bag. Seal bag and shake until salt and sugar dissolve. Add beef short ribs. Press out as much air as possible from the bag and seal. Refrigerate 6 to 8 hours.

3. Add beer to a large, deep saucepan or stockpot, and place over medium-high heat. Remove ribs from the bag, discard the bag and marinade, rinse ribs under cold water, and add to beer in the saucepan. If necessary, add water to saucepan to cover ribs by ½ inch. Bring almost to a simmer, reduce heat to medium-low, and cook, stirring once in a while, for 2 hours. Be careful not to let it come to a rapid boil.

4. Fire up the grill:

Barbecue Banter

Short ribs have a lot of fat, so when shopping for ribs, take a good look, and purchase the leanest, meatiest ribs you can find.

> *For a charcoal grill:* Open the bottom vents. Ignite 6 quarts or 2½ pounds charcoal briquettes or hardwood charcoal. When the coals are hot, set up for a single-level, medium heat fire (so you can hold your hand 5 inches above the cooking rack for only 4 to 5 seconds).
>
> *For a gas grill:* Turn each burner to high and ignite. Cover the grill. When hot, set all burners on medium heat.

5. When the grill is ready, using tongs, remove short ribs from cooking liquid and place on the grill bone-side down, not directly over coals or heat. Cover and grill for 20 to 30 minutes or until ribs are golden brown. Brush each rib on all sides, except for bone side, with barbecue sauce, and grill for 6 to 9 minutes, covered. Remove ribs from the grill, and serve immediately, passing additional barbecue sauce.

Lemon-Mustard Veal Chops

Serves: 4
Prep time: 10 to 12 minutes
Cook time: 18 to 19 minutes
Serving size: 1 chop

4 veal rib or loin chops, about 1-inch-thick

1 TB. chopped fresh thyme leaves or 1 tsp. dried thyme, crumbled

1 TB. Dijon mustard

2 tsp. fresh lemon juice

1 tsp. lemon-pepper seasoning

1 tsp. garlic powder

½ tsp. fresh-ground black pepper

1. Fire up the grill:

For a charcoal grill: Open the bottom vents. Ignite 6 quarts or 2½ pounds charcoal briquettes or hardwood charcoal. When the coals are hot, set up for a single-level, medium heat fire (so you can hold your hand 5 inches above the cooking rack for only 4 to 5 seconds).

For a gas grill: Turn each burner to high and ignite. Cover the grill. When hot, set all burners on medium heat.

Barbecue Banter

Crumbling a dried herb such as thyme, basil, or oregano helps bring out the herb's flavor. After you crumble a dried herb with your fingertips, smell your fingers and you'll know this works.

2. Trim any visible fat from veal chops.

3. In a small, nonmetallic bowl, whisk together thyme, Dijon mustard, lemon juice, lemon-pepper seasoning, garlic powder, and pepper.

4. *On a charcoal grill:* Grill chops on the rack of an uncovered grill directly over medium coals for 18 to 19 minutes, turning once halfway through, until juices run clear or internal temperature reaches 140°F when read in chop's center with an instant-read thermometer. Brush occasionally with sauce during the last 5 minutes of grilling. *On a gas grill:* Place chops on grill rack over medium heat, cover, and grill as directed for a charcoal grill.

Aromatic Rubbed, Baked, and Grilled Beef Back Ribs

4 or 5 lb. beef back ribs

6 TB. Aromatic and Savory Beef Rib Rub (recipe in Chapter 4)

Serves: 4
Prep time: 15 minutes, plus 1 hour, 45 minutes oven time
Cook time: 12 to 14 minutes
Serving size: 2 ribs

1. Place the oven rack in the middle position, and preheat oven to 300°F.

2. Separate rib racks into separate rib pieces, cutting out every other rib bone, and leaving full meat on either side of remaining ribs.

3. Line a 13×9-inch baking pan with foil. Rinse ribs under cold water, pat dry with paper towels, and place in a single layer in the baking pan. Coat all sides of ribs with rub. Cover the baking pan with foil, and bake for 1 hour, 45 minutes. Remove the baking pan from the oven, and remove foil cover (be careful, because steam will billow up). With tongs, remove ribs from baking pan and place on a clean tray to transport to the grill. Thirty minutes before ribs are done baking, begin heating grill.

4. Fire up the grill:

> *For a charcoal grill:* Open the bottom vents. Ignite 6 quarts or 2½ pounds charcoal briquettes or hardwood charcoal. When the coals are hot, set up for a single-level, medium heat fire (so you can hold your hand 5 inches above the cooking rack for only 4 to 5 seconds).
>
> *For a gas grill:* Turn each burner to high and ignite. Cover the grill. When hot, set half the burners on medium heat, and leave the remaining burners on high.

5. *On a charcoal grill:* Grill ribs, bone-side down, over medium-heat coals for 2 to 3 minutes or until golden. Turn ribs meat-side down and grill 2 to 3 minutes or until golden. *On a gas grill:* Grill ribs, bone-side down, covered, over medium heat until heated through, about 8 to 10 minutes. Serve immediately.

Barbecue Banter

If you want to do a little pregrilling prep work or prepare the ribs in the morning for dinner that night, remove the rib roasting pan from the oven at the end of baking time, cool the ribs to room temperature, and then cover and refrigerate the ribs for grilling at a later time.

Stuffed Steak Pinwheels

Serves: 4
Prep time: 35 minutes
Cook time: 12 to 14 minutes
Serving size: 2 pinwheels

8 slices lean bacon

1 (10-oz.) pkg. frozen chopped spinach, thawed and well drained

2 TB. unseasoned dry breadcrumbs

¾ tsp. lemon-pepper seasoning

½ tsp. dried thyme, crumbled

1 Dash plus ¼ tsp. salt

1 (1- to 1½-lb.) beef flank steak

3 oz. thinly sliced provolone cheese

1. In a large skillet, cook bacon slices over medium heat just until lightly golden but not crisp. Remove bacon from skillet, drain on paper towels, and set aside.

2. In a medium bowl, combine spinach, breadcrumbs, ¼ teaspoon lemon-pepper seasoning, thyme, and dash salt. Set aside.

3. Fire up the grill:

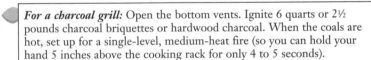
> **For a charcoal grill:** Open the bottom vents. Ignite 6 quarts or 2½ pounds charcoal briquettes or hardwood charcoal. When the coals are hot, set up for a single-level, medium-heat fire (so you can hold your hand 5 inches above the cooking rack for only 4 to 5 seconds).
>
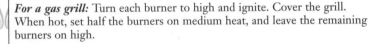
> **For a gas grill:** Turn each burner to high and ignite. Cover the grill. When hot, set half the burners on medium heat, and leave the remaining burners on high.

4. Trim any visible fat from steak. Score both sides of steak by making shallow, diagonal cuts at 1-inch intervals in a diamond pattern.

5. Place steak between 2 pieces of plastic wrap. Using the flat side of a meat mallet or a meat pounder and working from the center to the edges, pound steak into a 12×8-inch rectangle. Remove top piece of plastic wrap. Turn steak on the plastic so the grain goes from left to right. Sprinkle steak with remaining ½ teaspoon lemon-pepper seasoning and ¼ teaspoon salt. Arrange bacon lengthwise on steak.

6. Spread spinach and breadcrumb mixture over bacon and top, almost edge to edge, with provolone. Starting from short side, roll up steak. Secure with short bamboo skewers at 1-inch intervals, starting ½ inch from the end. Slice between toothpicks into 8 (1-inch) pinwheels. Thread 2 pinwheels onto each of 4 metal skewers.

Barbecue Banter

Don't have a meat mallet, or meat pounder? A rubber mallet, rolling pin, the bottom of a small iron skillet, or even baseball bat work almost as well.

7. *On a charcoal grill:* Grill pinwheels, uncovered, on the grill rack directly over medium coals for 12 to 14 minutes for medium-done, turning once halfway through. *On a gas grill:* Place pinwheels on the grill rack over heat. Cover and grill as directed for a charcoal grill. Remove skewers from the grill, and serve immediately with pinwheels still on the skewers.

Badman's Best Beef Back Ribs

½ cup kosher salt

5 TB. celery salt

¼ cup coarse-ground black pepper

2 TB. ground cayenne

1 tsp. cumin

10 lb. beef back ribs

1 cup apple cider vinegar

6 cups hickory or oak wood chips, soaked in warm water for 30 minutes

Barbecue sauce (your favorite homemade or store-bought)

Serves: 8
Prep time: 20 to 25 minutes
Cook time: 2 to 2½ hours
Serving size: 3 or 4 rib pieces

1. Fire up the grill:

> **For a charcoal grill:** Open the bottom vents. Ignite 6 quarts or 2½ pounds charcoal briquettes or hardwood charcoal. When the coals are hot, move briquettes into a circle around a drip pan in the center. Check for medium heat (you can hold your hand 5 inches above the cooking rack for only 4 to 5 seconds).
>
> **For a gas grill:** Turn each burner to high and ignite. Cover the grill. When hot, turn off the center burner, and set remaining burners to medium heat.

2. In a small mixing bowl, stir together salt, celery salt, pepper, cayenne, and cumin; set aside.

3. Using a paper towel to grip with, pull and remove membrane from back of rib slabs. Cut ribs apart into 3 to 4 rib sections. Rub ribs thoroughly with vinegar until moistened. Dry hands, and rub prepared spice mixture into meat, getting every surface covered well. (Either use disposable rubber gloves for this step, or wash your hands thoroughly with warm, soapy water and rinse them well afterward.)

4. *On a charcoal grill:* Start ribs bone-side down, positioned over the drip pan. Toss a few dampened wood chips on the coals, and if you have a cover, close it, and close all the vents about ⅓ to ½.

Barbecue Banter

Although they'll already be flavorful from the rub, you can still brush a sweet barbecue sauce on the ribs during their final 8 to 10 minutes on the grill.

Barbecue 2 to 2½ hours, turning ribs occasionally or until meat almost falls off bone. After 45 minutes, open the grill cover, with oven mitts (or other hand protection) lift out the grill rack and set it on a heat-safe surface. Spread 40 briquettes around the grill, placing them on the already lighted briquettes. Fanning the briquettes from time to time, get the added briquettes started. Add some more dampened wood chips and return grill rack with ribs and cover. Repeat after 45 minutes.

5. Start basting both sides of ribs with barbecue sauce the last 30 minutes. *On a gas grill:* Add wood chips according to manufacturer's directions. Grill as directed for a charcoal grill, except place ribs, fat-side up, in a roasting pan.

Barbecued Beef Ribs

Serves: 4 to 5
Prep time: 1 hour, 50 minutes (includes 90 minutes simmer time)
Cook time: 12 to 14 minutes
Serving size: 3 or 4 short ribs, depending on size

4 to 5 lb. beef short ribs

1 (8-oz.) can tomato sauce

¼ cup water

2 TB. dark brown sugar

2 TB. fresh lemon juice

1 TB. finely chopped onion

1 TB. Worcestershire sauce

1 tsp. crushed red pepper flakes

1. Trim fat from ribs, and cut ribs into serving-size pieces. Place ribs in a 6- to 8-quart pot or stock pot, and add enough water to cover. Bring to a boil over high heat and then reduce heat to low and slowly cook at a bare simmer, covered, about 1½ hours or until tender. Drain ribs.

2. While ribs simmer: in a small saucepan, combine tomato sauce, water, brown sugar, lemon juice, onion, Worcestershire sauce, and red pepper flakes. Bring to a boil over medium heat and then reduce heat to low and slowly simmer, uncovered, for 10 minutes, stirring occasionally. Set aside.

3. Fire up the grill:

> **For a charcoal grill:** Open the bottom vents. Ignite 6 quarts or 2½ pounds charcoal briquettes or hardwood charcoal. When the coals are hot, move briquettes into a circle around a drip pan in the center. Check for medium heat (you can hold your hand 5 inches above the cooking rack for only 4 to 5 seconds).
>
> **For a gas grill:** Turn each burner to high and ignite. Cover the grill. When hot, turn off a center burner and set remaining burners to medium heat.

4. *On a charcoal or gas grill:* Place ribs, bone-side down, on the grill rack over the drip pan. Brush with sauce. Cover and grill about 15 minutes or until browned, brushing occasionally with sauce. Brush with more sauce, remove from grill, and serve immediately, passing sauce.

Barbecue Banter

If you're watching your sodium intake, beware of the high sodium content of canned tomato sauces. If this is an issue for you, substitute a no-salt-added tomato sauce in this recipe.

Savory Barbecued Beef Brisket

1 (4- or 5-lb.) beef brisket, trimmed of excess fat

3 cloves garlic, cut into slivers

2 TB. vegetable oil

1 TB. kosher salt

1½ tsp. dried thyme, crumbled

1 tsp. fresh-ground black pepper

1 tsp. sweet paprika

1 tsp. ground cayenne

Barbecue sauce (your favorite homemade or store-bought)

Serves: 4 to 5
Prep time: 15 to 18 minutes
Cook time: 12 to 14 minutes
Serving size: 3 to 4 ounces

1. Fire up the grill:

> **For a charcoal grill:** Open the bottom vents. Ignite 6 quarts or 2½ pounds charcoal briquettes or hardwood charcoal. When the coals are hot, move briquettes into a circle around a drip pan in the center. Check for medium heat (you can hold your hand 5 inches above the cooking rack for only 4 to 5 seconds).
>
> **For a gas grill:** Turn each burner to high and ignite. Cover the grill. When hot, turn off the center burner, and set the remaining burners to medium heat.

2. Rinse brisket under cold water, and pat dry with paper towels. Make several slits in brisket's surface, and poke 1 garlic sliver into each one. Rub brisket with vegetable oil.

3. In a small bowl, stir together kosher salt, thyme, pepper, paprika, and cayenne, and rub over meat. Wash your hands thoroughly with warm, soapy water, and rinse them well afterward.)

4. *On a charcoal grill:* Place brisket, fat-side up, on the grill rack directly over a drip pan. Cover, close bottom and top vents ⅓, and cook 1 hour, turning once. About halfway through, uncover the grill, with oven mitts lift out the grill rack and set it on a heat-safe surface. Distribute 30 to 40 briquettes around the grill, placing them on the lighted briquettes. Fanning the briquettes from time to time, get the added briquettes started. Return the grill rack with brisket, brush with sauce, and cover. Cook 1 to 1¼ hours longer, turning and brushing lightly with sauce two or three times more until brisket is tender. Remove brisket from the grill and let rest for 10 minutes before serving. *On a gas grill:* Add wood chips according to manufacturer's directions. Grill as directed for a charcoal grill, except place meat, fat-side up, in a roasting pan. Remove brisket from the grill, and let rest for 10 minutes.

5. Slice brisket across the grain, and place on a platter. Pour sauce over brisket slices, and serve immediately, passing additional sauce.

Barbecue Banter

If you like corned beef, you'll love barbecued beef brisket. They're the same piece of meat but prepared in two very different ways.

Chapter 3

Bison

In This Chapter

- ◆ Bison's rise in popularity
- ◆ Fat content comparisons between bison and beef
- ◆ Bison grilling tips

One hundred years ago only about 1,000 bison (a.k.a. buffalo) were left in the United States. Today, 350,000 bison are being raised by more than 2,000 people—and that number is expected to increase at the rate of 20 percent a year.

Why is there such an increased interest in bison? Bison meat is leaner than beef, pork, or skinless chicken breast, for one thing. Plus, bison has a flavor similar to beef (they are genetic cousins), so it's easy to swap bison for beef if you're watching calories and fat.

Bison vs. Beef

According to the National Bison Association, bison are very hardy animals and, therefore, don't need feed with low-level amounts of antibiotics added. Most bison are born healthy and allowed to graze naturally. Growth hormones (which quickly increases muscle mass) are not used on bison, either. Antibiotics and steroids are common to American beef production. For these reasons alone, some folks choose bison.

The flavor difference between beef and bison is minimal, so if you like beef, you'll probably like bison, too. For convenience, all bison cuts—steaks, chops, prime rib, etc.—are labeled in exactly the same way as beef. If you know what a beef flank steak is, you know what a bison flank steak is.

Barbecue Banter

Bison is buffalo, but not all buffalo are bison. Asian water buffalo and African Cape buffalo aren't bison.

A bison steak has less fat than a beef steak, and depending on the cut, sometimes *much* less fat. This makes bison lower in calories, too.

Bison store most of their fat near their skin, where it keeps them warm during cold seasons. Beef fat is stored around the outside, like bison, but also in the muscles. Storing fat in muscle causes beef to, generally, have a higher fat content than bison.

Bison Grilling Considerations

Due to bison's fat content, grilling any cut of bison until well-done is a serious mistake because the end result will be dry and very tough. The best way to grill bison is to sear the outside quickly over medium-high heat to create a light flavor crust and then continue grilling over medium-high heat to quickly grill to rare or medium-rare.

Barbecue Banter

Unlike ground beef, no ground bison has ever been recalled for E. coli bacteria contamination, due in part, it appears, to a physiological difference between beef and bison. This doesn't mean, though, that ground bison bacterial contamination will never happen.

The USDA recommends cooking ground bison to the same temperature as ground beef—160°F—which guarantees its safety, but because bison can be very lean, it also dries it out. If you're willing to take the risk, a bison burger could be grilled medium-rare (145°F) and still, all things being equal, be safe to consume. Don't assume the ground bison is going to be very lean, though. Very lean ground meat is hard to work with, so most ground bison has had some fat added to it to make it less lean. Read the label, and buy whatever fits into your normal meal plans.

At rare or medium-rare, bison will be safely cooked, have all the flavor grilling imparts, but still be moist and tender. Herb and spice rubs work extremely well with bison, adding terrific flavor notes as well as bringing out bison's natural meat flavors.

Thanks to several bison grilling masters from the United States and Canada, it appears that a slightly different grilling technique produces the best end results. First, season and then brush or rub with oil all bison (except bison burgers) before it hits the grill. This helps grilling, because bison is almost free of natural fat. And grill bison over a medium-heat fire only. High heat cooks too fast, and low heat cooks too slowly.

Simple Grilled Bison Steaks

Serves: 4
Prep time: 5 minutes
Cook time: varies; see instructions
Serving size: 1 steak

4 (6- to 8-oz.) bison rib-eye steaks, at room temperature

Garlic salt

Lemon-pepper seasoning

Light olive oil or vegetable oil

1. Fire up the grill:

> *For a charcoal grill:* Open the bottom vents. Ignite 6 quarts or 2½ pounds charcoal briquettes or hardwood charcoal. When the coals are hot, set up for a one-level medium-heat fire (so you can hold your hand 5 inches above the cooking rack for only 4 to 5 seconds).
>
> *For a gas grill:* Turn each burner to high and ignite. Cover the grill. When hot, set burners to medium heat.

Barbecue Banter

Always remember bison or buffalo store little if any fat in the meat, making it a very lean protein source. That's what makes it healthier than other meats. But it also makes it trickier to grill, because it can dry out quickly.

2. While the grill heats, season both sides of each steak generously or to taste with garlic salt and lemon-pepper seasoning. Brush or rub oil on both sides.

3. Grill steaks, uncovered, over heat for 1 minute per side. *On a charcoal or gas grill:* Rotate steaks ¼ turn (do not turn over), look at your watch, note the time, and grill, uncovered, without moving steaks until pink-red juice droplets appear on the surface. Note the amount of time this takes. Turn over steaks, and grill for the same time as first side or until an instant-read thermometer inserted into the center of steaks reaches 125°F for rare or 135°F for medium-rare. Remove steaks from the grill, and let rest for 5 minutes. Serve.

Eye-Opener Bison Steaks

Serves: 4
Prep time: about 10 minutes
Cook time: varies; see instructions
Serving size: 1 bison steak

2 TB. coffee beans

2 TB. whole black peppercorns

1 TB. kosher salt

1 tsp. ground cumin

4 (6- to 8-oz.) boneless bison top loin (New York strip) steaks

2 TB. sweet (unsalted) butter, melted

1. Fire up the grill:

> *For a charcoal grill:* Open the bottom vents. Ignite 6 quarts or 2½ pounds charcoal briquettes or hardwood charcoal. When the coals are hot, set up for a one-level medium-heat fire (so you can hold your hand 5 inches above the cooking rack for only 4 to 5 seconds).
>
> *For a gas grill:* Turn each burner to high and ignite. Cover the grill. When hot, set the burners to medium heat.

2. While the grill heats, using an electric coffee or spice grinder, grind coffee beans and peppercorns until finely ground, transfer to a bowl, and stir together with kosher salt and cumin until combined. Generously season both sides of each steak with coffee mixture, pressing gently into steak's surface.

3. Grill steaks, uncovered, over heat for 1 minute per side. *On a charcoal grill:* Rotate steaks ¼ turn (do not turn over), look at your watch, note the time, and grill, uncovered, without moving steaks until pink-red juice droplets appear on surface. Note the amount of time this takes. Turn over steaks, and grill for the same time as first side or until an instant-read thermometer inserted into center of steaks reaches 125°F for rare or 135°F for medium-rare. When done, brush both sides of steaks with melted butter and remove from grill. Let rest for 5 minutes and serve.

Barbecue Banter

Most great steakhouses butter their steaks before serving because it both brings out the steak's flavor and adds a wonderful final flavor note.

Western Plains Bison Burger

2¼ lb. fresh-ground bison (80 percent lean)

2 tsp. salt

1 tsp. fresh-ground black pepper

6 (¾-oz.) slices sharp cheddar cheese

6 whole-grain hamburger buns

Smoky sweet barbecue sauce

Mustard

Pickles or pickle relish

Onion slices

Tomato slices

Lettuce leaves

Mayonnaise

Serves: 6
Prep time: 30 to 35 minutes
Cook time: 9 to 12 minutes
Serving size: 1 bison burger

1. Fire up the grill:

    For a charcoal grill: Open the bottom vents. Ignite 6 quarts or 2½ pounds charcoal briquettes or hardwood charcoal. When the coals are hot, set up for a two-level fire: one side high heat (so you can hold your hand 1 to 2 inches above cooking rack only 1 to 2 seconds) and the other medium heat (so you can hold your hand 1 to 2 inches above the cooking rack only 4 to 5 seconds).

    For a gas grill: Turn each burner to high and ignite. Cover the grill. When hot, leave half the burners on high heat, and set the other half on medium heat.

2. While the grill heats, place ground bison in a large mixing bowl, season with salt and black pepper, and, with clean hands, lightly mix seasonings into meat. Gently shape into 6 (½- to ¾-inch-thick) patties, being careful not to press too hard.

3. Grill burgers, uncovered, over high heat for 1 to 2 minutes per side. *On a charcoal grill:* Move burgers to medium heat, and grill 8 to 10 minutes total, turning every 2 minutes, until medium (155°F). *On a gas grill:* Move burgers to medium heat, and grill 4 to 5 minutes, covered. Turn and grill 5 to 6 more minutes, covered, until medium (155°F). Top burgers with cheese slices during last minute of grilling, remove burgers from the grill, and let rest for 5 minutes.

4. While bison burgers rest, lightly toast cut sides of buns on the grill's high heat side about 1 to 2 minutes. Place hamburgers on buns, and serve immediately, passing barbecue sauce, mustard, pickles, onion slices, tomato slices, lettuce, and mayonnaise.

Barbecue Banter

Just one of the many good things about ground bison: the condiments that make a beef hamburger taste even better also make a bison burger something special.

Bison Kabobs

½ cup soy sauce

½ cup vegetable oil

1 cup dry white wine

2 cloves garlic, peeled and minced, or pushed through a garlic press

1½ lb. bison sirloin steak, cut into 1-inch cubes

2 medium zucchini or yellow squash, rinsed under cold water, ends trimmed

1 large red bell pepper, stem end cut off, seeds and ribs discarded

1 large onion, peeled, root and stem end cut off, and cut into quarters

8 mushrooms, wiped with a damp paper towel with stem end trimmed

8 cherry tomatoes, rinsed under cold water

Serves: 4
Prep time: 30 to 35 minutes
Cook time: 8 to 12 minutes
Serving size: 2 kabobs

1. Add soy sauce, vegetable oil, white wine, and garlic to a reclosable plastic bag, and shake to combine. Pour ½ cup marinade into a small bowl, cover, and refrigerate. Add sirloin cubes to remaining marinade, push out air, seal the bag, and refrigerate for 8 to 24 hours, turning bag occasionally.

2. Fire up the grill:

   For a charcoal grill: Open the bottom vents. Ignite 6 quarts or 2½ pounds charcoal briquettes or hardwood charcoal. When the coals are hot, set up for a one-level medium-heat fire (so you can hold your hand 5 inches above the cooking rack for only 4 to 5 seconds).

   For a gas grill: Turn each burner to high and ignite. Cover the grill. When hot, set the burners to medium heat.

3. Cut squash and bell pepper into ½-inch-thick slices. Separate onion quarters into pieces. Remove sirloin cubes from marinade, and discard the bag and marinade. Alternate meat, squash, pepper, onion, and mushroom on each of 8 flat, metal skewers, ending each skewer with a cherry tomato.

4. *On a charcoal grill:* Grill kabobs directly above coals for 8 to 10 minutes, turning occasionally and brushing with reserved marinade. *On a gas grill:* Grill kabobs directly above heat source for 10 to 12 minutes, turning occasionally and brushing with reserved marinade. Serve.

Barbecue Banter

If your local supermarket or natural food store doesn't carry bison, head for the World Wide Web and do a search for the words "buy bison." Not only will you find mail-order sources, but you could also find a local source you didn't know existed as well.

Chapter 14

Lamb

In This Chapter

- ◆ Lamb vs. sheep
- ◆ Tips on getting the perfect cut
- ◆ From where in the world does our lamb come?

Throughout the Mediterranean region and East Asia, lamb has been cooked over hot coals and enjoyed for time long forgotten. Friends traveling to Greece tell stories of tiny, almost literally hole-in-the-wall storefronts where they tasted juicy lamb pieces quickly cooked over white-hot coals and served with a cool yogurt-based dip. It's surprising then, if lamb is really delicious and can be prepared so simply, that it's not more popular here.

I know some folks are just bothered that it's lamb: those cute little fluffy animals that frolic on hillsides and sacrifice their winter coats to give us lambswool sweaters. And yes, when cooking, lamb can have a strong aroma. But lamb also has a certain succulence that being licked by live flames brings out and intensifies. Live-fire cooking and lamb just seem to be made for each other.

The Difference Between Lamb and Sheep

The U.S. Department of Agriculture (USDA) defines *lamb* as the meat of sheep less than 12 months old. The majority of American lamb comes from 6- to 8-month-old sheep. Americans rarely consume lamb older than that mostly because of its strong flavor characteristics, even though it's available. If you see "Spring Lamb" on a label, you can safely assume it's only 4 months old.

Most of the lamb available in U.S. supermarkets actually comes from the United States. But you might find lamb that comes from other countries such as New Zealand, Australia, Canada, and even Iceland. American-raised lamb is excellent and has a balanced flavor and smooth texture. New Zealand lamb is fairly bland in flavor. Australian lamb has a better flavor than New Zealand, but it's also tougher. Canadian lamb is excellent.

The Right Cut

When we think of lamb chops, most of us visualize those two-bite, small loin chops that almost melt in your mouth. Some people even call them "lamb lollipops." Many folks are introduced to lamb when it's ground, spiced, grilled, and served in a gyros sandwich with onions, tomato, and yogurt.

Barbecue Banter

Searing the outer surface of lamb develops flavor and color through caramelization (sugar heated to the point that its color changes from white to golden brown), producing tastier

Not too many folks roast a leg of lamb for a holiday or weekend supper. Leg of lamb can be barbecued, but because it's a fairly large and dense piece of meat, it takes several long, low-heat cooking hours to prepare correctly. Most backyard chefs just aren't patient enough for that. If you have your heart set on grilling a whole lamb leg, the best way to do so is locate a butcher who'll butterfly it for you, making it less thick, lay flat, and take less time on the grill.

Barbecue Banter

A meat thermometer is the best tool to determine when to remove lamb from the grill. Insert an instant-read thermometer into the center of the meat, but do not touch any fat or bone. In general, cook ground lamb to an internal temperature of 155°F (for safety), while steaks and chops should be cooked to 130°F for rare, 145°F for medium, and 165°F for well. Resting for 5 minutes at the end of grilling allows the internal temperature to rise an additional 5°F.

Spiced Lamb Patties

3 TB. grated onion

2 TB. chopped fresh parsley

2 TB. chopped fresh basil

½ tsp. ground cumin

½ tsp. ground cinnamon

¼ tsp. salt

¼ tsp. ground cayenne

1 lb. ground lamb

Thinly sliced cucumber

Lemon wedges

Serves: 4
Prep time: 30 to 35 minutes
Cook time: 12 to 16 minutes
Serving size: 1 patty

1. Fire up the grill:

> *For a charcoal grill:* Open the bottom vents. Ignite 6 quarts or 2½ pounds charcoal briquettes or hardwood charcoal. When the coals are hot, set up for a one-level medium-heat fire (so you can hold your hand 5 inches above cooking rack for only 4 to 5 seconds).
>
> *For a gas grill:* Turn each burner to high and ignite. Cover the grill. When hot, set the burners to medium heat.

2. While grill heats, place ground lamb in a large mixing bowl, add parsley, basil, cumin, cinnamon, salt, and cayenne. With clean hands, lightly mix seasonings into meat. Gently shape into 4 (½-inch-thick) patties, being careful not to press too hard.

3. *On a charcoal grill:* Grill patties on the grill rack, uncovered, directly over medium coals for 12 to 16 minutes, turning once halfway through, until an instant-read thermometer inserted halfway into the center registers 140°F for medium-rare or 150°F for medium. *On a gas grill:* Grill, covered, 6 to 8 minutes per side or until an instant-read thermometer inserted halfway into the center registers 140°F for medium-rare or 150°F for medium.

4. Serve patties on a bed of cucumber slices, and garnish with lemon wedges.

Barbecue Banter

Lamb is just like any other meat: if it's grilled too long over too high a heat, it will turn gray and dry out. Lowering the heat of a grill—in essence slowing it down—extends the cooking time only a minute or two but gives you time to make the right decision as to when lamb or any other meat's done.

Brown Sugar–Glazed Shoulder Lamb Chops

Serves: 4
Prep time: 10 minutes, plus 20 to 30 minutes to marinate
Cook time: 8 to 14 minutes
Serving size: 1 lamb chop

4 lamb shoulder blade chops, cut ¾-inch thick

2 TB. soy sauce

1 TB. firmly packed brown sugar

6 cloves garlic, peeled and minced, or pushed through a garlic press

1½ tsp. grated fresh ginger

1 tsp. Oriental sesame oil

1. Trim all visible fat from chops, and set aside.

2. To a 1-gallon reclosable bag, add soy sauce, brown sugar, garlic, ginger, and sesame oil. Mix ingredients, and add lamb chops. Press as much air as possible out of the bag, and close the bag. When the grill's ready, drain chops, discarding bag and marinade.

3. Fire up the grill:

> *For a charcoal grill:* Open the bottom vents. Ignite 6 quarts or 2½ pounds charcoal briquettes or hardwood charcoal. When the coals are hot, set up for a one-level medium-heat fire (so you can hold your hand 5 inches above cooking rack for only 4 to 5 seconds).
>
> *For a gas grill:* Turn each burner to high and ignite. Cover the grill. When hot, set the burners to medium heat.

4. *On a charcoal grill:* Grill chops, uncovered, directly over medium coals for 8 to 10 minutes for rare (130°F), or 10 to 14 minutes for medium-rare (135°F), turning once halfway through. *On a gas grill:* Grill, covered, 5 to 6 minutes per side for rare (130°F) or 6 to 7 minutes per side for medium-rare (135°F). Let chops rest for 5 minutes. Serve.

Barbecue Banter

In 2002, the USDA estimated that 64,170 sheep ranches in the United States raised approximately 6.4 million sheep.

Herb-Crusted Lamb Chops

2 tsp. dried rosemary

1 tsp. fennel seed

1 TB. sweet paprika

2 tsp. fresh-ground black pepper

1 tsp. garlic powder

1 tsp. oregano, crumbled

1 tsp. dried basil, crumbled

½ tsp. thyme, crumbled

½ tsp. ground cayenne

½ tsp. salt

8 (5-oz.) loin lamb chops or 4 (6- to 7-oz.) shoulder blade lamb chops

1 to 2 TB. olive oil

Serves: 4
Prep time: about 20 minutes, plus 1 hour to marinate
Cook time: 6 to 12 minutes
Serving size: 2 loin lamb chops or 1 shoulder lamb chop

1. Coarsely grind rosemary and fennel seeds in an electric spice grinder. Add ground herbs to a small mixing bowl, and stir in paprika, black pepper, garlic powder, oregano, basil, thyme, cayenne, and salt.

2. Lightly coat lamb chops with olive oil. Then coat and rub lamb chops with herb mixture, and place on foil-covered platter or tray, covered with plastic wrap. Leave at room temperature for 1 hour.

3. Fire up the grill:

> *For a charcoal grill:* Open the bottom vents. Ignite 6 quarts or 2½ pounds charcoal briquettes or hardwood charcoal. When the coals are hot, set up for a one-level high-heat fire (so you can hold your hand 5 inches above cooking rack for only 1 to 2 seconds).
>
> *For a gas grill:* Turn each burner to high and ignite. Cover the grill. When hot, leave the burners on high heat.

4. Remove plastic from the platter or tray. *On a charcoal grill:* Grill chops, uncovered, directly over hot coals for 6 to 8 minutes for rare (130°F) or 8 to 10 minutes for medium-rare (135°F), turning once halfway through. *On a gas grill:* grill, covered, 4 to 5 minutes per side for rare (130°F) or 5 to 6 minutes per side for medium-rare (135°F). Remove the foil from the platter or tray, place chops on platter or tray, let rest 5 minutes, and serve.

Barbecue Banter

To keep grill flare-ups at a minimum, buy lamb that's been trimmed of most of the fat. If the lamb's not already trimmed, use a sharp knife and a cutting board to trim the fat and discard it before beginning any recipe.

Beer-Marinated Spicy Lamb Shoulder Chops

Serves: 4
Prep time: 18 to 20 minutes, plus 30 minutes to marinate
Cook time: 10 to 16 minutes
Serving size: 1 lamb chop

2 (12-oz.) bottles full-flavored beer or ale

4 cloves garlic, peeled and minced, or pushed through a garlic press

4 bone-in lamb shoulder chops, cut about ¾-inch thick

1 TB. chili powder

1 TB. firmly packed light brown sugar

1 tsp. kosher salt

1 tsp. fresh-ground black pepper

1 tsp. dried oregano, crumbled

½ tsp. ground cumin

1. Pour beer into 1-gallon reclosable plastic bag, and add garlic and lamb chops. Push out air, seal the bag, and let chops marinate for 30 minutes at room temperature, turning bag frequently.

2. Fire up the grill:

> *For a charcoal grill:* Open the bottom vents. Ignite 6-quarts or 2½ pounds charcoal briquettes or hardwood charcoal. When the coals are hot, set up for a one-level medium-heat fire (so you can hold your hand 5 inches above the cooking rack for only 4 to 5 seconds).
>
> *For a gas grill:* Turn each burner to high and ignite. Cover the grill. When hot, set the burners to medium heat.

3. While lamb marinates and grill heats, in a small bowl, stir together chili powder, brown sugar, kosher salt, pepper, oregano, and cumin.

4. Remove chops from marinade, and pat dry with paper towels. Discard the bag and marinade. Season chops with spice mixture, and rub into meat.

5. *On a charcoal grill:* Grill chops, uncovered, 10 to 14 minutes, turning once halfway through or until internal temperature of chops reaches 130°F for rare or 135°F for medium-rare. *On a gas grill:* Grill chops, covered, 6 to 8 minutes per side or until internal temperature of chops reaches 130°F for rare or 135°F for medium-rare. Remove chops from the grill and let rest 5 minutes. Serve.

Barbecue Banter

When shopping for lamb, be sure to look for meat that has a soft pink to red coloring with white marbling.

Lamb, Onion, and Peppers Shish Kabobs

1 medium onion, peeled and minced

2 cups dry red wine

3 TB. olive oil

2 lb. lamb sirloin, cut into 1-inch cubes

1 TB. grated lemon zest

1 TB. dried oregano, crumbled

½ TB. kosher salt

1 tsp. ground cumin

½ tsp. fresh-ground black pepper

1 medium onion, stem and root ends removed and quartered

2 large green bell peppers, stem ends removed, seeds and ribs discarded, and cut into 1-inch squares

Serves: 6
Prep time: 10 to 60 minutes, plus 3 to 12 hours to marinate
Cook time: 6 to 10 minutes
Serving size: 1 shish kabob

1. In a 1-gallion reclosable plastic bag, add onion, red wine, and olive oil. Seal the bag and shake until combined. Add lamb, push out air, seal the bag, and refrigerate for 3 hours and up to 12 hours, turning occasionally.

2. In a small bowl, stir together lemon zest, oregano, kosher salt, cumin, and pepper until combined.

3. Remove lamb from the plastic bag, and discard the bag and marinade. Coat lamb with seasoning mixture, cover, and let sit for 30 minutes.

4. Fire up the grill:

   For a charcoal grill: Open the bottom vents. Ignite 6 quarts or 2½ pounds charcoal briquettes or hardwood charcoal. When the coals are hot, set up for a one-level medium-heat fire (so you can hold your hand 5 inches above the cooking rack for only 4 to 5 seconds).

   For a gas grill: Turn each burner to high and ignite. Cover the grill. When hot, set the burners to medium heat.

5. Thread lamb cubes on 6 metal skewers, alternating with onions and green peppers.

6. *On a charcoal grill:* Grill kebobs, uncovered, over coals for 6 to 9 minutes, turning once a minute, for medium-rare (135°F). *On a gas grill:* Grill over heat for 7 to 10 minutes, turning once a minute, to cook on all sides for medium-rare (135°F). Serve.

Barbecue Banter

Rice makes the perfect bed for lamb shish kabobs. A rice pilaf, frequently made with a wide variety of herbs, spices, and seasonings adds color and interest. Properly prepared brown rice cooked in chicken or vegetable broth instead of water is also good. To my palate, wild rice (which isn't really rice, but a grass) does not go well with lamb kabobs.

Moroccan-Style Kefta Kabobs

Serves: 6
Prep time: 60 minutes (includes soaking time for bamboo skewers)
Cook time: 8 to 11 minutes
Serving size: 4 skewers

1 medium onion, peeled and quartered

¼ cup packed, fresh cilantro leaves

¼ cup packed, fresh parsley leaves (flat leaf preferred)

10 fresh mint leaves

2 tsp. dried marjoram, crumbled

2 lb. ground lamb

2 tsp. sweet paprika

1½ tsp. ground cumin

1½ tsp. salt

½ tsp. ground allspice

1 tsp. dried hot red pepper flakes (or to taste)

6 to 12 warm pita rounds

1. Soak 24 (10- to 12-inch) wooden skewers in warm water for 1 hour.

2. In the bowl of a food processor, add onion, cilantro, parsley, mint, and marjoram, and process, pulsing, until finely chopped. Transfer to a large mixing bowl, and add lamb, paprika, cumin, salt, allspice, and red pepper flakes. With a dinner fork, mix together until well combined. With clean hands, form mixture into 24 (2-inch) balls and then roll each ball into a 5-inch-long kefta (cigar shape).

3. Slide a skewer lengthwise through the center of each kefta and then pinch meat at each end to help it stick to the skewer.

4. Fire up the grill:

Barbecue Banter

Refrigerate or freeze lamb as soon as you bring it home from the store. Use an ice chest or ask the butcher for a plastic bag filled with ice to transport the meat if you won't be able to refrigerate the lamb within an hour.

> *For a charcoal grill:* Open the bottom vents. Ignite 6 quarts or 2½ pounds charcoal briquettes or hardwood charcoal. When the coals are hot, set up for a one-level medium-heat fire (so you can hold your hand 5 inches above the cooking rack for only 4 to 5 seconds).
>
> *For a gas grill:* Turn each burner to high and ignite. Cover the grill. When hot, set the burners to medium heat.

5. *On a charcoal grill:* Lightly oil the grill rack (do not use aerosol oil), and grill kefta, uncovered, turning once, 8 to 10 minutes total for medium. *On a gas grill:* Lightly oil the grill rack (do not use aerosol oil), and grill kefta, uncovered, turning once, 9 to 11 minutes total for medium. Serve with warm pita.

Part 5

Poultry and the Other White Meat—Pork

Chicken, turkey, and duck all taste better when prepared on a grill, especially if it's been rubbed, marinated, brined, or sauced. Just one of things you'll discover in Part 5 is how to use poultry's skin to protect the meat and then what to do after that so it not only looks great when it gets to the table but also tastes great, too. First you'll learn how to work with a whole, half, or quarter chicken. Then, I cover poultry pieces/parts and create grilled food that plays off the strengths of each of those parts.

Plus, we plunge into pork here, too. By the end of this part, if you aren't the neighborhood go-to person for ribs, then someone else got to this book before you did! Ribs aren't the whole story when it comes to: "p-i-g, hog," as TV cook Justin Wilson used to say. There's still ham, chops, tenderloins, roasts, and kabobs!

Chicken: Whole, Halves, and Quarters

In This Chapter

- Types of chickens
- Grilling issues unique to chicken
- Chicken cooking temperatures
- Tips on boosting flavor with sauces, marinades, and brines

Many Americans love chicken, and they enjoy it prepared in a gazillion different ways, from roasted whole to fried chicken fingers. On average, Americans consume more than 2 pounds of chicken per person, in one form or another, every week.

Chicken meat, for the most part, is both lean and tasty, which makes it fit into just about everybody's food plan. And because chicken spends more time on the fire than hamburgers and steaks, it comes away from the grill with a lot more flavor.

A Chicken in Every Pot

You'll find a variety of chicken available. The smallest and youngest chicken is called a Rock Cornish game hen, a special breed of chicken that weighs 12 ounces to 2 pounds whole. These young chickens are brought to market in 6 weeks. For grilling, whether whole or cut up, we'll be using broiler-fryer chickens, which are 9- to 12-week-old chickens that weigh 2½ to 3½ pounds when sold whole.

Roasting chickens, still a tender chicken, range in age from 12 to 20 weeks, and weigh between 3½ to 6 pounds. Roasting chickens, because of their size, are difficult to cook over a live fire without charring the outside before the inside is done, making them ideal for oven-roasting.

Next comes a chicken rarely seen these days, the stewing hen chicken. They're older than roasters, weigh about 5 to 6 pounds, and are perfect to use as a slow-cooking chicken stew chicken or to slow-simmer for chicken stock or broth. Neither roasting chickens nor stewing hen chickens are good for grilling.

Finally, you have the king of chickens: the capon. A capon is a neutered male chicken, younger than 32 weeks old, 5 to 8 pounds, and very meaty and tender. Unless you want to spend a lot of time at the grill, turning a capon and feeding more charcoal to your grill, a capon is best left to oven-roasting.

Barbecue Banter _____

For several years now, there's been a raging debate over whether regular, store-bought (caged) chicken tastes as good as what's called "free-range" (never caged) chicken. In my opinion, free-range chicken has more flavor and tastes better. But there's a price to be paid, too. Free-range chicken generally costs more than regular chicken—sometimes significantly more. But if you've never tasted a free-range before, grill one and see what you think. Organic free-range chickens are also available, and to my palate they taste better. But the breast meat sometimes ends up a little tougher, so the choice is up to you.

Unique Chicken Grilling Issues: Fat and Flavor

The majority of the fat in a chicken resides in the skin. And that's a good news/ bad news situation. When grilling a chicken, whether whole or in parts, you'll want to leave the skin on because it protects the meat and keeps the grill's heat from drying it out. This helps produce moist grilled chicken. That's the good news.

The bad news: as the chicken starts to cook over the flames, the fat in the skin begins to melt and drip into the fire, causing the fire to both smoke and flare up. Grill flames can ultimately burn chicken skin and produce an off-flavor. So you're always going to have a battle between keeping the flames away from your grilling chicken and leaving the chicken's skin on to protect the meat from the heat.

Flames may harm a chicken, but flavored smoke, on the other hand, enhances the chicken's flavor. For a charcoal grill, you'll want to soak anywhere from 2 to 4 cups woods chips for 20 to 30 minutes before using them on the grill.

You will need to distribute these wood chips directly onto the coals from time to time throughout the grilling process to produce a tasty smoke flavor. You'll also need to keep the grill covered so smoke collects inside the grill and can then be absorbed by the chicken. Hickory, oak, and mesquite chips work best.

To flavor chicken with smoke on your gas grill, you'll use a different technique:

1. Lay 2 sheets of 12×18-inch heavy-duty aluminum foil one directly on top of the other.

2. Soak 2 cups of your favorite wood chips for 20 to 30 minutes, drain, and then place in a rectangular shape in the center of the foil.

3. Bring the sides nearest and farthest from you up and roll together. On the left and right, fold the ends under to make a packet.

4. Poke 12 to 24 small holes in the top of the packet.

5. When starting your grill on high heat, remove one of the cooking grates and rest the packet across two burners, holes side up.

By the time you're ready to grill, smoke should be coming from the packet and should last 30 minutes. Have another packet ready before the first one stops smoking.

Aren't You Done Yet?

Always check chicken for doneness before serving. The first and best way to tell if a whole or half (split) chicken is done is by inserting an instant-read thermometer into a thick section of the thigh without touching the bone. Then check the following table to see the correct temperature.

Barbecue Banter

A *half chicken* and a *split chicken* are the same thing. A *whole chicken* is split or cut in half by removing the back bone and cutting through the breast bone lengthwise. Each piece of the two halves is approximately equal in weight to the other.

Chicken Part	Internal "Done" Temperature
Whole chicken or leg meat parts	180°F
Bone-in breast	170°F
Skinless, boneless breast	160°F
Coarsely and finely ground chicken	at least 165°F

The second and slightly less reliable method is to pierce the meat of the breast or thigh. If the liquid that comes out is clear, it's probably done; if it's pink, it's not done and needs more grill time. Also, the leg, when wiggled, should feel loose, not tight.

Flavor Boosters: Sauces, Marinades, and Brines

Because of the sugar content in almost every barbecue sauce, whether store-bought or homemade, whether high-fructose corn syrup (which acts like sugar) or natural sugar (remember, tomatoes are a fruit), barbecue sauce can burn very easily. I don't mean burn as burst into flames; a grill's high-heat output cooks sugar very fast and turns it much too quickly from brown to black. To avoid pulling a blackened mess from your grill, wait until the final 5 to 6 minutes of grill time before you start brushin' on the sauce.

If you remember from Chapter 5, a marinade is a flavored liquid, usually containing some form of acid such as vinegar or lemon juice. This marinade doesn't just add flavor, though. It also tenderizes the chicken. Brines, as you remember from Chapter 6, are very salty liquids, sometimes flavored with sugars as well as herbs and spices. Brining helps water migrate into the chicken to boost its moisture content, and the flavors in that liquid migrate into the chicken, too. What a great process!

Because chicken needs to be grilled to such high internal temperatures—around 180°F—marinating and brining can add moisture and flavor that won't disappear on the grill. If you don't believe me (and you should!), turn back to Chapters 5 and 6 if you haven't looked at those chapters already and pick out a few marinades and brines to try on your next chicken.

Chicken Safety

I don't give you a temperature to grill a rare chicken breast because no one likes rare chicken. In fact, a chicken breast could be cooked rare, but it would *not* be guaranteed safe to consume. Bacteria that may be present anywhere on or in a chicken will definitely be killed when the chicken exceeds 140°F. But for a whole chicken to reach at least 140°F, including the thickest part, other parts could be well above 140°F. So it comes down to when a chicken is "done," meaning properly and safely finished cooking.

And rinsing a chicken under cold water doesn't solve the "safety" issue either. In fact, the current opinion is not to rinse a chicken under cold water before preparing it, because that risks potentially contaminating everything with which that water comes in contact, and the rinsing water doesn't penetrate the surface like cooking will. So be certain the chicken you cook on your grill—or anywhere else for that matter—comes to the correct temperatures listed in the previous table before you serve it.

Harrison's E-Z No-Charcoal Grilled Chicken

Serves: 4
Prep time: 13 to 15 minutes
Cook time: 2 hours
Serving size: ¼ chicken

1 whole (3- to 3½-lb.) broiler-fryer chicken, split

6 TB. onion powder

3 TB. fresh-ground black pepper

3 TB. granulated sugar

3 TB. garlic powder

3 TB. ground allspice

1 TB. plus 1 tsp. dried thyme, crumbled

1 TB. plus 1 tsp. ground cinnamon

2 tsp. ground nutmeg

1½ tsp. ground cayenne

1. Fire up the grill: *On a gas grill:* Turn each burner to high and ignite. Cover the grill.

2. Rinse chicken halves under cold water, and pat both sizes dry with paper towels. Set on a foil-covered tray.

3. In a medium mixing bowl, stir together onion powder, pepper, sugar, garlic powder, allspice, thyme, cinnamon, nutmeg, and cayenne until combined. Coat chicken halves all over with seasoning mixture. (Any leftover mixture may be kept frozen; see Chapter 4.)

4. When the grill's hot, shut off one side and turn the other to its lowest setting. Place chicken halves, skin side up, on the "off" side of the grill. Close the cover, and grill for 1 hour. Open the cover, turn chicken halves over (should now be skin side down), close the cover, and grill for 1 hour. Test thigh for doneness by inserting an instant-read thermometer into thigh's thickest part without touching bone to check for 180°F; about 180°F is okay. Or pull the wing, which should come off easily. Remove chicken from the grill, and let it rest for 10 minutes before serving. Cut each half in chicken half and serve.

Barbecue Banter

A thin membrane between the skin and the flesh holds moisture in the meat while keeping the fat out. So remove the skin from the chicken after cooking, instead of before cooking, to get juicy flavor with less fat.

Milwaukee's Best Charcoal-Grilled Chicken on a Can

1 (3½-lb.) whole broiler-fryer chicken

1 cup kosher salt or ½ cup table salt

1 cup granulated sugar

2 qt. water (bottled, if tap water isn't very tasty)

3 TB. spice rub (your choice from those given in Chapter 4)

1 (12-oz.) can beer (your choice)

Serves: 4 to 6
Prep time: 18 to 20 minutes, plus 3 hours to brine
Cook time: 70 to 90 minutes
Serving size: ¼ chicken

1. Remove *giblet* bag from inside chicken cavity and discard, and rinse chicken inside and out with cold water. Set aside.

2. Add kosher salt, sugar, and water to a 1-gallon, reclosable plastic bag, seal the bag, and shake until salt and sugar dissolve. Immerse chicken in liquid, press as much air out of the bag as possible, and seal the bag. Refrigerate 3 hours.

3. Fire up the grill: *On a charcoal grill:* Open the bottom vents. Ignite 6 quarts or 2½ pounds charcoal briquettes or hardwood charcoal.

4. Remove chicken from salt solution, discarding the bag and solution. Rinse chicken inside and out under cold, running water, and pat dry with paper towels. With clean hands, massage chicken inside and out with your choice of spice rub (pick from those given in Chapter 4). From the cavity end, lift chicken skin away from breast, and massage spice rub directly onto chicken meat.

5. Open beer can and remove ¼ cup. Using a "church key"–style can opener, poke 2 more holes in the can top. Slide the can up into chicken's cavity so drumsticks exceed can's bottom and chicken stands upright.

6. Using long-handled tongs, divide the hot coals in half, forming two piles near the edge on opposite sides of the grill. Position a drip pan in the center between the coals. Put the food rack in position, and place chicken and the beer can on the grill rack over the drip pan, using chicken legs to securely balance chicken. Cover, open the cover vents halfway, and grill 30 minutes. Quickly but carefully, uncover, turn chicken 90 degrees, cover, and grill 30 more minutes or until an instant-read thermometer reads 170°F to 175°F when inserted into thigh's thickest part. The total cook time should be between 70 to 90 minutes.

Grill Guide

Giblets are the chicken's heart, liver, and gizzard. Most folks use the giblets and neck as the foundation for chicken gravy.

7. Using a large wad of paper towels for each hand, pick up chicken with the can and place on a tray. Carefully lift chicken off the can, and place chicken on a serving platter. Discard the can and whatever beer remains inside. Cut chicken into quarters and serve.

Honey-Soy Grilled Chicken

Serves: 4
Prep time: 15 minutes, plus 6 to 24 hours to marinate
Cook time: 75 to 90 minutes
Serving size: ¼ chicken

1 (3- to 4-lb.) whole broiler-fryer chicken

¼ cup water

¼ cup soy sauce

¼ cup dry sherry

1 green onion, trimmed and sliced

2 cloves garlic, peeled and minced, or pushed through a garlic press

½ tsp. Chinese five-spice powder

1 TB. vegetable oil

1 TB. honey

1. Remove neck and giblets from chicken and discard. Rinse chicken under cold running water inside and out. Pat dry with paper towels. With toothpicks, secure neck skin to back. Twist wing tips under back, and tie legs to tail with kitchen twine. Place chicken in a plastic bag set in a deep bowl.

2. In a small bowl, stir together water, soy sauce, sherry, green onion, garlic, and Chinese five-spice powder. Pour mixture over chicken, push out air, seal the bag, and refrigerate for 6 to 24 hours, turning bag occasionally.

3. Drain chicken, discarding the bag and marinade, and pat dry with paper towels. Brush chicken with oil.

4. Fire up the grill:

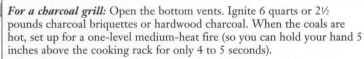

For a charcoal grill: Open the bottom vents. Ignite 6 quarts or 2½ pounds charcoal briquettes or hardwood charcoal. When the coals are hot, set up for a one-level medium-heat fire (so you can hold your hand 5 inches above the cooking rack for only 4 to 5 seconds).

For a gas grill: Turn each burner to high and ignite. Cover the grill. When hot, set the burners to medium heat.

5. *On a charcoal grill:* Arrange medium-hot coals around a drip pan. Add 12 to 15 briquettes onto the hot coals. Test for medium heat above the pan. Place chicken, breast side up, on the grill rack over the drip pan. Cover and grill for 1¼ to 1½ hours or until chicken is no longer pink and drumsticks move easily, brushing with honey during the last 10 minutes of grilling. *On a gas grill:* Place chicken on a rack in a roasting pan, and place on grill. Cover and grill as directed for a charcoal grill.

6. Remove chicken from the grill. Cover with foil, and let stand 10 minutes before carving. Serve.

Flame Point

Never use marinade in which raw chicken has been soaking on cooked chicken. Do not brush marinade that's come in contact with raw chicken on cooking chicken. If you want to brush marinade on grilling chicken, set about ¼ prepared marinade aside, covered and chilled, and use what remains to marinate the chicken. Marinade can be rendered "safe" by pouring it into a saucepan and bringing it to a boil over high heat. When it boils, turn heat down and boil for 8 to 10 minutes.

Grilled Garlic-Head Chicken

2 whole garlic heads

8 cups cold water

½ cup granulated sugar

½ cup table salt

¼ cup hot pepper sauce

3 medium bay leaves, crumbled

1 whole (3- to 3½-lb.) chicken, back removed (ask your butcher to do this)

2 TB. olive oil

1 tsp. fresh-ground black pepper

Serves: 4
Prep time: 15 to 20 minutes
Cook time: 40 minutes, plus 10 minutes rest
Serving size: ¼ chicken

1. Break all garlic cloves off garlic heads. Place in a quart-size reclosable plastic bag, press as much air out of the bag as possible, seal the bag and place on a cutting board. Using a rubber mallet or a meat mallet, pound garlic cloves until they're crushed. Pour 1 cup cold water into the bag, swish it around, and pour contents of bag

into a 1-gallon, reclosable plastic bag. Add sugar, salt, hot pepper sauce, bay leaves and enough cold water to make 2 quarts (7 more cups). Seal the bag, and shake it until salt and sugar dissolve. Add chicken, press as much air out as possible, seal, and refrigerate for 2 to 4 hours.

2. Fire up the grill:

> *For a charcoal grill:* Open the bottom vents. Ignite 6 quarts or 2½ pounds charcoal briquettes or hardwood charcoal. When the coals are hot, set up for a one-level medium-low-heat fire (so you can hold your hand 5 inches above the cooking rack for only 4 to 5 seconds).
>
> *For a gas grill:* Turn each burner to high and ignite. Cover the grill. When hot, set the burners to medium-low heat.

Barbecue Banter

To visually check chicken for doneness, pierce it with the tines of a fork or a knife point. The juices should run clear—not pink—when the fork or knife meets no resistance when inserted.

3. Remove chicken from brine, and pat both sides dry with paper towels. Open chicken where back has been removed, spread chicken open, bone side down, and use the heal of your hand to flatten the breast bone. Place a triple layer of paper towels over chicken, cover with plastic wrap, and with a rubber mallet, pound chicken until it's close to evenly flat. Remove plastic wrap and paper towel, brush both sides with olive oil, and season with pepper.

4. When the grill's hot, grill chicken, skin side down, over the coals for 30 to 40 minutes or until an instant-read thermometer reads 170°F to 175°F when inserted into the thickest part of thigh. Transfer chicken to cutting board, cover with single sheet of foil, and let it rest 10 minutes. Carve into 8 pieces and serve.

Herb and Mustard–Coated Chicken

2 TB. Dijon mustard

1 TB. chopped fresh parsley

1 TB. chopped fresh oregano or 1 tsp. dried oregano, crumbled

1 TB. water

⅛ tsp. ground cayenne

1 (3- to 3½-lb.) whole broiler-fryer

1 TB. vegetable oil

Serves: 4		
Prep time: 15 to 20 minutes		
Cook time: 75 to 90 minutes		
Serving size: ¼ chicken		

1. Fire up the grill:

> *For a charcoal grill:* Open the bottom vents. Ignite 6 quarts or 2½ pounds charcoal briquettes or hardwood charcoal. When the coals are hot, set up for a one-level medium-heat fire (so you can hold your hand 5 inches above the cooking rack for only 4 to 5 seconds).
>
> *For a gas grill:* Turn each burner to high and ignite. Cover the grill. When hot, set the burners to medium heat.

2. In a small bowl, stir or whisk together Dijon mustard, parsley, oregano, water, and cayenne. Cover and set aside.

3. Remove neck and giblets from chicken and discard. Rinse chicken under cold running water inside and out. Pat dry with paper towels. With toothpicks, secure neck skin to back, twist wing tips under back, and tie legs to tail with kitchen twine. Brush vegetable oil over chicken.

4. *On a charcoal grill:* Arrange medium-hot coals around a drip pan. Place chicken, breast side up, on the grill rack over the drip pan, cover, and grill for 1¼ to 1½ hours or until chicken is no longer pink and drumsticks move easily, brushing with mustard sauce during last 10 minutes of grilling. *On a gas grill:* Place chicken on a rack in a roasting pan and place on the grill. Cover and grill as directed for a charcoal grill. Remove chicken from the grill. Cover with foil, and let stand for 10 minutes before carving. Serve.

Barbecue Banter

You can safely thaw chicken in cold water (never use warm water thinking it'll defrost faster). Place chicken in its original wrap or water-tight plastic bag, and submerge in cold water. Change the water often. It will take about 2 hours to thaw a whole chicken and slightly less for chicken parts.

Korean-Style Grilled Chicken

Serves: 4
Prep time: 10 to 12 minutes plus 3 hours to marinate
Cook time: 40 to 50 minutes
Serving size: ¼ chicken

1 (3- to 3½-lb.) broiler-fryer chicken, cut into quarters

½ cup light vegetable oil

½ cup dark corn syrup

½ cup soy sauce

½ cup sesame seeds

1 small onion, peeled and sliced

1 clove garlic, peeled and crushed

½ tsp. ground ginger

½ tsp. fresh-ground black pepper

1. Rinse chicken quarters under cold water, and pat dry with paper towels.

2. Add vegetable oil, corn syrup, soy sauce, sesame seeds, onion, garlic, ginger, and pepper to a 1-gallon, reclosable plastic bag. Seal the bag, and shake until combined. Immerse chicken quarters in liquid, press as much air out as possible, and seal the bag. Refrigerate 3 hours, turning once.

3. Fire up the grill:

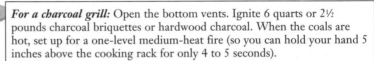

For a charcoal grill: Open the bottom vents. Ignite 6 quarts or 2½ pounds charcoal briquettes or hardwood charcoal. When the coals are hot, set up for a one-level medium-heat fire (so you can hold your hand 5 inches above the cooking rack for only 4 to 5 seconds).

For a gas grill: Turn each burner to high and ignite. Cover the grill. When hot, set the burners to medium heat.

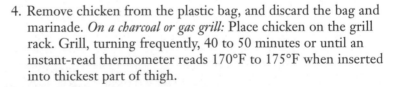

Barbecue Banter

Never leave grilled chicken at room temperature for more than 2 hours. If not eaten immediately, keep grilled chicken either hot (at or above 140°F) or refrigerated.

4. Remove chicken from the plastic bag, and discard the bag and marinade. *On a charcoal or gas grill:* Place chicken on the grill rack. Grill, turning frequently, 40 to 50 minutes or until an instant-read thermometer reads 170°F to 175°F when inserted into thickest part of thigh.

5. Transfer grilled chicken to a serving platter or tray, cover with a single foil sheet, and let it rest 10 minutes. Serve.

Jamaican-Style Jerk Chicken

½ **cup red wine vinegar**

½ **cup distilled white vinegar**

½ **cup soy sauce**

½ **cup olive oil**

½ **cup orange juice, not from concentrate**

1 **TB. firmly packed dark brown sugar**

1 **TB. fresh thyme or 1 tsp. dried thyme, crumbled**

1 **TB. grated fresh ginger**

1 **tsp. coarse-ground black pepper**

1 **tsp. ground cinnamon**

½ **tsp. ground nutmeg**

½ **tsp. ground cayenne**

6 **green onions, trimmed and finely chopped**

¼ **cup minced onion**

2 **cloves garlic, peeled and minced or pushed through a garlic press**

1 **large jalapeño chili pepper, stem top cut off and finely chopped, including seeds and ribs**

1 **(3- to 3½-lb.) broiler-fryer chicken, quartered**

Serves: 4
Prep time: 30 minutes, plus 4 to 6 to marinate
Cook time: 40 to 60 minutes
Serving size: ¼ chicken

1. To a 1-gallon, reclosable plastic bag, add red wine vinegar, white vinegar, soy sauce, olive oil, orange juice, brown sugar, thyme, ginger, pepper, cinnamon, nutmeg, cayenne, green onions, minced onion, garlic, and jalapeño pepper. Seal the bag, and shake until combined. Measure out ½ cup marinade from the bag, cover, and chill. Rinse chicken under cold running water and pat dry with paper towels. Immerse chicken quarters in remaining liquid, press out air, seal the bag, and refrigerate for at least 4 and up to 6 hours.

2. Fire up the grill:

> *For a charcoal grill:* Open the bottom vents. Ignite 6 quarts or 2½ pounds charcoal briquettes or hardwood charcoal. When the coals are hot, set up for a one-level medium-heat fire (so you can hold your hand 5 inches above cooking rack for only 4 to 5 seconds).
>
> *For a gas grill:* Turn each burner to high and ignite. Cover the grill. When hot, set the burners to medium heat.

3. Remove chicken quarters from marinade, and discard the bag and marinade. *On a charcoal grill:* Grill chicken directly over coals, uncovered, for 40 to 50 minutes, turning and basting with reserved jerk sauce every 15 minutes. *On a gas grill:* Grill chicken, covered, for 50 to 60 minutes, turning and basting with reserved jerk sauce every 15 minutes.

4. Transfer grilled chicken to a serving platter or tray, cover with a single sheet of foil, and let it rest 10 minutes. Serve.

Barbecue Banter

Always grill chicken well-done, not medium or rare. If you're using a meat thermometer, the internal temperature should reach 175° to 189°F for whole chicken and 160° to 170°F for bone-in parts and boneless parts. See the table earlier in this chapter.

Grilled Lemon Chicken

Serves: 4
Prep time: 10 minutes, plus 8 to 24 hours to marinate
Cook time: 40 to 60 minutes
Serving size: ¼ chicken

1 TB. finely grated fresh lemon zest

½ cup fresh lemon juice (from about 2 to 3 large lemons)

½ cup mayonnaise

1 TB. salt

1 tsp. poultry seasoning

¼ tsp. ground white pepper

1 (3- to 3½-lb.) broiler-fryer chicken, quartered

1. To a 1-gallon, reclosable plastic bag, add lemon zest, lemon juice, mayonnaise, salt, poultry seasoning, and white pepper. Seal the bag, and shake until combined. Rinse chicken under cold running water and pat dry with paper towels. Immerse chicken quarters in liquid, press out air, seal the bag, and refrigerate for at least 8 and up to 24 hours.

2. Fire up the grill:

> *For a charcoal grill:* Open the bottom vents. Ignite 6 quarts or 2½ pounds charcoal briquettes or hardwood charcoal. When the coals are hot, set up for a one-level medium-heat fire (so you can hold your hand 5 inches above the cooking rack for only 4 to 5 seconds).
>
> *For a gas grill:* Turn each burner to high and ignite. Cover the grill. When hot, set the burners to medium heat.

3. Bring chicken to room temperature 30 minutes before grilling, and discard the bag and marinade. *On a charcoal grill:* Grill chicken directly over coals, uncovered, for 40 to 50 minutes or until an instant-read thermometer inserted into the thickest part of the breast registers 170°F, turning and basting with reserved marinade every 15 minutes. *On a gas grill:* Grill chicken, covered, 50 minutes to 1 hour or until an instant-read thermometer inserted into the thickest part of the breast registers 170°F, turning and basting with reserved sauce every 15 minutes.

4. Transfer grilled chicken to a serving platter or tray, cover with a single sheet of foil, and let rest 10 minutes. Serve.

Barbecue Banter

Myth: Yellow-skinned chicken has more fat than lighter-skinned chicken. *Truth:* The differences in skin color are caused by what the chickens are fed. Skin color does not affect nutritional value, flavor, tenderness, or fat content.

Barbecue Sauce–Glazed Chicken

3 large onions (about 1 lb.) peeled, stem and root ends cut off, and finely chopped (about 2¾ cups)

4 cloves garlic, peeled and minced

¼ cup olive oil

1 cup distilled white vinegar

1 cup canned tomato purée

½ cup mild honey

¼ cup steak sauce

1 TB. Worcestershire sauce

¾ tsp. salt

¼ tsp. fresh-ground black pepper

1 (3- to 3½-lb.) broiler-fryer chicken, split in half

Serves: 4	
Prep time: 25 to 30 minutes	
Cook time: 55 to 75 minutes	
Serving size: ¼ chicken	

1. Fire up the grill:

   > *For a charcoal grill:* Open the bottom vents. Ignite 6 quarts or 2½ pounds charcoal briquettes or hardwood charcoal. When the coals are hot, set up for a one-level medium-heat fire (so you can hold your hand 5 inches above the cooking rack for only 4 to 5 seconds).
   >
   > *For a gas grill:* Turn each burner to high and ignite. Cover the grill. Leave the burners set to high heat and set the remaining burners to medium.

2. Cook onions and garlic in olive oil in a 4-quart heavy saucepan over medium-low heat, covered, stirring occasionally, until soft, 12 to 14 minutes (reduce heat to low if onions begin to brown). Stir in vinegar, tomato purée, honey, steak sauce, Worcestershire sauce, salt, and pepper, and bring to a boil. Remove sauce from heat, and reserve 1 cup for basting and 1½ cups for serving.

3. Rinse chicken under cold water, pat dry with paper towels, and season with salt and pepper.

4. *On a charcoal grill:* Grill chicken directly over coals, uncovered, for 10 to 15 minutes or until golden brown. Move chicken to the side of the grill with no coals underneath, arranging skin-side up, and grill, covered, brushing with sauce and turning every 10 minutes, until cooked through, 45 minutes to 1 hour or until an instant-read thermometer inserted into the thickest part of the breast registers 170°F. *On a gas grill:* Sear chicken over high-heat burners on lightly oiled grill rack, uncovered, turning, until golden brown, about 10 to 15 minutes total. Move chicken to the medium-heat side of the grill, arranging skin-side up, and grill, covered, brushing with sauce and turning every 10 minutes, until cooked through, about 25 to 35 minutes or until an instant-read thermometer inserted into the thickest part of the breast registers 170°F. Serve chicken, passing warmed reserved sauce.

Barbecue Banter

Play it safe by always thawing chicken in the refrigerator or in warm water—not on your kitchen countertop. It takes about 24 hours to thaw a 4-pound chicken in the refrigerator, and cut-up chicken parts takes 3 to 9 hours to thaw.

Mopped and Grilled Chicken

Serves: 4
Prep time: about 15 minutes
Cook time: 50 to 60 minutes
Serving size: ¼ chicken

¼ **cup distilled white vinegar**

1 **TB. plus 1 tsp. firmly packed light brown sugar**

½ **tsp. salt**

¼ **tsp. fresh-ground black pepper**

¼ **cup plus 2 TB. water**

¼ **cup plus 1 TB. ketchup**

1½ **TB. butter**

1 **tsp. lemon juice**

1 **(3- to 3½-lb.) broiler-fryer chicken, split**

1. In a small saucepan over medium-high heat, stir together vinegar, brown sugar, salt, and pepper, stirring until sugar dissolves. Stir in water, ketchup, butter, and lemon juice, and bring to a low boil. Reduce heat to low and simmer 5 minutes. Remove from heat, and set aside.

2. Fire up the grill:

> *For a charcoal grill:* Open the bottom vents. Ignite 6 quarts or 2½ pounds charcoal briquettes or hardwood charcoal. When the coals are hot, set up for a one-level medium-heat fire (so you can hold your hand 5 inches above the cooking rack for only 4 to 5 seconds).
>
> *For a gas grill:* Turn each burner to high and ignite. Cover the grill. Leave the burners set to high heat.

3. Rinse chicken under cold, running water and pat dry with paper towels. Place chicken halves, skin-side up, on the grill. *On a charcoal grill:* Grill uncovered over coals for about 20 minutes, without turning, mopping with prepared sauce every 5 minutes. Grill 30 to 40 more minutes or until an instant-read thermometer inserted into the thickest part of the breast registers 170°F, turning every 5 to 10 minutes, ending with chicken skin-side down to crisp, mopping with sauce at each turn. *On a gas grill:* Reduce all burners to medium, and grill chicken halves starting skin-side up over medium heat for about 15 minutes, covered, without turning, mopping with sauce every 5 minutes. Grill 30 to 40 more minutes total or until an instant-read thermometer inserted into the thickest part of the breast registers 170°F, turning three times and mopping with sauce on each turn. Arrange chicken on a platter and serve.

Flame Point

When barbecuing chicken outdoors, keep the chicken refrigerated until no more than 30 minutes before you're ready to cook it. Do not place cooked chicken on the same plate or tray you used to transport raw chicken to the grill. To avoid that, I place a layer of foil on the plate or tray I use for transportation. After the chicken's on the grill, I ball up the foil and discard it and use the same plate or tray to transport the cooked chicken to the table.

Chapter 16

Bawk, Gobble, and Quack: More Poultry

In This Chapter

- The lowdown on chicken parts
- Hints for keeping your poultry fresh
- Bone and skin or boneless and skinless?
- Tips on applying sauce to your bird
- A look at nonchicken poultry: turkey and duck

Years ago, if you wanted to cook just chicken legs, you either had the butcher cut up your chicken and figure out what to make for another meal with everything but the legs, or you took the whole chicken home and cut it up yourself.

Today, you can find chickens cut into parts, including breasts (with or without skin and bones), legs or drumsticks, thighs (with or without skin and bones), wings, and drummettes (the small second joint of the chicken wing, with skin pulled back). Depending on where you shop, sometimes the wing comes attached to the breast, and if you're buying chicken quarters, the leg and thigh can come attached. Much of the same is true for turkey and duck parts. No matter which you pick, they're all made for the grill.

Freshness Counts

Okay, so you're off to the store to pick up skin-on, bone-in chicken parts. How do you know the chicken parts you're buying are as fresh and safe as they can be? Figuring this out is not as easy as it might seem, but here are some general rules for checking freshness:

Buy poultry as close to when you're going to grill it as is reasonably possible. Don't try to be efficient and pick up your chicken on Monday for next Saturday's grilling get-together, even if it's on sale. Plus, if you're running a lot of errands, and the day's warm, too, it's a good idea to take along a cooler with ice in it to keep your poultry safely cool.

Don't freeze your chicken. By freezing, you may keep a "fresh" chicken from spoiling; that's good. But although "fresh" chicken should never have been frozen, most "fresh" chicken has actually been frozen or close to it (chicken truckers and stores, erring to the safe side, tend to keep chicken too cold rather than too warm). If you take it home on Monday and freeze it for Saturday, you may be freezing that chicken for the second time. Freezing causes moisture loss.

Give your chicken the sniff test. Open the package and smell the chicken. Chicken spoils from the bone out, not the skin in, so give the bones a sniff. If it smells sweet, it's fine. If it smells off or odd, there's a good chance it's well on its way to spoiling. Either return it to the store or discard it.

When you get your chicken home, immediately refrigerate it in the coldest part of your refrigerator, usually the area in the lower third. And keeping it in the lower third makes certain that if the package leaks, it's not going to drip down through the refrigerator contaminating other foods.

Always wash your hands with warm soapy water and rinse them well before and after handling chicken. And always rinse your chicken under cold water and pat it dry with paper towels before beginning to work with it.

> **Barbecue Banter**
>
> Follow the crowd. The more chicken a store sells, the higher the likelihood what you buy there will be fresh.

Bone In or Boned?

When it comes to grilling cut-up poultry, I prefer leaving the bone in and the skin on, for good reason. Leaving these parts intact keeps the meat from drying out and delivers more flavor.

When coals glow and their heat and flames rise up to tickle the chicken, the chicken's skin and sometimes the bones (think chicken breast) act as a firewall. Because the fat's located between the meat and the skin, with the skin on, the chicken bastes itself when that fat begins to melt.

Also, some of the fat and chicken juices drip down on the coals or the metal or lava rocks of a gas grill and produce smoke. That smoke can imbue a flavor that doesn't exist without it. This "skin" advantage is one that steaks, burgers, and chops don't have, and ribs only have their bones for partial flame protection.

Saucing Up the Bird

The best way I've found to sauce cut-up poultry grilled with the skin on is to remove the skin just before it's done and add the sauce then. At that point, the poultry's skin has done its job and protected the meat throughout almost all the grilling process.

Removing the skin is easy to do with tongs, and most of the time, the skin should simply slip off. Quickly pull the skin off and discard, and then brush on barbecue sauce during the final 5 or 6 minutes of grill time, keeping the poultry away from the highest-heat areas. You want to virtually melt the sauce on by using the fire's heat to liquefy the sugar, not burn it.

Flame Point _____

Almost every commercial barbecue sauce, and even many made at home, have some or a lot of sugar. The sugar comes from added sugar, high-fructose corn syrup in ketchup, and the natural sugar in tomatoes. Sugar can turn from glaze to burned in a few seconds at temperatures far lower than a grill's high heat. So wait until the end to sauce your bird.

Checking for Doneness

No one likes rare chicken. If you don't have an instant-read thermometer, get one before cooking chicken! It's a necessity. A meat thermometer works, too, but it takes too long to register the temperature. (Hey, you're working near the flames, so you gotta move quickly.)

Each part of a chicken is done at a different temperature. The first and best way to tell if chicken is done is by inserting an instant-read thermometer into the thickest part without touching the bone. Then check the following table to see the correct temperature.

Part	Internal Take-It-Off-the Grill Temperature
Chicken	
Bone-in breast	165°F
Skinless and boneless breast	160°F
Leg and thigh meat	170°F
Duck	
Whole duckling	175°F
Breast or parts	165°F

Barbecue Banter

The USDA's Food Safety and Inspection Service (FSIS) recommends cooking whole chicken to 180°F as measured in the thigh using a food thermometer. This is certainly a safe temperature to consider chicken or chicken parts safely done. However, a slightly lower temperature produces a more moist chicken and is no less safe. Also, for example, if the thigh temperature is 170°F when it's taken off the grill, due to retained heat, over the next 5 minutes it will rise to 175°F.

As mentioned in Chapter 15, the second and slightly less reliable method is to pierce the meat of the breast, thigh, or leg. If the juice that comes out is clear, it's probably done. If it's pink, it's not done and needs more grill time.

Flame Point

Remember these important rules for grilling safety:

◆ Never leave a grill with lighted briquettes or charcoal unattended.

◆ Never use a grill in a garage or enclosed area.

◆ Never move a grill when it's in use or hot.

◆ Never use a grill unless all the unit's parts are firmly in place and the grill is level and absolutely stable.

Turkey and Duck

You don't have to wait for Thanksgiving to enjoy turkey, especially turkey on the grill. All the rules for chicken hold true for turkey and duck:

- It's generally better to grill turkey or duck with the skin on and bones in. As with chicken, these can act as your firewall.
- Buy from stores with a lot of shoppers, and buy it as near as possible to the time you're going to grill it.
- Freeze turkey or duck to keep it from spoiling only as a last resort. Or buy it already frozen and defrost it slowly in the refrigerator.
- Be sure the bird passes the sniff test.
- Keep poultry cold (below 40°F) as soon as it gets home until you're ready to use it.
- Keep your hands clean (it's better to wash them too frequently than not enough). Rinse turkey and duck under cold water, and pat it dry with paper towels before beginning to work with it.

Okay, let's grill some poultry.

Citrus-Flavored Chicken Breasts

Serves: 6
Prep time: about 20 minutes, plus 2 to 3 hours to marinate
Cook time: 10 to 12 minutes
Serving size: 1 breast

6 skinless, boneless chicken breast halves (about 2 lb.)

½ cup fresh lemon juice (from 2 to 3 large lemons)

½ cup orange juice, not from concentrate

2 cloves garlic, peeled and minced or pushed through a garlic press

1 TB. grated fresh ginger

1 tsp. dried tarragon, crumbled

½ tsp. salt

¼ tsp. fresh-ground black pepper

1. Rinse chicken breasts under cold water, pat dry with paper towels, and pound between plastic wrap to ½-inch thick.

2. Two to three hours before grilling, prepare marinade. Place chicken breasts in a 1-gallon, resealable plastic bag. In a small bowl, stir together lemon juice, orange juice, garlic, ginger, tarragon, salt, and pepper. Reserve ½ cup marinade, and pour remainder over chicken, push out air, seal the bag, and refrigerate, turning occasionally, for 2 to 3 hours.

3. Fire up the grill:

> *For a charcoal grill:* Open the bottom vents. Ignite 6 quarts or 2½ pounds charcoal briquettes or hardwood charcoal. When the coals are hot, set up for a one-level medium-heat fire (so you can hold your hand 5 inches above the cooking rack for only 4 to 5 seconds).
>
> *For a gas grill:* Turn each burner to high and ignite. Cover the grill. When hot, set the burners to medium heat.

4. Remove chicken from marinade, pat dry with paper towels, and discard the bag and marinade. *On a charcoal grill:* Arrange chicken on the grill over the coals. Grill chicken, uncovered, turning two or three times and brushing with reserved marinade, until chicken is no longer pink in the center, about 10 to 12 minutes or until an instant-read thermometer inserted into center of the thickest part registers 160°F. *On a gas grill:* Arrange chicken on the grill over heat. Grill, 10 to 12 minutes, covered, turning once halfway through, brushing with reserved marinade, until chicken is no longer pink in center or until an instant-read thermometer inserted into center of the thickest part registers 160°F. Remove chicken from the grill and serve.

Barbecue Banter

"Didn't you just write that the best chicken is grilled with skin on and bones in? Yes, but skinless and boneless is easier to work with when you haven't done this before. We're starting with some easy preparations first. And the marinade makes up for the flavor loss without the skin.

Rum and Lime–Marinated Caribbean Chicken Breasts

6 skinless, boneless chicken breast halves (about 2 lb. total)

⅔ cup light rum

½ medium onion, peeled and minced

Juice of 2 limes

1 TB. vegetable oil

Salt

Lime wedges, for garnish

Serves: 6
Prep time: about 20 minutes, plus 2 to 3 hours to marinate
Cook time: 10 to 12 minutes
Serving size: 1 breast

1. Rinse chicken breasts under cold water, pat dry with paper towels, and pound between plastic wrap to ½-inch thick.

2. Two hours before grilling, prepare marinade. Place chicken breasts in a 1-gallon, resealable plastic bag. In a small bowl, stir together rum, onion, lime juice, and vegetable oil. Pour marinade over chicken, push out air, seal the bag, and refrigerate, turning occasionally, for 2 hours.

3. Fire up the grill:

> *For a charcoal grill:* Open the bottom vents. Ignite 6 quarts or 2½ pounds charcoal briquettes or hardwood charcoal. When the coals are hot, set up for a one-level medium-heat fire (so you can hold your hand 5 inches above the cooking rack for only 4 to 5 seconds).
>
> *For a gas grill:* Turn each burner to high and ignite. Cover the grill. When hot, set the burners to medium heat.

4. Remove chicken from marinade, drain, and discard the bag and marinade. Season chicken with salt, and let it sit at room temperature until the grill's ready.

5. *On a charcoal grill:* Grill chicken, uncovered, 5 to 6 minutes per side, until chicken is no longer pink in the center or until an instant-read thermometer inserted into the center of the thickest part registers 160°F. *On a gas grill:* Grill chicken, covered, 10 to 12 minutes, turning once halfway through, until chicken is no longer pink in the center or until an instant-read thermometer inserted into the center of the thickest part registers 160°F. Remove chicken from the grill, and serve.

Barbecue Banter

To add authenticity, you could serve a Caribbean hot sauce as a condiment with these chicken breasts. Caribbean hot sauces are generally a fragrant combination of high-heat habañero or scotch bonnet chilies with a touch of mustard. Use them a few drops at a time.

Grilled Garlic Chicken Breasts

Serves: 4
Prep time: 15 minutes, plus 1 hour to marinate
Cook time: 12 to 16 minutes
Serving size: 1 chicken breast

4 skinless, boneless chicken breasts (about 1½ lb.)

4 cloves garlic, peeled and minced or pushed through a garlic press

1 tsp. kosher salt

½ cup chopped fresh cilantro leaves

2 TB. fresh lime juice

2 TB. coarse-ground black pepper

1. Rinse chicken breasts under cold water, and pat dry with paper towels.

2. One hour before grilling, prepare marinade. Place chicken breasts in a 1-gallon, resealable plastic bag. Chop and mash garlic with kosher salt to make paste. To a small stainless-steel or glass bowl, add garlic purée, cilantro, lime juice, and pepper, stirring to combine. Pour marinade over chicken, push out air, seal the bag, and refrigerate, turning occasionally, for 1 hour.

3. Fire up the grill:

> ***For a charcoal grill:*** Open the bottom vents. Ignite 6 quarts or 2½ pounds charcoal briquettes or hardwood charcoal. When the coals are hot, set up for a one-level medium-heat fire (so you can hold your hand 5 inches above the cooking rack for only 4 to 5 seconds).
>
> ***For a gas grill:*** Turn each burner to high and ignite. Cover the grill. When hot, set the burners to medium heat.

4. Remove chicken from the bag, and discard the bag and marinade. *On a charcoal grill:* Grill chicken, uncovered, 6 to 8 minutes per side, until chicken is no longer pink in the center or until an instant-read thermometer inserted into the center of the thickest part registers 160°F. *On a gas grill:* Grill chicken, covered, 12 to 16 minutes, turning once halfway through, until chicken is no longer pink in the center or until an instant-read thermometer inserted into the center of the thickest part registers 160°F. Remove chicken from the grill, and serve.

Barbecue Banter

When preparing to mash garlic and kosher salt to a paste, push the garlic cloves through a garlic press. The press does almost all the work and takes much less time than if you started with whole garlic cloves and used a knife to mince them first before adding the salt.

Black Olive and Blue Cheese–Stuffed Chicken Breasts

4 skinless, boneless chicken breast halves (about 1½ lb.)

3 oz. blue cheese, crumbled

¼ cup chopped black olives

1 TB. unsalted butter, melted

2 TB. chopped fresh cilantro leaves

¼ tsp. salt

¼ tsp. fresh-ground black pepper

Serves: 4
Prep time: 12 minutes
Cook time: about 15 minutes
Serving size: 1 chicken breast

1. Rinse chicken breasts under cold water, and pat dry with paper towels.

2. Fire up the grill:

> *For a charcoal grill:* Open the bottom vents. Ignite 6 quarts or 2½ pounds charcoal briquettes or hardwood charcoal. When the coals are hot, set up for a one-level medium-heat fire (so you can hold your hand 5 inches above the cooking rack for only 4 to 5 seconds).
>
> *For a gas grill:* Turn each burner to high and ignite. Cover the grill. When hot, set the burners to medium heat.

3. In a small bowl, use a fork to mix blue cheese and black olives together.

4. Place each chicken breast between 2 pieces of plastic wrap. Use the flat side of a meat mallet to pound chicken into rectangles about ¼- to ⅜-inch thick. Remove plastic wrap. Season chicken with salt and pepper. Divide blue cheese mixture evenly among pounded breasts, spread mixture on chicken, fold in sides of each chicken breast, roll up chicken, and secure with wooden toothpicks. Brush with melted butter.

5. *On a charcoal or gas grill:* Grill chicken rolls, seam sides down, about 15 minutes, covered with all the vents open, turning after 10 minutes until juice of chicken is no longer pink when centers of thickest pieces are pierced. Serve dusted with cilantro.

Barbecue Banter
You can find several different kinds of black olives. Canned California black olives look perfect but taste more like salt than olives. Black (almost dark-purple) Greek kalamata olives have a big flavor that leaps over the salt. And tiny, black French Nicoise olives pack a big flavor punch for their diminutive size.

Turkey and Penne Caesar Salad

Serves: 4
Prep time: about 25 minutes
Cook time: 12 to 15 minutes
Serving size: about 2 cups

1 (6-oz.) pkg. uncooked penne pasta

4 turkey breast tenderloin steaks, cut ½-inch thick (about 1 lb. total)

¾ cup bottled Caesar salad dressing

6 cups rinsed, torn, and spun dry, romaine lettuce

12 cherry tomatoes, washed under cold running water and halved

¼ cup fine-shredded Parmesan cheese

Fresh-ground black pepper to taste

1. Cook pasta according to package directions. Drain, rinse under running cold water, drain again, and chill.

2. Rinse turkey steaks under cold water, and pat dry with paper towels.

3. Fire up the grill:

 For a charcoal grill: Open the bottom vents. Ignite 6 quarts or 2½ pounds charcoal briquettes or hardwood charcoal. When the coals are hot, set up for a one-level medium-heat fire (so you can hold your hand 5 inches above the cooking rack for only 4 to 5 seconds).

 For a gas grill: Turn each burner to high and ignite. Cover the grill. When hot, set the burners to medium heat.

4. *On a charcoal grill:* Grill turkey steaks, uncovered, over prepared coals for 12 to 15 minutes until no longer pink or until an instant-read thermometer when inserted into the center of the thickest part registers 160°F, turning and brushing once with ¼ cup salad dressing halfway through. *On a gas grill:* Place turkey on the grill rack over heat, cover, and grill as directed for a charcoal grill. Transfer cooked turkey to a cutting board, and cool slightly.

5. In a large salad bowl, toss together cooked pasta, romaine lettuce, and tomatoes. Add remaining salad dressing, and toss gently to coat. Slice turkey diagonally across the grain, and arrange on greens mixture. Sprinkle with Parmesan cheese and black pepper and serve.

 **Lean Note** ___

Most bottled salad dressings are very high in fat—14 to 18 fat grams per 2 tablespoons. Most reduced-fat (not fat-free) salad dressings taste very good and can fool almost anyone. Try this salad with a reduced-fat Caesar dressing.

Middle-Eastern Grilled Chicken Breasts

4 skinless, boneless chicken breasts (about 1½ lb. total)

1 (8-oz.) carton plain yogurt

1 small onion, stem and root ends trimmed, peeled, and finely chopped

1 tsp. dried oregano, crumbled

3 cloves garlic, peeled and minced or pushed through a garlic press

1 tsp. sesame seeds

½ tsp. ground cumin

¼ tsp. ground turmeric (optional)

⅛ tsp. salt

1 small cucumber, peeled, seeded and chopped (about ⅔ cup)

Serves: 4
Prep time: 25 to 30 minutes, plus 3 or more hours to marinate
Cook time: 15 to 18 minutes
Serving size: 1 breast

1. Rinse chicken breasts under cold water, and pat dry with paper towels.

2. In a medium bowl, stir together yogurt, onion, oregano, garlic, sesame seeds, cumin, turmeric (if using), and salt. Transfer ½ yogurt mixture to a small bowl, and stir in cucumber. Cover and chill until ready to serve. Add chicken breasts to remaining yogurt mixture, stirring and tossing to coat. Cover and refrigerate at least 3 hours or overnight.

3. Fire up the grill:

   > *For a charcoal grill:* Open the bottom vents. Ignite 6 quarts or 2½ pounds charcoal briquettes or hardwood charcoal. When the coals are hot, set up for a one-level medium-heat fire (so you can hold your hand 5 inches above the cooking rack for only 4 to 5 seconds).
   >
   > *For a gas grill:* Turn each burner to high and ignite. Cover the grill. When hot, set the burners to medium heat.

4. *On a charcoal grill:* Arrange hot coals around a drip pan. Place chicken on the grill rack over the drip pan, cover, and grill for 15 to 18 minutes, turning once halfway through, until chicken is no longer pink or until an instant-read thermometer inserted into the center of the thickest part registers 165°F. *On a gas grill:* Place chicken on the grill over heat. Cover and grill as directed for a charcoal grill. Serve, passing cucumber-yogurt mixture.

Barbecue Banter

Sour cream and yogurt certainly seem similar, but their flavors couldn't be less alike. Sour cream, although sour, has an underlying sweetness; yogurt stays tangy. Don't try to substitute them in this recipe.

Chicken Fajitas with Guacamole

<table>
<tr><td>

Serves: 4

Prep time: 35 to 40 minutes (including guacamole), plus 1 hour to marinate

Cook time: 12 to 16 minutes

Serving size: 2 prepared tortillas

</td></tr>
</table>

3 skinless, boneless chicken breasts (about 18 oz. total)

¼ cup chopped fresh cilantro

¼ cup olive oil

1 tsp. grated lemon zest

2 TB. fresh lemon juice (from 1 medium lemon)

1 tsp. chili powder

½ tsp. ground cumin

½ tsp. fresh-ground black pepper

1 recipe Pure and Simple Guacamole (recipe follows)

8 (8-inch) flour tortillas

2 cups shredded iceberg lettuce

1 cup shredded sharp cheddar cheese (about 4 oz.)

1 large tomato, cored and chopped

½ cup sliced pitted ripe (black) olives

1. Rinse chicken breasts under cold water, and pat dry with paper towels.

2. Place chicken in a shallow stainless-steel or glass bowl. In a small bowl, stir together cilantro, olive oil, lemon zest, lemon juice, chili powder, cumin, and pepper until combined. Pour marinade over chicken, and turn to coat. Cover and chill for 1 hour, turning chicken once.

3. Prepare guacamole, cover, and chill.

4. Fire up the grill:

> *For a charcoal grill:* Open the bottom vents. Ignite 6 quarts or 2½ pounds charcoal briquettes or hardwood charcoal. When the coals are hot, set up for a one-level medium-heat fire (so you can hold your hand 5 inches above the cooking rack for only 4 to 5 seconds).
>
> *For a gas grill:* Turn each burner to high and ignite. Cover the grill. When hot, set the burners to medium heat.

Barbecue Banter

Normally you discard any marinade that's come in contact with raw chicken, but in this recipe, the grill's heat will cook the marinade, making it safe. If you're not cooking it, though, always discard and never reuse marinade once grilling's completed.

5. Stack tortillas and wrap in foil. Drain chicken, reserving marinade. *On a charcoal grill:* Place tortillas on the grill and heat, turning stack over every 2 to 3 minutes until warmed, about 6 to 8 minutes. Grill chicken, uncovered, directly over coals for 12 to 16 minutes, turning chicken once and brushing with marinade halfway through, until chicken is no longer pink or until an instant-read thermometer inserted into the center of the thickest part registers 160°F. *On a gas grill:* Place chicken and tortillas on the grill rack over heat. Cover and grill as directed for a charcoal grill.

6. To serve, cut chicken into bite-size strips. Serve, passing tortillas, lettuce, cheese, tomato, olives, and prepared guacamole.

Pure and Simple Guacamole

2 ripe California avocados, peeled, pits removed and reserved

2 cloves garlic, peeled and minced or pushed through a garlic press

½ tsp. kosher salt

¼ tsp. fresh-ground black pepper or to taste

1 TB. fresh lemon juice

Serves: 4 (about 1½ cups)
Prep time: 15 to 20 minutes
Serving size: 1 tablespoon

1. On a cutting board, mash avocados well with a silver or stainless-steel fork, and place in a small stainless-steel or glass bowl. With the side of a large kitchen knife, mash minced or pressed garlic with kosher salt until garlic becomes a paste. Add puréed garlic, pepper, and lemon juice to mashed avocados, and stir until combined. Press avocado pits into guacamole, lay plastic wrap over the bowl, pressing the wrap into the exposed surface of guacamole, and refrigerate.

2. Remove and discard the plastic wrap and pits. Smooth surface of guacamole and serve.

Barbecue Banter

The avocado pits help keep the guacamole from oxidizing and turning brown during refrigeration. The lemon juice adds flavor, but it also slows the guacamole's oxidation. The plastic wrap keeps oxygen from coming into contact with the guacamole's surface.

Chicken and Scallion Skewers

Serves: 4 (as a snack)
Prep time: 60 to 75 minutes
Cook time: 12 to 16 minutes
Serving size: 3 skewers

1½ lb. skinless, boneless chicken thighs (about 6)

12 (8-inch) bamboo skewers

½ cup soy sauce

½ cup granulated sugar

1 (1½-in.) piece fresh ginger, peeled and sliced

2 cloves garlic, peeled and minced or pushed through a garlic press

1 TB. bourbon or other whiskey

3 bunches green onions, washed and trimmed

1. Rinse chicken under cold water, pat dry with paper towels, and cut into 1-inch pieces (you'll need 36 pieces total).

2. Soak bamboo skewers in warm water for 30 minutes.

3. Bring soy sauce, sugar, ginger, garlic, and bourbon to a boil in a 1-quart saucepan over medium-high heat, stirring until sugar dissolves. Reduce heat to medium, and simmer, uncovered, stirring occasionally, about 5 minutes. Remove from heat, reserving 1½ tablespoons sauce in a small bowl for brushing after skewers are grilled.

4. Cut white and pale green parts of green onions crosswise into ½-inch pieces. Reserve green leaves for another use. You'll need 36 pieces.

5. Fire up the grill:

Barbecue Banter

If you've never been to an Asian market, it's worth an hour on Saturday afternoon to go. You'll see lots of things, and almost all labels have English translations on them. One thing to check out: soy sauce. There are many, many different kinds and brands, and the prices are better than in supermarkets.

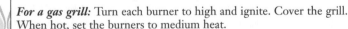

For a charcoal grill: Open the bottom vents. Ignite 6 quarts or 2½ pounds charcoal briquettes or hardwood charcoal. When the coals are hot, set up for a one-level medium-heat fire (so you can hold your hand 5 inches above the cooking rack for only 4 to 5 seconds).

For a gas grill: Turn each burner to high and ignite. Cover the grill. When hot, set the burners to medium heat.

6. While the grill heats, thread each skewer alternately with chicken and onions, using 3 pieces of each and piercing onions crosswise through their center. Brush both sides of all skewers generously with sauce. *On a charcoal or gas grill:* Place skewers on the grill rack above the coals or heat, and grill 6 to 8 minutes per side or until slightly charred or until an instant-read thermometer when inserted into the center of the thickest part of thigh meat registers 165°F, brushing occasionally with sauce. Just before serving, coat skewers a final time with reserved sauce, using a clean brush. Serve.

Jamaican Jerk Chicken

4 skinless, boneless chicken breasts (about 1½ lb. total)

½ cup chopped yellow onion

2 TB. fresh lime juice, from 1 lime

1 tsp. salt

1 tsp. crushed red pepper flakes

½ tsp. ground allspice

¼ tsp. fresh-ground black pepper

¼ tsp. curry powder

¼ tsp. ground ginger

⅛ tsp. dried thyme, crumbled

⅛ tsp. ground cayenne

2 cloves garlic, peeled

1 medium green sweet bell pepper, seeds and ribs discarded, and cut into 1½-inch pieces

1 small zucchini, ends trimmed and sliced ½-inch thick

4 (12-inch) metal skewers

1 TB. peanut oil

¼ tsp. coarse-ground black pepper

Serves: 4
Prep time: 35 to 40 minutes, plus 30 minutes to marinate
Cook time: 12 to 16 minutes
Serving size: 1 chicken breast and 1 vegetable kabob

1. Rinse chicken breasts under cold water, and pat dry with paper towels.

2. In a food processor, process onion, lime juice, salt, crushed red pepper flakes, allspice, pepper, curry powder, ginger, thyme, cayenne, and garlic until smooth.

3. Place chicken breasts in a shallow stainless-steel or glass dish. Pour onion mixture over chicken, turn chicken to coat both sides, cover, and marinate in the refrigerator for 30 minutes.

4. Fire up the grill:

> *For a charcoal grill:* Open the bottom vents. Ignite 6 quarts or 2½ pounds charcoal briquettes or hardwood charcoal. When the coals are hot, set up for a one-level medium-heat fire (so you can hold your hand 5 inches above the cooking rack for only 4 to 5 seconds).
>
> *For a gas grill:* Turn each burner to high and ignite. Cover the grill. When hot, set the burners to medium heat.

5. While chicken marinates and the grill heats, thread sweet pepper and zucchini pieces onto metal skewers. Brush with peanut oil, and sprinkle with coarse-ground pepper.

6. Drain chicken, reserving onion mixture. *On a charcoal grill:* Grill chicken (about 6 to 8 minutes per side) and vegetable kabobs (about 10 minutes), uncovered, directly over coals until chicken is no longer pink or until an instant-read thermometer when

Barbecue Banter

When an herb such as basil, thyme, or oregano is dried, the flavor becomes more concentrated. If a recipe requires 1 tablespoon fresh chopped basil, you'll get the same flavor kick if you substitute 1 teaspoon dry basil.

inserted into the center of the thickest part registers 160°F, and vegetables are tender, turning and brushing once with onion mixture halfway through. After brushing, discard remaining onion mixture. *On a gas grill:* Place chicken and vegetable kabobs on the grill rack over heat. Cover and follow directions for a charcoal grill. Remove chicken and kabobs from the grill and serve.

Chicken and Italian Sausage Kabobs

Serves: 8
Prep time: 40 to 45 minutes, plus 2 to 8 hours to marinate
Cook time: 12 to 16 minutes
Serving size: 1 kabob and 1 pita

4 skinless, boneless chicken breasts (about 1½ lb. total)

1 cup dry red wine

½ cup olive oil

¼ cup red wine vinegar

¼ cup orange juice, not from concentrate

2 TB. fresh lemon juice

1 tsp. dried, rubbed sage, crumbled

2 or 3 sprigs fresh parsley

3 large cloves garlic, peeled and minced or pushed through a garlic press

10 black peppercorns

2 medium bay leaves

1 lb. uncooked sweet Italian sausage links

8 (12- to 16-in.) metal skewers

8 pita bread rounds

1. Rinse chicken breasts under cold water, pat dry with paper towels, and cut into 1-inch pieces.

2. To a 1-gallon, reclosable plastic bag, add wine, olive oil, vinegar, orange juice, lemon juice, sage, parsley, garlic, peppercorns, and bay leaves. Seal the bag, and shake to combine. Add chicken pieces, push out air, seal the bag, and marinate in the refrigerator for 2 to 8 hours, turning the bag occasionally.

3. Fire up the grill:

> *For a charcoal grill:* Open the bottom vents. Ignite 6 quarts or 2½ pounds charcoal briquettes or hardwood charcoal. When the coals are hot, set up for a one-level medium-heat fire (so you can hold your hand 5 inches above the cooking rack for only 4 to 5 seconds).
>
> *For a gas grill:* Turn each burner to high and ignite. Cover the grill. When hot, set the burners to medium heat.

4. While the grill heats, drain chicken, reserving marinade. Cut sausage into 1-inch chunks (there should be 16 pieces). Alternately thread sausage and chicken on metal skewers, leaving a ¼-inch space between pieces.

5. *On a charcoal grill:* Grill kabobs, uncovered, on the grill rack directly over coals for 12 to 16 minutes or until chicken and sausage are no longer pink or until an instant-read thermometer when inserted into the center of the thickest part of the chicken registers 165°F, turning and brushing once with marinade halfway through. (Discard remaining marinade after this point.) *On a gas grill:* Place kabobs on the grill rack over heat. Cover and follow as directed for a charcoal grill. Remove kabobs from the grill.

6. During kabob's final 3 to 4 minutes, warm pita rounds on the grill or until lightly toasted, turning once halfway through. Serve kabobs with pita bread.

Barbecue Banter

Here's a quick lesson in grilling and cooking with wine: never use cooking sherry or cooking wine because its flavor is terrible and is made worse by the addition of salt. Always cook or grill with wine you would or do drink.

Wranglers Special Barbequed Chicken Drumsticks

12 chicken legs (drumsticks) (about 3½ lb. total)

1 TB. unsalted butter

1 medium onion, peeled, trimmed, and finely chopped

2 cloves garlic, peeled and minced or pushed through a garlic press

1 tsp. chili powder

¼ tsp. dried, rubbed sage, crumbled

½ cup ketchup

2 TB. water

2 TB. apple cider vinegar

1 TB. granulated sugar

1 TB. fresh lemon juice

1 TB. Worcestershire sauce

½ tsp. salt

½ tsp. hot pepper sauce

¼ tsp. coarse-ground black pepper

Serves: 6
Prep time: 40 minutes
Cook time: 20 to 30 minutes
Serving size: 2 chicken drumsticks

1. Rinse chicken legs under cold water, and pat dry with paper towels.

2. Fire up the grill:

For a charcoal grill: Open the bottom vents. Ignite 6 quarts or 2½ pounds charcoal briquettes or hardwood charcoal. When the coals are hot, set up for a one-level medium-heat fire (so you can hold your hand 5 inches above the cooking rack for only 4 to 5 seconds).

For a gas grill: Turn each burner to high and ignite. Cover the grill. When hot, set the burners to medium heat.

3. While the grill heats, make sauce. Add butter to a 2-quart saucepan and melt over medium-high heat. When butter melts, add onion, garlic, chili powder, and sage, and cook, stirring occasionally, until onion is tender, about 6 minutes. Stir in ketchup, water, vinegar, sugar, lemon juice, Worcestershire sauce, salt, hot pepper sauce, and pepper. Bring to boil, reduce heat to low, and simmer, uncovered, for 5 minutes, stirring occasionally. Remove from heat.

4. *On a charcoal grill:* Grill chicken on the rack of an uncovered grill directly over coals for 20 to 30 minutes until tender and when pricked juices run clear or until an instant-read thermometer when inserted into the center of the thickest part registers 170°F, turning once and brushing with some sauce during the last 10 minutes of grilling. *On a gas grill:* Place chicken, skin-side down, on the grill rack over heat, cover, and follow directions for a charcoal grill. Serve, passing remaining sauce.

Barbecue Banter

Chili powder is a mixture of ground dried chilies, oregano, cumin, garlic, and salt.

Honey Mustard–Glazed Drumsticks

Serves: 4
Prep time: 15 minutes
Cook time: 20 to 30 minutes
Serving size: 2 chicken drumsticks

8 chicken legs (about 2¼ lb. total)

3 TB. clover honey

3 TB. Dijon mustard

1 tsp. fresh lemon juice

1. Rinse chicken legs under cold water, and pat dry with paper towels.

2. Fire up the grill:

For a charcoal grill: Open the bottom vents. Ignite 6 quarts or 2½ pounds charcoal briquettes or hardwood charcoal. When the coals are hot, set up for a one-level medium-heat fire (so you can hold your hand 5 inches above the cooking rack for only 4 to 5 seconds).

For a gas grill: Turn each burner to high and ignite. Cover the grill. When hot, set the burners to medium heat.

3. While the grill heats, make sauce. In a small stainless-steel or glass bowl, stir together honey, Dijon mustard, and lemon juice. Set aside.

4. *On a charcoal grill:* Grill chicken legs on the grill rack, uncovered, directly over coals for 20 to 30 minutes until juices run clear when pricked or until an instant-read thermometer when inserted into the center of the thickest part registers 170°F, turning once halfway through and brushing with sauce during last 10 minutes of grilling. *On a gas grill:* Place chicken legs on the grill rack over heat, cover, and follow directions for a charcoal grill. Serve, passing remaining sauce.

Barbecue Banter

Although they all have "Dijon mustard" on the label, what's inside the jar can have a different flavor and texture unlike any other. From time to time, purchase a different brand of Dijon mustard until you find one your palate appreciates.

Sweet, Nutty, and Smoky Chicken Thighs

2 lb. skin-on, bone-in chicken thighs

½ cup bottled sweet and smoky flavored barbecue sauce

¼ cup smooth peanut butter

1 to 2 TB. orange juice, not from concentrate

½ tsp. grated orange zest

Serves: 6
Prep time: 15 minutes
Cook time: 20 to 30 minutes
Serving size: 1 thigh

1. Rinse chicken under cold water, and pat dry with paper towels.

2. Fire up the grill:

For a charcoal grill: Open the bottom vents. Ignite 6 quarts or 2½ pounds charcoal briquettes or hardwood charcoal. When the coals are hot, set up for a one-level medium-heat fire (so you can hold your hand 5 inches above the cooking rack for only 4 to 5 seconds).

For a gas grill: Turn each burner to high and ignite. Cover the grill. When hot, set the burners to medium heat.

3. While the grill heats, make sauce. In a small saucepan over medium heat, stir together barbecue sauce, peanut butter, 1 tablespoon orange juice, and orange zest. Bring to a simmer, remove from heat and thin, if necessary, with added orange juice until it reaches a brushable consistency. Set aside.

4. *On a charcoal grill:* Grill chicken thighs on the grill rack, uncovered, directly over coals for 20 to 30 minutes until the juices run clear when pricked or until an instant-read thermometer when inserted into the center of the thickest part registers 170°F, turning once halfway through. Five to ten minutes before chicken is done, using tongs, remove and discard skin, and brush with sauce during the last few minutes. *On a gas grill:* Place chicken on the grill rack over heat, cover, and follow directions for a charcoal grill. Serve, passing any remaining sauce.

> **Barbecue Banter**
>
> All peanut butters will blend in to this sauce, but natural peanut butters, in which the oil separates, may not work quite as well.

Stick-to-Your-Fingers BBQ Chicken Thighs

Serves: 6	
Prep time: 60 minutes, plus 2 to 4 hours to marinate	
Cook time: 50 to 60 minutes	
Serving size: 2 chicken thighs	

12 (about 4 lb.) skin-on, bone-in chicken thighs

1½ cups dry sherry

1 cup finely chopped onion

¼ cup fresh lemon juice

6 cloves garlic, peeled and minced or pushed through a garlic press

2 medium bay leaves

1 (15-oz.) can tomato purée

¼ cup clover honey

3 TB. molasses (not blackstrap or strong)

1 tsp. salt

½ tsp. dried thyme, crumbled

½ tsp. ground cayenne

¼ tsp. fresh-ground black pepper

2 TB. distilled white vinegar

1. Rinse chicken under cold water, and pat dry with paper towels.

2. Place chicken in a 1-gallon reclosable plastic bag set in a shallow dish. In a medium bowl, stir together sherry, onion, lemon juice, garlic, and bay leaves. Pour marinade over chicken, push out air, seal the bag, and refrigerate for 2 to 4 hours, turning bag occasionally. Drain chicken, reserving marinade. Place chicken on foil-lined tray, and cover until ready to grill.

3. In a saucepan, stir together reserved marinade, tomato purée, honey, molasses, salt, thyme, cayenne, and pepper. Bring to a boil over medium-high heat, reduce heat to low, and simmer, uncovered, stirring occasionally for 30 minutes or until slightly thickened. Remove from heat, remove bay leaves, and stir in vinegar.

4. Fire up the grill:

> *For a charcoal grill:* Open the bottom vents. Ignite 6 quarts or 2½ pounds charcoal briquettes or hardwood charcoal. When the coals are hot, set up for a one-level medium-heat fire (so you can hold your hand 5 inches above the cooking rack for only 4 to 5 seconds).
>
> *For a gas grill:* Turn each burner to high and ignite. Cover the grill. When hot, set the burners to medium heat.

5. *On a charcoal grill:* Arrange coals around a drip pan. Place chicken pieces, bone side down, on the grill rack over the drip pan. Cover, with vents open, and grill for 50 to 60 minutes until juices run clear when pricked or until an instant-read thermometer when inserted into the center of the thickest part registers 170°F, brushing with some sauce during the last 15 minutes of grilling. *On a gas grill:* Turn off the center burner, place chicken on the grill over the turned-off burner, cover, and grill as directed for a charcoal grill. Reheat remaining sauce, and pass with chicken.

Barbecue Banter

The charcoal briquettes most folks use are made from burned wood, but they generally also contain coal dust, mineral carbon, limestone, starch (as a binder), borax, sodium nitrate, and sawdust.

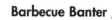

Bison City Wings

4 lb. chicken wings (about 24)

1 cup apple cider vinegar

2 TB. vegetable oil

2 TB. plus 2 tsp. Worcestershire sauce

2 TB. chili powder

1 TB. hot red pepper sauce

1½ tsp. kosher salt

1¼ tsp. fresh-ground black pepper

1 tsp. red pepper flakes

⅔ cup reduced-fat sour cream

½ cup mayonnaise

1 large clove garlic, peeled and minced or pushed through a garlic press

1 cup (about 4 oz.) crumbled blue cheese

Salt to taste

2 TB. milk

Celery sticks

> *Serves: 4 as main course, 6 to 8 as appetizer*
>
> **Prep time:** 40 minutes, plus 6 hours to marinate
>
> **Cook time:** 25 to 30 minutes
>
> **Serving size:** 4 to 6 wings

1. Rinse chicken under cold water, and pat dry with paper towels.

2. In a medium mixing bowl, stir together vinegar, vegetable oil, 2 tablespoons Worcestershire sauce, chili powder, red pepper sauce, kosher salt, 1 teaspoon pepper, and red pepper flakes until combined. Place chicken wings in a 1-gallon reclosable plastic bag, and pour in marinade. Press out air, seal the bag, massage the bag gently to distribute marinade. Set the bag in a large bowl, and refrigerate for 6 hours, turning and massaging the bag occasionally.

3. Fire up the grill:

> *For a charcoal grill:* Open the bottom vents. Ignite 6 quarts or 2½ pounds charcoal briquettes or hardwood charcoal. When the coals are hot, set up for a one-level medium-heat fire (so you can hold your hand 5 inches above the cooking rack for only 4 to 5 seconds).
>
> *For a gas grill:* Turn each burner to high and ignite. Cover the grill. When hot, set the burners to medium heat.

4. While the grill heats, make sauce. In a medium mixing bowl, whisk together sour cream, mayonnaise, garlic, remaining 2 teaspoons Worcestershire sauce, and remaining ¼ teaspoon black pepper until combined. Stir in blue cheese. Taste and season with salt, if necessary. Thin sauce with milk to make it the consistency of salad dressing. Cover and refrigerate.

5. Remove wings from marinade, reserving marinade. *On a charcoal grill:* Grill wings, uncovered, on the gill rack above coals, turning frequently and brushing occasionally with reserved marinade for first 15 minutes (discard remaining marinade at that point) until cooked through, 25 to 30 minutes. *On a gas grill:* Place chicken on the grill rack over heat, cover, and grill as directed for a charcoal grill. Serve with dipping sauce and celery sticks.

Barbecue Banter

Always be aware of the possibility of the contamination of grilled poultry or meats by their raw counterparts. I always place uncooked poultry or meat on a tray lined with two layers of foil. When the poultry or meat goes on the grill, I remove the first foil layer and discard it, leaving a fresh, clean layer to put the grilled meat or poultry on at the end.

Bourbon-Flavored Turkey Breast Fillets

6 (5- to 6-oz.) turkey breast fillet sections

¾ cup bourbon or other similar American whiskey

2 TB. white wine Worcestershire sauce

½ tsp. fresh-ground black pepper

1 TB. clover (or other mild) honey

1 TB. unsalted butter

Serves: 6
Prep time: 30 minutes, plus 2 to 8 hours to marinate
Cook time: 10 to 20 minutes
Serving size: 1 breast fillet

1. Rinse turkey under cold water, pat dry with paper towels, and pound between plastic wrap to ½- to ¾-inch thick.

2. At least 2 hours and up to 8 hours before you plan to grill, make marinade. To a 1-gallon resealable plastic bag, add bourbon, Worcestershire sauce, and pepper. Seal the bag, and shake until combined. Add turkey breast fillets, push out air, seal the bag, and refrigerate for 2 to 8 hours, turning bag occasionally.

3. Remove the plastic bag from the refrigerator, and drain marinade into a small saucepan. Blot any excess liquid from fillets with paper towels, and let turkey sit, covered, at room temperature for 20 to 30 minutes.

4. Fire up the grill:

> *For a charcoal grill:* Open the bottom vents. Ignite 6 quarts or 2½ pounds charcoal briquettes or hardwood charcoal. When the coals are hot, set up for a one-level medium-heat fire (so you can hold your hand 5 inches above the cooking rack for only 4 to 5 seconds).
>
> *For a gas grill:* Turn each burner to high and ignite. Cover the grill. When hot, set the burners to medium heat.

5. While the grill heats, bring marinade to a boil over medium-high heat, taking care to keep it away from any open flames (alcohol in marinade could flame up, so be very careful), boiling for 3 to 4 minutes. Remove marinade from heat, and immediately stir in honey and butter. Set aside.

6. *On a charcoal grill:* Grill breast fillets, uncovered, over coals for 5 to 6 minutes per side until opaque but still juicy or until an instant-read thermometer registers 160°F when inserted into the center of the thickest part. Brush turkey with sauce in

Barbecue Banter

Reduce your frustration and hassle factor by always having extra charcoal available or a second LP tank for your gas grill.

last couple minutes of grilling and again after it comes off the grill. *On a gas grill:* Grill breast fillets, uncovered, over heat for 9 to 10 minutes or until an instant-read thermometer registers 160°F when inserted into the center of the thickest part, turning once halfway through and brushing with sauce at the end. Serve breast fillets thinly sliced, passing remaining sauce.

Grilled Turkey Pasta Salad

Serves: 6 as a lunch salad
Prep time: 25 minutes, plus 1 hour to chill
Serving size: 1½ cups salad

Flame Point

If a marinade recipe calls for vinegar, lemon juice, or lime juice, always use a plastic bag or a stainless-steel or glass bowl. Never use iron or aluminum because the acids in those liquids can react with those containers and give your food a "metallic" flavor.

1 qt. canned low-fat, lower-sodium chicken broth

6 oz. uncooked shell-shaped pasta

1 cup calorie-reduced mayonnaise

½ tsp. celery salt

½ tsp. Dijon mustard

⅓ tsp. fresh-ground black pepper

1½ lb. leftover grilled turkey breast, cut into bite-size pieces

2 celery ribs, strings removed and cut crosswise into ¼-inch slices

1 cup baby peas, cooked briefly, drained, and cooled

1 cup seedless red grapes, rinsed, dried, and sliced in half

Romaine lettuce leaves or ripe tomato slices

1. Add chicken broth to a medium saucepan over medium-high heat, and bring to a boil. Stir uncooked pasta shells into broth, return broth to a boil, stirring, and cook following pasta package directions. Drain and cool (do not rinse).

2. In a medium mixing bowl, whisk together mayonnaise, celery salt, Dijon mustard, and pepper. Stir or fold in turkey, celery, peas, and grapes until coated with dressing. Cover and refrigerate for 1 hour. Serve over chilled Romaine lettuce leaves or ripe tomato slices.

Grilled and Glazed Duck Breasts

4 skinless, boneless, duck breasts (about 1½ to 2 lb.)

½ cup orange marmalade

½ cup canned cranberry sauce

1 TB. distilled white vinegar

1 tsp. grated fresh ginger

2 tsp. vegetable oil

Serves: 4
Prep time: 22 to 25 minutes
Cook time: 25 to 35 minutes
Serving size: 1 duck breast

1. Rinse duck under cold water, and pat dry with paper towels.

2. Add marmalade, cranberry sauce, vinegar, and ginger to a small saucepan and place over medium-low heat. Bring to a simmer, stirring, and remove from heat. Set aside.

3. Brush oil over both sides of duck breasts.

4. Fire up the grill:

> *For a charcoal grill:* Open the bottom vents. Ignite 6 quarts or 2½ pounds charcoal briquettes or hardwood charcoal. When the coals are hot, set up for a one-level medium-heat fire (so you can hold your hand 5 inches above the cooking rack for only 4 to 5 seconds).
>
> *For a gas grill:* Turn each burner to high and ignite. Cover the grill. When hot, set the burners to medium heat.

5. *On a charcoal grill:* Grill duck breasts directly over coals, uncovered, for 25 to 35 minutes, until tender and no longer pink or until an instant-read thermometer registers 165°F when inserted into the center of the thickest part, turning once and brushing frequently with orange and cranberry glaze during last 5 to 7 minutes. *On a gas grill:* Grill directly over heat source, covered, 12 to 17 minutes per side, until tender and no longer pink or until an instant-read thermometer registers 165°F when inserted into the center of the thickest part, brushing frequently with orange and cranberry glaze during last 5 to 7 minutes. Serve.

Barbecue Banter

If it's a windy day, place your grill out of the wind. Neither the grill nor the food will stay as hot as it should because the fast-moving air will keep cooling your grill.

Barbecue Duckling

1 (4- to 6-lb.) duckling

1 stick unsalted butter

½ cup chopped yellow onion

2 TB. orange juice, not from concentrate

2 TB. Worcestershire sauce

1 TB. fresh lemon juice

½ tsp. hot pepper sauce

½ tsp. garlic salt

½ tsp. fresh-ground black pepper

1 yellow onion, peeled and quartered

1 orange, quartered

1. Rinse duckling inside and out with cold water, and pat dry with paper towels.

2. Fill a pot large enough to comfortably hold duckling half full with cold water. Place on stove over high heat, and bring to a boil. Prick skin of duck all over with sharp fork tines to allow fat to render. Immerse duckling in water, reduce heat to medium-low, and cook for 15 to 20 minutes to render some fat from duck. Remove duck from water, and cool to room temperature.

3. Fire up the grill:

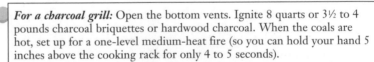

> *For a charcoal grill:* Open the bottom vents. Ignite 8 quarts or 3½ to 4 pounds charcoal briquettes or hardwood charcoal. When the coals are hot, set up for a one-level medium-heat fire (so you can hold your hand 5 inches above the cooking rack for only 4 to 5 seconds).
>
>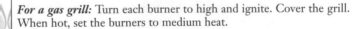
>
> *For a gas grill:* Turn each burner to high and ignite. Cover the grill. When hot, set the burners to medium heat.

4. Place butter in a medium saucepan over medium heat. When butter melts, add onion and cook until soft, about 7 or 8 minutes. Stir in orange juice, Worcestershire sauce, lemon juice, hot pepper sauce, garlic salt, and pepper, mixing well. Remove the pan from heat.

5. Season duckling inside and out with salt and pepper. Stuff duckling with quartered onion and quartered orange. Make a slit in the lower side of each breast.

6. *On a charcoal grill:* Divide the coals between two sides of the grill, and place a deep drip pan in the center. Grill duckling, covered, for 1½ to 2½ hours, or until an instant-read thermometer inserted into the thickest part of the thigh registers 175°F, basting with prepared sauce every 15 minutes. After 45 minutes, open the grill cover, lift duckling off the grill to a clean tray,

with oven mitts (or other hand protection) lift the grill rack out and set on a heat-safe surface. Spread 40 to 50 briquettes around the grill, placing them on the already lighted briquettes. Fanning the briquettes from time to time, get the added briquettes started. Put the grill rack back in place, return duckling to the rack and cover. Repeat after 1 hour. *On a gas grill:* Place duckling on a rack in a roasting pan, and place the roasting pan in the center of the grill. Grill, covered for 1½ to 2½ hours or until an instant-read thermometer inserted into the thickest part of the thigh registers 175°F, basting every 15 minutes with prepared sauce. Remove duckling from the grill to a cutting board, and let rest for 10 minutes. Carve into serving pieces and serve.

Turkey Kabobs with Cranberry Sauce

1¼ lb. turkey breast fillet sections

1 TB. dried thyme, crumbled

1 tsp. dried rubbed sage, crumbled

1 tsp. kosher salt

½ tsp. fresh ground black pepper

½ tsp. ground white pepper

1 cup fresh or frozen cranberries, thawed

¼ cup granulated sugar

¼ cup chicken broth

4 TB. red wine

2 TB. orange juice, not from concentrate

1 small clove garlic, peeled and minced or pushed through a garlic press

1 large tart apple, such as Granny Smith

1 medium onion, peeled, root and stem ends trimmed, quartered, and layers separated

3 very lean raw bacon slices, cut into 1-inch pieces

6 (12- to 16-inch) metal skewers

Serves: 4 to 6
Prep time: 45 to 50 minutes
Cook time: 8 to 12 minutes
Serving size: 1 to 1 ½ kabobs

1. Rinse turkey under cold water, pat dry with paper towels, pound between plastic wrap to 1-inch thick, and then cut into 1-inch cubes.

2. The night before you plan to grill, prepare herb and spice rub. Add thyme, sage, kosher salt, black pepper, and white pepper to a medium mixing bowl, and stir together until combined. Add turkey cubes to the bowl, stirring and tossing until coated with spice mixture. Cover and refrigerate.

3. Fire up the grill:

> **For a charcoal grill:** Open the bottom vents. Ignite 6 quarts or 2[1/2] pounds charcoal briquettes or hardwood charcoal. When the coals are hot, set up for a one-level medium-heat fire (so you can hold your hand 5 inches above the cooking rack for only 4 to 5 seconds).
>
> **For a gas grill:** Turn each burner to high and ignite. Cover the grill. When hot, set the burners to medium heat.

4. While grill heats, prepare sauce. To a small saucepan, add cranberries, sugar, chicken broth, red wine, orange juice, and garlic. Place saucepan over medium-high heat, and bring to a boil. Lower heat and simmer until cranberries pop and sauce thickens but is still thin enough to brush.

5. Cut apple into quarters, trim out core, and cut into chunks slightly smaller than turkey cubes, leaving peel attached. Thread turkey cubes on skewers interspersed with apple, onion, and bacon pieces.

6. *On a charcoal grill:* Grill kabobs, uncovered, over coals for 8 to 10 minutes, turning on all sides, until turkey cubes are opaque or until an instant-read thermometer when inserted into the center of a turkey piece registers 160°F. Brush kebobs with cranberry sauce in the last minutes of grilling and again when they come off grill. *On a gas grill:* Grill kabobs over heat, covered, for 10 to 12 minutes or until an instant-read thermometer when inserted into the center of a turkey piece registers 160°F., turning once halfway through and brushing with sauce at the end.

Flame Point

Grilling on a wooden deck or porch requires extra safety precautions. Place a metal sheet or several sheets of wide, heavy-duty aluminum foil under your grill to catch any hot ashes that might fall through an open vent and land on the wood.

Chapter 17

Oh, Dem Ribs!

In This Chapter

- Before you grill: rib prep
- Chef's secret: oven-roasting
- Sauces and rubs, sauces and rubs
- Tips on cutting ribs

Done right, barbecued pork ribs may be the finest food to ever come off a backyard grill. It doesn't matter whether they're spareribs (the largest bones with the least meat), baby back ribs (the smallest bones with the most meat), or country-style ribs (small bones with a lot of meat and fat). If the soft, luxurious meat melts in your mouth and brings smoky pork combined with sweet and tangy barbecue sauce flavors to your palate, you know you've got something special.

The best commercial barbecued ribs are slow-cooked over real wood fires, mopped with a liquid mixture that keeps them from drying out, and at the end glazed with a sauce made from a recipe that usually remains a secret forever.

In Chapter 7, you'll find numerous superb barbecue sauces you can simmer up at home and then brush on your ribs at the end of their grill time to make them almost as good as the world's best—even if you don't sweat for hours over a huge, live-wood fire to prepare them.

Rib Prep

Before you ever start to grill your ribs, you have some definite kitchen work to do. First, remove the ribs from the plastic package and rinse them under cold running water to get rid of any small bone chips and other debris that can cling to them. Then pat the slabs dry with paper towels. Next, pull the thin yet tough and, unfortunately, slippery membrane from the back of the rib slabs. I've found two keys to doing this easily and successfully:

1. To start, use a sharp-tipped paring knife to lift the corner of the membrane away from the meat and bone.
2. Then use a paper towel to grab the membrane you've separated and hold on to it (I'm not kidding—few people can hold it tight enough to keep it from slipping through their fingers) and pull it away from the meat and bones all the way to the end.

Not only is that membrane slippery, but it's also tough, and no length of cooking softens it up. Cooking it just makes it more elastic and difficult to deal with.

To Oven-Roast or Not to Oven-Roast?

The very best commercial ribs are slow-slow cooked over glowing coals—the result of burning down large wood chunks until they're just glowing embers—at low heat for hours. Some have been seasoned with an herb-and-spice rub applied before the ribs headed to the fire; others head to the coals with just meat and bones.

Because it takes so long to get to that final moment when the barbecue sauce is slathered on, I'm going to share a preparation method with you that, although true barbecue connoisseurs may quibble with, produces ribs with delicious and flavorful, fall-off-the-bone meat and requires little effort and no perspiration on your part: dry rubbed ribs that are first oven-roasted.

Some folks simmer their ribs in water or beer before they head for the grill, but I believe that washes out and waters down most of the flavor of the ribs. Sometimes I coat my ribs with any one of the excellent rubs you'll find in Chapter 4 or just leave them alone and dust them with only salt and fresh-ground black pepper. Using wide, heavy-duty aluminum foil, I line a pan large enough to comfortably hold the ribs. Then, I place the rubbed or plain ribs into the pan on the foil and bring the foil up and together, tightly enclosing the ribs, sealing in moisture and flavor. Next, the ribs go into a 300°F oven for 90 minutes to 2 hours.

When you open the foil, you'll see ribs that look quite different from the ones you wrapped up. At the bottom of the pan will be a lot of liquid fat that's melted off the ribs. The meat will have shrunk down and, consequently, their flavor will be concentrated. At this point, you could cool down the ribs, place them in plastic bags, and refrigerate for later use. Or head out to the grill now!

Gettin' Saucy! (or Using Rubs)

The final grilling works well with ribs that have been rubbed and baked or just baked. A rub, if it has enough sugar added to it, will actually melt on the grill's high heat and cause the ribs to look and taste as if they've been sauced. Or adding sauce to already lightly seasoned and baked ribs on the grill will help deepen the flavor of the ribs.

This is a personal preference. Some like to rub ribs and then sauce them; others like to rub them and leave the sauce alone (that's how they do it in Memphis, Tennessee); others like to rub, bake, grill, and sauce their ribs at the end for additional flavor layering. Try it different ways to see which you prefer.

Right and Wrong Time to Lay On the Sauce

Almost every barbecue sauce—except for those made in eastern North Carolina (where they use vinegar, water, salt, and pepper only)—have a little to a lot of sugar. Ketchup usually plays a major role in many homemade and bottled barbecue sauces, and ketchup's second ingredient is high-fructose corn syrup, a less-expensive sweetener similar to sugar (take a look at the label). Many sauces also have added sugar such as granulated sugar or brown sugar. Some barbecue sauces use molasses (made from sugar) for flavor and sweetness, while others contain honey (a sugar made by bees).

No matter where the sugar comes from, when sugar gets too hot for too long, it burns. When your barbecue-sauced ribs get too close to the hot coals for too long, they turn black. That's burned sugar.

Barbecue Banter

You want the fire's heat to melt the sugar in the sauce and produce a tasty glaze, not a charcoal crust the same color as your briquettes.

The only way to keep that from happening is to brush the sauce on the ribs near the end of the grill time. Brush the sauce on during the last 10 minutes, and keep the ribs close enough to the heat to melt the sugar but far enough away to keep it from burning.

Sauces: Supermarket vs. Homemade

It still amazes me how many commercial sauces are available on my local supermarket's shelves. Many of them are good, and certainly they all make grilling ribs a cinch because all you have to do is open the bottle and begin brushing.

But making your own homemade sauce gives you total control over its flavor and consistency because you select the ingredients. You can use fresh onions, not dehydrated or frozen onions. You can buy the freshest and best-quality herbs and spices. You can decide how sweet, how smoky, how salty, or how tangy to make it.

You can take any barbecue sauce recipe and make it your own by adjusting, adding, and subtracting ingredients until it tastes just right. At that point, it's your own.

The Meatiest Way to Cut Apart Ribs

When I first began grilling ribs, I'd cut each slab in half and serve those portions. For my portion, I always took a sharp knife and cut apart the ribs by slicing through the meat from top to bottom halfway between each of the bones. This left meat on either side of the bones. This works, but it's not the best way. Here's a better way:

1. Starting with the first bone, begin cutting at the top right next to the bone, leaving as little meat on the bone as possible, and cut along the bone from top to bottom.

2. On the other side of that bone, cut, as close to the bone as possible, from the top to the bottom. You should have an almost meatless bone in your hand. Discard it.

3. Skip the meat, the next bone, and the meat attached to that bone's other side, and cut out that next bone on both sides, again, leaving as little meat on it as possible.

4. Repeat until no more bones remain.

When you're done, you should have a small pile of meatless bones and a nice pile of bones with a huge amount of meat attached to either side.

Classic Good Ol' American Barbecued Spareribs

2 slabs *pork spareribs* (about 6 lb.), brisket flap and chine bone removed

Salt

Fresh-ground black pepper

Barbecue sauce (your favorite; try some given in Chapter 7)

Serves: 4
Prep time: 8 to 10 minutes
Cook time: 1½ hours
Serving size: ⅓ to ½ rib rack

1. Use a knife to lift the corner of membrane on back of ribs. Using a paper towel to grip, completely pull off membrane and discard. Rinse rib slabs under cold running water, and pat dry with paper towels. Cut racks in half along the edge of a center bone.

2. Fire up the grill:

> *For a charcoal grill:* Open the bottom vents. Ignite 8 quarts or 3½ to 4 pounds charcoal briquettes or hardwood charcoal. When the coals are hot, set up for a one-level medium-heat fire (so you can hold your hand 5 inches above the cooking rack for only 4 to 5 seconds).
>
> *For a gas grill:* Turn each burner to high and ignite. Cover the grill. When hot, set the burners to medium heat.

3. While the grill heats, season ribs generously on both sides with salt and pepper.

4. *On a charcoal grill:* Arrange hot coals around both sides of a centered drip pan. Put the grill rack in place over the coals, clean the rack, and place ribs on the rack over the drip pan. Cover the grill, and open the cover vent. Grill 1 hour, turning once, and at the same time (the 30-minute mark) add 16 to 20 charcoal briquettes (8 or 10 to each side) on top of the coals, and briefly fan briquettes on both sides to get the briquettes just started. At the end of the hour brush top of ribs with barbecue sauce, cover, and grill for 15 minutes. Turn ribs, brush with sauce, cover, and grill for 10 to 15 minutes or until done. *On a gas grill:* Turn the center burner off, place spareribs on the grill over the center burner, close the cover, and grill as directed for a charcoal grill. Serve, passing sauce.

Barbecue Banter

Pork spareribs have had the brisket flap and chine bone removed from the spareribs. If the available spareribs have not had those removed, have your butcher or the butcher at the supermarket remove those two pieces.

Rubbed and Mopped Barbecued Spareribs

Serves: 4
Prep time: 20 to 25 minutes, plus 90 minutes to bake
Cook time: 20 minutes
Serving size: ½ rib rack

2 full racks pork spareribs (about 6 lb. total), brisket flap and chine bone removed

4½ TB. granulated sugar

3 TB. fresh ground black pepper3 TB. sweet paprika

2 TB. ground cumin

2 TB. kosher salt

1 TB. chili powder

1¾ cups white vinegar

1 TB. hot pepper sauce

1 tsp. *liquid smoke*

1. Place the oven rack in the center position, and preheat oven to 300°F. Use a knife to lift the corner of membrane on back of ribs. Using a paper towel to grip, completely pull off membrane and discard. Rinse rib racks under cold running water, and pat dry with paper towels. Cut racks in half along the edge of a center bone.

2. In a small bowl, stir together 2½ tablespoons sugar, 1½ tablespoon pepper, paprika, cumin, 1 tablespoon salt, and chili powder. Rub mixture all over ribs, coating well.

3. Line an oven-safe pan large enough to comfortably hold spareribs with foil. Place ribs on the foil in the pan, and, using another piece of foil, cover and seal the pan. Bake 90 minutes. Remove the pan from the oven, carefully remove the foil cover (steam will billow up), remove ribs to a pan or a tray to take to the grill, and discard liquid in the pan.

4. In a mixing bowl, stir together vinegar, remaining 2 tablespoons sugar, hot pepper sauce, remaining 1 tablespoon salt, re-maining 1½ tablespoons pepper, and liquid smoke until sugar dissolves.

5. Fire up the grill:

> *For a charcoal grill:* Open the bottom vents. Ignite 6 quarts or 2½ pounds charcoal briquettes or hardwood charcoal. When the coals are hot, set up for a one-level medium-heat fire (so you can hold your hand 5 inches above the cooking rack for only 4 to 5 seconds).
>
> *For a gas grill:* Turn each burner to high and ignite. Cover the grill. When hot, set the burners to medium heat.

6. *On a charcoal or gas grill:* Place ribs on the grill rack over coals or heat, brush with mop sauce, cover, and grill 5 minutes. Turn ribs, brush with mop sauce, cover, and grill 5 minutes. Repeat once. Before removing ribs from the grill, brush with sauce. Cut racks into single-rib pieces, and serve, passing sauce.

Grill Guide

Liquid smoke is an entirely natural product produced from smoke; no artificial flavors or colors. Liquid smoke can easily overwhelm other flavors if you use too much. Start with a small amount, taste, and add more if necessary.

Chinese-Style Barbecued Spare Ribs

2 full racks pork spareribs (about 6 lb. total), brisket flap and chine bone removed

1½ cups water

1 cup soy sauce

½ cup granulated sugar

4 tsp. minced garlic

4 tsp. plus 2 TB. hoisin sauce

Serves: 4
Prep time: about 20 minutes, plus 90 minutes to bake
Cook time: 20 minutes
Serving size: ½ rib rack

1. Use a knife to lift the corner of membrane on back of ribs. Using a paper towel to grip, completely pull off membrane and discard. Rinse racks under cold running water, and pat dry with paper towels. Cut racks in half along the edge of a center bone.

2. Add water, soy sauce, sugar, garlic and 4 teaspoons hoisin sauce to a reclosable, plastic bag large enough to hold all ribs. Seal the bag, and shake until sugar dissolves. Place ribs in the bag, push air out, seal the bag, and refrigerate, turning occasionally, for 6 hours.

3. Place the oven rack in the center position, and preheat the oven to 300°F. Remove ribs from the plastic bag, reserving marinade.

4. Line an oven-safe pan large enough to comfortably hold spareribs with foil. Place ribs on the foil in the pan, and, using another piece of foil, cover and seal the pan. Bake 90 minutes. Remove the pan from the oven, carefully remove the foil cover (steam will billow up), remove ribs to a pan or a tray to take to the grill, and discard liquid in the pan.

5. While ribs bake, pour reserved marinade and 2 remaining tablespoons hoisin sauce into a small saucepan and bring to a boil over medium heat. Reduce heat and simmer for 5 minutes. Remove from heat.

6. Fire up the grill:

   > *For a charcoal grill:* Open the bottom vents. Ignite 6 quarts or 2½ pounds charcoal briquettes or hardwood charcoal. When the coals are hot, set up for a one-level medium-heat fire (so you can hold your hand 5 inches above the cooking rack for only 4 to 5 seconds).
   >
   > *For a gas grill:* Turn each burner to high and ignite. Cover the grill. When hot, set the burners to medium heat.

7. *On a charcoal or gas grill:* Place ribs on the grill rack over coals or heat, brush with heated sauce, cover, and grill 5 minutes. Turn ribs, brush with sauce, cover, and grill 5 minutes. Repeat once. Before removing ribs from the grill, brush with sauce. Serve, passing sauce.

Barbecue Banter

To learn more about grilling ribs, see if there's a rib-cooking contest held during the summer within easy driving distance. Go to the contest but to watch, talk, share, and learn—and, oh yeah, to have some fun and some great-tasting ribs!

Beer and Brown Sugar–Soaked BBQ Ribs

Serves: 2 to 3
Prep time: 35 to 40 minutes, plus 24 hours to marinate and 90 minutes to bake
Cook time: 20 minutes
Serving size: ½ to ⅓ rack

1 (3½-lb.) rack spareribs, brisket flap and chine bone removed

1 qt. full-flavored beer

2 cups firmly packed dark brown sugar

1 cup apple cider vinegar

1 TB. chili powder

2 tsp. crushed red pepper flakes

1 tsp. ground cumin

1 tsp. dry mustard

1. Use a knife to lift the corner of membrane on back of ribs. Using a paper towel to grip, completely pull off membrane and discard. Rinse racks under cold running water, and pat dry with paper towels. Cut racks in half along the edge of a center bone.

2. In a large saucepan, stir together beer, brown sugar, vinegar, chili powder, red pepper flakes, cumin, and dry mustard until sugar dissolves. Place the saucepan over medium-high heat, and bring beer mixture to a boil, stirring occasionally. Remove from heat, and let cool to room temperature.

3. Place ribs in a large, shallow, nonaluminum roasting pan. Pour cooled marinade over ribs, cover, and refrigerate for 24 hours, turning ribs over in marinade from time to time.

4. After 24 hours, place the oven rack in the center position and preheat the oven to 300°F.

5. Line an oven-safe pan large enough to comfortably hold spareribs with foil. Remove ribs from marinade, reserving marinade. Place ribs on the foil in the pan, and, using another piece of foil, cover and seal the pan. Bake 90 minutes. Remove the pan from the oven, carefully remove the foil cover (steam will billow up), remove ribs to a pan or a tray to take to the grill, and discard liquid in the pan.

6. While ribs bake, pour reserved marinade into a medium saucepan and bring to a boil over medium heat. Reduce heat to low, and simmer for 10 minutes, stirring occasionally. Remove from heat.

7. Fire up the grill:

> ***For a charcoal grill:*** Open the bottom vents. Ignite 6 quarts or 2½ pounds charcoal briquettes or hardwood charcoal. When the coals are hot, set up for a one-level medium-heat fire (so you can hold your hand 5 inches above the cooking rack for only 4 to 5 seconds).
>
> ***For a gas grill:*** Turn each burner to high and ignite. Cover the grill. When hot, set the burners to medium heat.

8. *On a charcoal or gas grill:* Place ribs on the grill rack over coals or heat, brush with heated marinade, cover, and grill 5 minutes. Turn ribs, brush with marinade, cover, and grill 5 minutes. Repeat once. Before removing ribs from the grill, brush with marinade. Serve, passing marinade.

Barbecue Banter
Another way to flavor grilled foods is to sprinkle the hot coals with soaked and drained dried herbs or lay sprigs of fresh herbs on the hot coals and close the cover.

Basic Barbecued Baby Back Pork Ribs

2 racks (about 5 to 6 lb. total) pork baby back ribs

½ cup firmly packed dark brown sugar

½ cup sweet paprika

¼ cup fresh-ground black pepper

¼ cup garlic salt

¼ cup chili powder

2 TB. dry mustard

Bottled or homemade barbecue sauce

Serves: 4
Prep time: about 25 minutes, plus 12 hours (overnight) to marinate and 90 minutes to bake
Cook time: 20 minutes
Serving size: ½ rack

1. Use a knife to lift the corner of membrane on back of ribs. Using a paper towel to grip, completely pull off membrane and discard. Rinse racks under cold running water, and pat dry with paper towels. Cut racks in half along the edge of a center bone.

2. In a medium mixing bowl, stir together brown sugar, paprika, black pepper, garlic salt, chili powder, and dry mustard until combined and all brown sugar lumps are pressed out. Rub both sides of ribs with a thick coat of seasoning rub. Place ribs in a 1-gallon reclosable plastic bag, push out air, seal the bag, and refrigerate overnight.

3. Place the oven rack in the center position, and preheat the oven to 300°F. Remove ribs from the plastic bag, and discard the bag.

Barbecue Banter

The most reliable way to tell whether your spareribs or baby back ribs are done is to use a "pull-apart" or "tear" test: toward the middle of the slab, take hold of two adjacent bones and give them a pull. If the meat offers a bit of resistance and then tears or pulls apart easily, the ribs are ready.

4. Line an oven-safe pan large enough to comfortably hold ribs with foil. Place ribs on the foil in the pan, and, using another piece of foil, cover and seal the pan. Bake 90 minutes. Remove the pan from the oven, carefully remove the foil cover (steam will billow up), remove ribs to a pan or a tray to take to the grill, and discard liquid in the pan.

5. Fire up the grill:

> *For a charcoal grill:* Open the bottom vents. Ignite 6 quarts or 2½ pounds charcoal briquettes or hardwood charcoal. When the coals are hot, set up for a one-level medium-heat fire (so you can hold your hand 5 inches above the cooking rack for only 4 to 5 seconds).
>
> *For a gas grill:* Turn each burner to high and ignite. Cover the grill. When hot, set the burners to medium heat.

6. *On a charcoal or gas grill:* Place ribs on the grill rack over coals or heat, cover, and grill 5 minutes. Turn ribs, cover, and grill 5 minutes. Repeat once. Serve, passing sauce.

KC-Style Barbecued Baby Back Ribs

Serves: 4
Prep time: about 25 minutes, plus 90 minutes to bake
Cook time: 25 minutes (including brushing time)
Serving size: ½ rack

2 racks (about 5 or 6 lb. total) pork baby back ribs

2 TB. firmly packed dark brown sugar

2 TB. sweet paprika

1 TB. garlic powder

1 TB. fresh-ground black pepper

1 TB. chili powder

2 tsp. kosher salt

1 tsp. celery seed

½ cup apple cider vinegar

1 tsp. liquid smoke

Kansas City–Style Barbecue Sauce (recipe in Chapter 7)

1. Use a knife to lift the corner of membrane on back of ribs. Using a paper towel to grip, completely pull off membrane and discard. Rinse racks under cold running water, and pat dry with paper towels. Cut racks in half along the edge of a center bone.

2. In a small bowl, stir together brown sugar, paprika, garlic powder, black pepper, chili powder, kosher salt, and celery seed together until combined. Sprinkle seasoning rub evenly over ribs, and rub

in with your fingers. Place ribs in a 1-gallon reclosable plastic bag, push out air, seal the bag, and refrigerate overnight.

3. Place the oven rack in the center position, and preheat oven to 300°F. Remove ribs from the plastic bag, and discard the bag.

4. Line an oven-safe pan large enough to comfortably hold back ribs with foil. Place ribs on the foil in the pan, and, using another piece of foil, cover and seal the pan. Bake 90 minutes. Remove the pan from the oven, carefully remove foil cover (steam will billow up), remove ribs to a pan or a tray to take to the grill, and discard liquid in the pan.

5. In a small bowl, whisk together vinegar and liquid smoke, and take to the grill with a brush and ribs.

6. Fire up the grill:

> *For a charcoal grill:* Open the bottom vents. Ignite 6 quarts or 2½ pounds charcoal briquettes or hardwood charcoal. When the coals are hot, set up for a one-level medium-heat fire (so you can hold your hand 5 inches above the cooking rack for only 4 to 5 seconds).
>
> *For a gas grill:* Turn each burner to high and ignite. Cover the grill. When hot, set the burners to medium heat.

7. *On a charcoal or gas grill:* Place ribs on the grill rack over coals or heat, cover, and grill 5 minutes. Turn ribs over, cover, and grill 5 minutes. Repeat once. Brush ribs with vinegar mixture before and after each turnover. Serve, passing barbecue sauce.

Barbecue Banter

Rib racks let you cook ribs on their sides, vertically, instead of flat on the grill. You'll be able to cook at least twice as many ribs with a rib rack than without.

Mustard and Honey–Glazed Baby Back Ribs

Serves: 4
Prep time: about 30 minutes, plus 90 minutes to bake
Cook time: about 20 minutes
Serving size: ½ rack

2 racks (about 5 or 6 lb. total) pork baby back ribs

Salt to taste, plus ½ tsp.

Fresh-ground black pepper to taste

2 TB. vegetable oil

1 small onion, peeled, root and stem ends trimmed, chopped

1 cup honey

1 cup Dijon mustard

½ cup apple cider vinegar

1 tsp. ground cloves

1. Use knife to lift the corner of membrane on back of ribs. Using a paper towel to grip, completely pull off membrane and discard. Rinse racks under cold running water, and pat dry with paper towels. Cut racks in half along the edge of a center bone.

2. Place the oven rack in the center position, and preheat the oven to 300°F.

3. Line an oven-safe pan large enough to hold ribs with foil. Salt and pepper ribs on both sides. Place ribs on foil in pan, and, using another piece of foil, cover and seal the pan. Bake 90 minutes. Remove the pan from the oven, carefully remove the foil cover, remove ribs to a pan or a tray to take to the grill, and discard liquid in the pan.

4. While ribs bake, make sauce. In a medium saucepan over medium heat, add oil. Add onion and cook until soft, about 5 minutes, stirring occasionally. Add honey, Dijon mustard, vinegar, ½ teaspoon salt, and cloves. Stir well and bring to a boil. Reduce heat to low, and simmer for 5 minutes, stirring. Remove from heat and set aside.

5. Fire up the grill:

> *For a charcoal grill:* Open the bottom vents. Ignite 6 quarts or 2½ pounds charcoal briquettes or hardwood charcoal. When the coals are hot, set up for a one-level medium-heat fire (so you can hold your hand 5 inches above the cooking rack for only 4 to 5 seconds).
>
> *For a gas grill:* Turn each burner to high and ignite. Cover the grill. When hot, set the burners to medium heat.

6. *On a charcoal or gas grill:* Place ribs on the grill rack over coals or heat, brush with sauce, cover, and grill 5 minutes. Turn ribs, brush with sauce, cover, and grill 5 minutes. Repeat once. Before removing ribs from the grill, brush with sauce. Serve, passing sauce.

Barbecue Banter

When measuring out anything sticky such as honey, molasses, or even peanut butter, spray the inside of the measuring cup with vegetable oil spray before measuring. The sticky stuff will slide right out.

Spicy Beer-Brined Baby Back Ribs with Beer 'n' Honey BBQ Sauce

2 racks (about 5 or 6 lb. total) pork baby back ribs

3 (12-oz.) bottles imported beer (½ cup reserved)

3 TB. kosher salt

3 TB. firmly packed dark brown sugar

1 TB. ground cayenne

1 TB. celery seeds

2 tsp. fresh-ground black pepper

1 tsp. liquid smoke

1 TB. vegetable oil

⅓ cup chopped onion

1 clove garlic, pushed through a garlic press

¾ cup bottled chili sauce (I prefer Heinz)

¼ cup honey

2 TB. Worcestershire sauce

1 TB. Dijon mustard

Serves: 4
Prep time: 55 minutes
Cook time: about 90 minutes
Serving size: ½ rack

1. Use a knife to lift the corner of membrane on back of ribs. Using a paper towel to grip, completely pull off membrane and discard. Rinse racks under cold running water, and pat dry with paper towels. With a sharp knife, remove every other bone in rib racks and discard. (You should be left with bones with a full compliment of meat on either side of each.)

2. In a 1-gallon reclosable plastic bag, add 3 bottles beer, kosher salt, brown sugar, cayenne, celery seeds, pepper, and liquid smoke. Seal the bag, and shake until salt and sugar dissolve. Add bones with attached meat to brine, push out air, seal the bag, and refrigerate for 4 to 6 hours, turning bag occasionally.

3. Place a medium saucepan over medium heat, and add vegetable oil. When oil is hot, add onion and garlic and cook, stirring frequently, until onion is softened, about 5 or 6 minutes. Stir in chili sauce, ½ cup reserved beer, honey, Worcestershire sauce, and Dijon mustard. Bring to a boil, reduce heat to low, and simmer, stirring occasionally, for 20 minutes or until slightly thickened.

4. Fire up the grill:

> *For a charcoal grill:* Open the bottom vents. Ignite 8 quarts or 3½- to 4 pounds charcoal briquettes or hardwood charcoal. When the coals are hot, set up on one side of grill for a one-level medium-heat fire (so you can hold your hand 5 inches above the cooking rack for only 4 to 5 seconds).
>
> *For a gas grill:* Turn each burner to high and ignite. Cover the grill. When hot, set the burners to medium heat and turn off center burner.

5. *On a charcoal grill:* Place ribs on the grill rack away from coals, cover, positioning cover vent over ribs, and fully open vent. Grill for 1½ hours, or until ribs are tender. After 45 minutes, open the grill cover, with oven mitts (or other hand protection) lift grill rack with ribs out and set on a heat-safe surface. Spread 20 to 30 briquettes around grill, placing them on the already lighted briquettes. Fanning the briquettes from time to time, get the added briquettes started. Put the grill rack back in place, and cover. Brush with sauce during last 10 minutes. *On a gas grill:* Place ribs over the center burner and cook for 1½ hours, brushing with sauce during the last 10 minutes. Serve ribs, passing remaining sauce.

Barbecue Banter

Over time, you'll learn how many briquettes you'll need to reach the proper heat required for that day's grilling. You'll soon know how to build the right height and size pyramid of charcoal to cook your food evenly and quickly. You'll also get a feel for where the hot and cool spots are on your grill, so you can move food from one to another to control cooking speed.

Chapter 18

Beyond Ribs: Piggin' Out

In This Chapter

- ◆ The other white meat: pork!
- ◆ Pork grilling safety
- ◆ Loins, and ribs, and chops—so many options!
- ◆ Fun with kabobs

Grilling pork includes much more than just ribs—although pork ribs coming off the grill, shiny with sauce, taste mighty good. Pork chops taste much better seasoned and grilled than fried in a skillet. Pork roasts can be oven-roasted, but brining a roast to add flavor and moisture and seasoning it with herbs and spices before grilling adds new dimensions of flavor. (Plus chilled and thin-sliced grill-roasted pork makes terrific sandwiches.)

Seasoned and grilled pork tenderloin is a new favorite for many grilling enthusiasts. Pork tenderloin is naturally lean but also tender at the same time (hence the name), as long as it's not grilled too long, as that will dry it out. And for some fun, pork kabobs taste great, too!

New Pork, Lean Issues

Due to modern breeding methods, pork is now 30 percent leaner than it was 20 years ago. For your health, that's good news. For your grill, that's not such good news.

When pork contained more fat, you could overcook a pork chop some and still have a juicy chop. But that's not so today. Overcook today's lean pork, and you'll get something that matches the toughness of the bottoms of your running shoes. So it's more important than ever today to watch the temperature of your cooked pork and get it off the fire at just the right moment so it's done—and done right.

Safety First

These days we don't worry as much about cooking anything pork to the well-done point, 180°F, because trichinosis, the reason we were always told to essentially overcook pork, has almost vanished. This is true for two reasons:

- Trichinosis is extremely rare in today's world; thanks to significant pig farm and pork-processing changes.
- Even if trichinosis is present, pork only needs to be heated to an internal temperature of 150°F (it will rise to 155° to 160°F after it's removed from the grill), making it perfectly safe to consume.

This Little Piggy Went to the Grill …

When you're in the mood to cook something pork on the grill, you have several options. From steaks to ribs to chops, your butcher's case has many choices available.

Let's start with ham steaks. A ham steak is exactly what its name implies: a thick slice of steak-size ham. Grilling a ham steak works well because all ham steaks have "water added," which means, even though they're lean, they won't dry out as fast on the grill.

Next up, let's look at pork chops. Four different cuts of chops come from a whole pork loin:

- **Blade chops.** Blade chops have the most fat, flavor, and juice. Unfortunately, they're also the toughest.
- **Rib chops.** Rib chops have some fat, are relatively tender and juicy, and have a great flavor.

- **Center-cut chops.** Center-cut chops have very little fat, a large piece of tenderloin on one side (they look like miniature T-bone steaks), a good flavor, but are less juicy.

- **Sirloin chops.** Sirloin chops (usually the least expensive) are tough, dry, and have little flavor.

The best chops for grilling are rib chops and center-cut chops. Rib chops are my first choice.

I asked a Canadian friend of mine who is absolutely crazy about grilling what his favorite thing to grill is. His answer: pork tenderloin. Or more precisely: marinated pork tenderloin. And that makes sense. Pork tenderloin is very lean yet tender, and even juicy if cooked right. There are no bones to cut around and virtually no fat to trim off. And because it's not good to overcook pork tenderloin, if it's cooked right, it's on and off the grill in no time.

Barbecue Banter

Try this variation sometime when you're in the mood for something different from your pork tenderloin: slice pork tenderloin into ¾-inch-thick rounds, and pound them flat between 2 sheets of plastic wrap. These cook at lightening speed and offer nice wide surfaces for marinating, seasoning, or basting.

Barbecue Banter

In preparing pork tenderloin for the grill, you'll need to trim the silverskin, the thin, silvery-looking membrane attached to the tenderloin. If you're using a sharp, thin knife, it's easy to do: slip the tip of your knife at one end under the silverskin and start slicing back and forth with the edge of the blade angled slightly upward (you don't want to cut through it, just cut under it), keeping the membrane tight as you cut, repeating this process until all the silverskin is removed.

Pork loin roasts come in four types: blade-end roast, center-cut roast, sirloin roast, and *tenderloin roast*. The best roast for grilling is the blade-end roast because it's both moist and flavorful. The recognized second choice would be a center-cut roast. It has a milder flavor but less fat, so it can easily dry out on the grill.

Grill Guide

A **tenderloin roast** is actually two tenderloins tied together. If you're going to grill tenderloins, you might as well grill them separately so they can cook quicker and not dry out.

Finally, pork spareribs come from the belly or the side of the hog. They're the least tender and have more meat than back ribs. Back ribs are cut from the blade (as in shoulder blade) and center section of the loin (think pork chops). They're more tender, but less meaty than spareribs. Country-style ribs cut from the rib end of the loin are the meatiest (and unfortunately fattest) of pork ribs.

Kabobs—Easier Than You Might Think

Even though you have to spend some time getting all the pieces together—buying the skewers (plus soaking the bamboo or wooden ones), cutting the meat into cubes as well as the vegetables (or fruit), and then threading everything onto the skewers—making kabobs is still a lot of fun to do. Mostly all you need to remember is to make all the pieces the same size so they'll all grill at the same rate. Leave about ¼ inch between each piece, which lets the fire get all around each piece to cook them evenly and quickly.

Plus, marinating pork not only adds flavor but can tenderize, too, which means the meat can be done at the same time as the other ingredients. Kabobs are fun and great eating!

Barbecue Banter

You'll see some of the following recipes call for roasted garlic. This is pretty easy to do: heat the oven to 350°F. Trim off the pointed end of a head of garlic just barely exposing the cloves. Place on a 12×12-inch square of foil, drizzle a little olive oil onto the exposed cloves, bring the foil up from all corners, and twist to seal. Bake for 1 hour. Open foil (be careful—hot steam will be released) and cool to room temperature, cover, and refrigerate. To remove roasted cloves, push and press up from the bottom of the clove. It should pop right out.

Sweet Whiskey-Flavored Ham Steaks

2 (1-lb.) fully cooked, bone-in ham steaks, about ½-inch thick

3 TB. honey

2 TB. bourbon or other whiskey

1 TB. soy sauce

2 cloves garlic, roasted, peel removed, and mashed

1 tsp. dry mustard

Serves: 4	
Prep time: 6 to 7 minutes	
Cook time: 6 to 9 minutes	
Serving size: ½ ham steak	

1. Rinse ham steaks under cold running water, and pat dry with paper towels. To prevent ham from curling, with a sharp knife, make shallow cuts around the edge at 1-inch intervals.

2. In a medium mixing bowl, stir together honey, bourbon, soy sauce, garlic, and dry mustard until combined.

3. Fire up the grill:

For a charcoal grill: Open the bottom vents. Ignite 6 quarts or 2½ pounds charcoal briquettes or hardwood charcoal. When the coals are hot, set up for a one-level high-heat fire (so you can hold your hand 5 inches above the cooking rack for only 1 to 2 seconds).

For a gas grill: Turn each burner to high and ignite. Cover the grill. When hot, leave the burners on high heat.

4. *On a charcoal grill:* Grill steaks on a lightly oiled rack, uncovered, over coals for 7 to 9 minutes, turning once halfway through and brushing with glaze. Brush with glaze again in the last couple minutes. *On a gas grill:* Grill steaks on a lightly oiled rack, covered, over heat for 6 to 8 minutes, turning once halfway through and brushing with glaze. Brush with glaze again in the last couple minutes. Cut steaks in half and serve, passing remaining glaze.

Barbecue Banter

When cooking ham steaks, oiling the rack is very important. Most hams have been infused with a "curing" liquid that frequently contains some type of sugar. If a ham steak hits an unoiled grill rack, expect some sticking because the sugar in the steak will caramelize and make it difficult to remove from the grill.

Spicy Rubbed and Q'd Pork Chops

<table>
<tr><td>

Serves: 6

Prep time: 18 to 20 minutes, plus 1 to 8 hours to marinate

Cook time: 17 to 23 minutes

Serving size: 1 pork chop

</td></tr>
</table>

6 (10- to 11-oz.) bone-in center-cut pork chops

3 TB. hot paprika

1 TB. sweet paprika

1 TB. kosher salt

1 TB. ground cayenne

1 tsp. ground cumin

¾ tsp. granulated sugar

Vegetable oil spray

Bottled or homemade sweet and smoky barbecue sauce

1. Rinse pork chops under cold running water, and pat dry with paper towels.

2. In a small bowl, stir together hot paprika, sweet paprika, kosher salt, cayenne, cumin, and sugar until combined.

3. From 1 hour to 8 hours before you plan to grill pork chops, coat chops with seasoning rub, place them in a 1-gallon, reclosable plastic bag, push out air, seal the bag, and refrigerate.

4. Fire up the grill:

 For a charcoal grill: Open the bottom vents. Ignite 6 quarts or 2½ pounds charcoal briquettes or hardwood charcoal. When the coals are hot, set up for a one-level medium-heat fire (so you can hold your hand 5 inches above the cooking rack for only 4 to 5 seconds).

 For a gas grill: Turn each burner to high and ignite. Cover the grill. When hot, set the burners to medium heat.

Barbecue Banter

One way to keep from overcooking pork chops whether on the grill or in the kitchen is to buy thick—not thin—chops. Today's pork is so lean, thin chops cook fast—very fast—so being off by a minute or two can ruin them.

5. Remove chops from the refrigerator, and let them sit, covered, at room temperature for about 30 minutes. Remove chops from the bag, and discard the bag and marinade. Lightly spray chops with vegetable oil and transfer them to the grill.

6. *On a charcoal grill:* Grill chops, uncovered, over coals 17 to 20 minutes, turning once halfway through, or until an instant-read thermometer registers 150°F when inserted horizontally into chop's center. *On a gas grill:* Grill chops over heat, covered, for 20 to 23 minutes, turning several times, or until an instant-read thermometer registers 150°F when inserted horizontally into chop's center. Remove chops from the grill, let rest for 5 minutes, and serve, passing barbecue sauce.

Maple-Glazed Pork Chops

4 (10- to 11-oz.) bone-in center-cut pork chops

½ cup plus 2 TB. *pure maple syrup*

4 TB. olive oil

3 TB. balsamic vinegar

2 green onions, trimmed and thinly sliced

1 TB. gin

3 large cloves garlic, peeled and minced or pushed through a garlic press (about 2 tsp.)

1½ tsp. dried rubbed sage, crumbled

4 bay leaves, crumbled

1 tsp. fresh-ground black pepper

Kosher salt

Serves: 4
Prep time: 25 minutes, plus 6 hours or more to marinate
Cook time: 12 to 17 minutes
Serving size: 1 pork chop

1. Rinse pork chops and pat dry with paper towels.

2. To a 1-gallon, reclosable plastic bag, add ½ cup syrup, 3 tablespoons olive oil, 2 tablespoons vinegar, onions, gin, garlic, sage, bay leaves, and pepper. Seal the bag, and shake until combined. Add chops, push out the air, seal the bag, and marinate in the refrigerator at least 6 hours or overnight, turning bag occasionally.

3. Fire up the grill:

> *For a charcoal grill:* Open the bottom vents. Ignite 6 quarts or 2½ pounds charcoal briquettes or hardwood charcoal. When the coals are hot, set up for a one-level medium-heat fire (so you can hold your hand 5 inches above the cooking rack for only 4 to 5 seconds).
>
> *For a gas grill:* Turn each burner to high and ignite. Cover the grill. When hot, set the burners to medium heat.

4. Remove chops from the refrigerator, and let them sit, covered, at room temperature for about 30 minutes. Remove chops from the bag, and discard the bag and marinade. Season with kosher salt.

5. In a small bowl stir together remaining 2 tablespoons syrup, 1 tablespoon olive oil, and 1 tablespoon vinegar until combined.

6. *On a charcoal grill:* Grill chops, uncovered, over coals 12 to 16 minutes, turning once halfway through. Brush chops with syrup, and grill 2 to 3 minutes more or until an instant-read thermometer registers 150°F when inserted horizontally into chop's center. *On a gas grill:* Grill chops over heat, covered, for 7 to 9 minutes, turning once and grilling 6 to 8 minutes more. Brush chops with syrup, and grill 2 to 3 minutes more or until an instant-read thermometer registers 150°F when inserted horizontally into chop's center. Remove chops from the grill, let rest for 5 minutes, and serve, passing syrup.

Grill Guide

Pure maple syrup is made from maple tree sap, with nothing added. Maple-flavored syrup is made with corn syrup and high fructose corn syrup and maple flavoring. The only maple in maple-flavored syrup is on the label. If you can buy "Grade B" pure maple syrup, you'll save money and enjoy a maple syrup with a bigger flavor and slightly darker color than "Grade A."

Grilled Pork Chop Sandwiches

Serves: 4
Prep time: about 30 minutes, plus 6 to 8 hours to marinate
Cook time: 25 to 30 minutes
Serving size: 1 sandwich

4 boneless pork loin chops, about 1¼ to 1½ inches thick

1 TB. chili powder

1 TB. vegetable oil

1¼ tsp. ground cumin

¼ tsp. salt

¼ tsp. ground cayenne

1 large clove garlic, peeled and minced or pushed through a garlic press

⅓ cup bottled chili sauce (I like Heinz)

½ tsp. curry powder

4 kaiser rolls, or other good-quality roll, split and toasted on a hot grill

Romaine lettuce leaves (optional)

1. Rinse pork chops under cold running water, and pat dry with paper towels.

2. In a small bowl stir together chili powder, vegetable oil, 1 teaspoon cumin, salt, cayenne, and garlic until combined.

3. Cut the outer edge of fat on pork chops diagonally at 1-inch intervals (do not cut into meat) so chops stay flat on the grill. Spread rub evenly on both sides of chops. Place chops in a 1-gallon reclosable plastic bag, push out air, seal the bag, and refrigerate for 6 to 8 hours.

4. Fire up the grill:

> **For a charcoal grill:** Open the bottom vents. Ignite 8 quarts or 3½ to 4 pounds charcoal briquettes or hardwood charcoal. When the coals are hot, set up for a one-level medium-heat fire (so you can hold your hand 5 inches above the cooking rack for only 4 to 5 seconds).
>
> **For a gas grill:** Turn each burner to high and ignite. Cover the grill. When hot, set the burners to medium heat.

5. While the grill heats, make topping. In a small bowl, stir together chili sauce, curry powder, and remaining ¼ teaspoon cumin. Set aside.

6. Remove chops from the bag, and discard the bag and marinade. Place chops on a foil-lined pan or tray, and take to the grill. *On a charcoal grill:* Place chops on the grill rack directly over coals and sear, about 3 minutes per side. Move chops away from coals, cover, open top vent halfway, and grill for 22 to 25 minutes until chops are slightly pink in center and juices run clear or until an instant-read thermometer registers 150°F when inserted into the

Barbecue Banter

There isn't just one blend for chili powder; there are many. The one with which you're probably most familiar is from your supermarket. However, herb and spice stores (look on the Internet) make a variety of flavorful chili powders, some without salt. Check Appendix B for a source.

center of the thickest part, turning once and brushing occasionally with sauce during final 10 minutes. *On a gas grill:* Follow charcoal grilling instructions, except for vent. Remove chops from the grill.

7. Trim fat from chops and slice chops thinly. Top toasted rolls with sliced pork, some sauce, and Romaine lettuce (if using) and serve.

Grilled Garlic and Rosemary Pork Tenderloin

2 (¾-lb.) pork tenderloins

2 large cloves garlic, peeled and minced or pushed through a garlic press

2 tsp. kosher salt

4 tsp. minced fresh rosemary leaves or 2 tsp. dried rosemary, broken up or chopped

½ tsp. fresh-ground black pepper

2 TB. olive oil

Serves: 4
Prep time: 10 to 12 minutes, plus 20 to 30 minutes to marinate
Cook time: 20 to 30 minutes
Serving size: ½ tenderloin, sliced

1. Rinse tenderloins under cold running water, and pat dry with paper towels.

2. On a cutting board, mix garlic with kosher salt, and mash to a paste using the side of a large, heavy knife. In a small bowl, stir together garlic paste, rosemary, pepper, and olive oil. Brush marinade all over tenderloins. Marinate, uncovered, at room temperature for 20 to 30 minutes.

3. Fire up the grill:

> *For a charcoal grill:* Open the bottom vents. Ignite 6 quarts or 2½ pounds charcoal briquettes or hardwood charcoal. When the coals are hot, set up for a one-level medium-heat fire (so you can hold your hand 5 inches above the cooking rack for only 4 to 5 seconds).
>
> *For a gas grill:* Turn each burner to high and ignite. Cover the grill. When hot, set the burners to medium heat.

4. *On a charcoal or gas grill:* Grill tenderloins on lightly oiled grill rack, directly over coals or heat, 20 to 30 minutes, turning occasionally, or until an instant-read thermometer registers 150°F when inserted horizontally into center of tenderloin. Transfer tenderloins to a cutting board, and let stand 5 minutes. Slice and serve.

Barbecue Banter

When you purchase pork tenderloins, they come packaged in a plastic pouch. Those pouches hold two tenderloins, even though it looks like one large one. Many times the two tenderloins are not identical, one being larger and heavier than the other. Take this into consideration when estimating grilling time.

Cuban-Style Grilled Pork Tenderloin

Serves: 4
Prep time: 20 minutes, plus 2 to 3 hours to marinate
Cook time: 13 to 23 minutes
Serving size: ½ pork tenderloin

2 (¾-lb.) pork tenderloins

1½ cups orange juice, not from concentrate

¼ cup fresh lime juice

6 TB. olive oil

⅓ cup chopped fresh parsley

1 TB. dried oregano, crumbled

1 tsp. salt

2 large cloves garlic, peeled and minced or pushed through a garlic press

Sliced *avocado*

Ripe tomato slices

1. Rinse tenderloins under cold water, and pat dry with paper towels.

2. Two to three hours before you plan to grill tenderloins, make marinade. Add orange juice, lime juice, olive oil, parsley, oregano, salt, and garlic to a 1-gallon, reclosable plastic bag. Seal the bag, and shake until mixed well. Pour off ¾ cup marinade and reserve. Place tenderloins in the bag, push out air, seal the bag, and refrigerate for 2 to 3 hours, turning occasionally.

3. Fire up the grill:

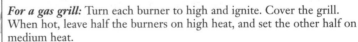

For a charcoal grill: Open the bottom vents. Ignite 6 quarts or 2½ pounds charcoal briquettes or hardwood charcoal. When the coals are hot, set up for a two-level fire: one side high heat (so you can hold your hand 1 to 2 inches above the cooking rack for only 1 to 2 seconds) and the other medium heat (so you can hold your hand 1 to 2 inches above the cooking rack for only 4 to 5 seconds).

For a gas grill: Turn each burner to high and ignite. Cover the grill. When hot, leave half the burners on high heat, and set the other half on medium heat.

4. Remove pork from the refrigerator and drain it. Let pork sit, covered, at room temperature for 20 to 30 minutes.

5. *On a charcoal or gas grill:* Transfer tenderloins to grill over high-heat coals or heat, arranging them so the thin ends are angled away from the hottest part of fire. Grill tenderloins, uncovered, for 3 minutes, turning them on all sides. Move tenderloins to medium heat for 10 to 12 minutes for smaller tenderloins and up to 20 minutes for larger. Continue turning tenderloins on all sides for even cooking until an instant-read thermometer registers 150°F when horizontally inserted into tenderloin. Remove pork from grill, and place on cutting board. Let rest 5 minutes.

6. Carve tenderloins into thin slices, garnish with avocado and tomato, and serve hot, accompanied by reserved sauce.

Barbecue Banter

An **avocado** is a fruit grown on a tree and has more protein and oil content than any other fruit. The avocado ripens off the tree and, if picked fully grown and firm, takes 1 to 2 weeks in a warm room to ripen. Avocadoes are ripe when they are faintly but perceptibly squashy, especially at the stem end. If they give too much when squeezed, they're overripe.

Asian-Inspired Pork Tenderloin

2 (¾-lb.) pork tenderloins

½ cup soy sauce

¼ cup Oriental sesame oil

¼ cup unseasoned rice wine vinegar

1 (2-in.) piece fresh ginger, peeled and sliced

1 bunch cilantro, rinsed well under cold running water, spun dry, and minced

6 to 8 garlic cloves, peeled and minced or pushed through a garlic press, about 2 TB.

2 TB. firmly packed dark brown sugar

½ cup water

Serves: 4
Prep time: 18 to 20 minutes, plus 2 to 12 hours to marinate
Cook time: 20 to 30 minutes
Serving size: ½ tenderloin

1. Rinse tenderloins under cold running water, and pat dry with paper towels.

2. Add soy sauce, sesame oil, vinegar, ginger, cilantro, garlic, brown sugar, and water to a 1-gallon, reclosable plastic bag. Seal and shake until combined. Add tenderloins, push out air, seal the bag, and refrigerate for 2 to 12 hours, turning occasionally.

3. Fire up the grill:

   For a charcoal grill: Open the bottom vents. Ignite 6 quarts or 2½ pounds charcoal briquettes or hardwood charcoal. When the coals are hot, set up for a one-level medium-heat fire (so you can hold your hand 5 inches above the cooking rack for only 4 to 5 seconds).

   For a gas grill: Turn each burner to high and ignite. Cover the grill. When hot, set the burners to medium heat.

4. Remove tenderloins from marinade, reserving marinade. *On a charcoal or gas grill:* Grill tenderloins on lightly oiled grill rack, directly over coals or heat, turning occasionally, brushing with reserved marinade during the first 10 minutes (discard remaining marinade after that point), for 20 to 30 minutes total or until an instant-read thermometer registers 150°F when inserted diagonally into center of tenderloin. Transfer tenderloins to a cutting board, and let stand 5 minutes. Slice and serve.

Barbecue Banter

This recipe requires *unseasoned* rice wine vinegar, which is milder vinegar than cider vinegar. Seasoned rice wine vinegar has added salt and sugar. A variety of different flavors of rice wine vinegars are now available. Experiment and check out a few next time you go shopping.

Cajun Pork Roast

Serves: 4 to 6

Prep time: 50 minutes

Cook time: about 60 minutes

Serving size: 3 ounces

1 (2½- to 3-lb.) boneless blade-end pork loin roast, tied with butcher's twine or netted in oven-safe netting

2 TB. unsalted butter

½ medium yellow onion, peeled and finely chopped

1 (12-oz.) can full-flavored beer

½ cup vegetable oil

½ cup cider vinegar

2 TB. dry mustard

1 TB. Worcestershire sauce

2 jalapeño chili peppers, finely chopped

2 cloves garlic, peeled and minced or pushed through a garlic press

3 TB. sweet paprika

1 TB. garlic powder

2 tsp. dried oregano, crumbled

2 tsp. dried thyme, crumbled

½ tsp. ground cayenne

½ tsp. kosher salt

½ tsp. ground white pepper

½ tsp. ground cumin

½ tsp. grated nutmeg

1. Rinse pork roast under cold running water, and pat dry with paper towels.

2. In a medium saucepan over medium heat, melt butter. Add onion and cook until soft, about 5 to 7 minutes. Add beer, vegetable oil, vinegar, dry mustard, Worcestershire sauce, jalapeño pepper, and chopped garlic. Bring to a simmer, reduce heat to low, and simmer 10 minutes, stirring occasionally.

3. While baste simmers, make seasoning rub. In small mixing bowl, stir together paprika, garlic powder, oregano, thyme, cayenne, kosher salt, white pepper, cumin, and nutmeg until combined. Apply liberally to roast.

4. Fire up the grill:

> *For a charcoal grill:* Open the bottom vents. Ignite 6 quarts or 2½ pounds charcoal briquettes or hardwood charcoal. When the coals are hot, set up for a one-level medium-heat fire (so you can hold your hand 5 inches above the cooking rack for only 4 to 5 seconds).
>
> *For a gas grill:* Turn each burner to high and ignite. Cover the grill. When hot, set all the burners to medium heat, except turn the center burner off.

5. *On a charcoal grill:* Place a drip pan in the grill's center and, using tongs, place hot coals around the pan. Add and evenly distribute 8 to 10 new briquettes on started coals, put the food grill rack in position, and place roast on the grill rack over the drip pan. Baste roast, cover, open the grill cover vent halfway, and grill for 30 minutes. Open the grill. Using tongs, turn roast 180 degrees, baste, close cover, and grill 30 minutes. Open the grill, baste roast, and insert an instant-read thermometer halfway into roast's center. If the thermometer registers 150°F, remove roast from the grill. If it has not reached 150°F yet, baste roast, cover, and grill 15 minutes more and check temperature again. *On a gas grill:* Except for coal position and drip pan, follow as directed for a charcoal grill. When done, remove roast from grill, tent roast with foil, and allow meat to rest 10 minutes before carving into thin slices. Serve.

> **Barbecue Banter**
> The best paprika, either sweet or hot, comes to the United States from Hungary. Fortunately, most supermarkets carry an excellent, imported Hungarian paprika.

Caribbean Pork Roast

1 (2½- to 3-lb.) boneless blade-end pork loin roast, tied with butcher's twine or netted in oven-safe netting	1 TB. minced onion
	2 tsp. granulated sugar
3 TB. soy sauce	2 tsp. dried thyme, crumbled
2 TB. olive oil	1 tsp. ground allspice
2 TB. apple cider vinegar	1 tsp. ground cayenne
2 TB. water	½ tsp. ground cinnamon
	½ tsp. ground nutmeg

Serves: 4 to 6
Prep time: 15 minutes, plus 8 hours or overnight to marinate
Cook time: about 60 minutes
Serving size: 3 ounces

1. Rinse pork roast under cold running water, and pat dry with paper towels. With a sharp fork or knife, poke 8 or 10 holes in roast.

2. To a 1-gallon, reclosable plastic bag, add soy sauce, olive oil, vinegar, water, onion, sugar, thyme, allspice, cayenne, cinnamon, and nutmeg. Seal and shake the bag to mix. Add roast, press out air, seal the bag, and refrigerate 8 hours or overnight.

3. Fire up the grill:

> **For a charcoal grill:** Open the bottom vents. Ignite 6 quarts or 2½ pounds charcoal briquettes or hardwood charcoal. When the coals are hot, set up for a one-level medium-heat fire (so you can hold your hand 5 inches above the cooking rack for only 4 to 5 seconds).
>
> **For a gas grill:** Turn each burner to high and ignite. Cover the grill. When hot, set all the burners to medium heat, except turn the center burner off.

4. Remove roast from the refrigerator, remove roast from the bag, and discard the bag and marinade.

5. *On a charcoal grill:* Place a drip pan in the grill's center and, using tongs, place hot coals around the pan. Add and evenly distribute 8 to 10 new briquettes on started coals, put the food grill rack in position, and place roast on the grill rack over the drip pan. Cover the grill, open the grill cover vent halfway, and grill for 30 minutes. Open the grill. Using tongs, turn roast 180 degrees, cover, and grill 30 minutes. Open the grill, insert an instant-read thermometer halfway into roast's center. If the thermometer registers 150°F, remove roast from the grill. If it has not reached 150°F yet, close cover and grill 15 minutes more and check temperature again. *On a gas grill:* Except for coal position and drip pan, follow as directed for a charcoal grill. When done, remove roast from the grill, tent roast with foil, and allow meat to rest 10 minutes before carving into thin slices. Serve.

> **Barbecue Banter**
>
> A roast rests to allow its internal temperature to rise 5 to 10 degrees. Also, the roast's juices redistribute themselves, and the roast will lose less liquid when sliced when allowed to rest. This holds true for any large piece of cooked meat.

Marinated Pork Kabobs

Serves: 4
Prep time: about 25 minutes, plus 4 hours or overnight to marinate
Cook time: 20 to 35 minutes
Serving size: 1 kabob

1 (2-lb.) pork shoulder
¾ cup vegetable oil
½ cup cider vinegar
1 clove garlic, peeled and minced or pushed through a garlic press
½ tsp. kosher salt
½ tsp. dried basil, crumbled

½ tsp. dried oregano, crumbled
3 green bell peppers, stem ends cut off, seeds and ribs discarded, and cut into 1-inch pieces
1 (16-oz.) can pineapple chunks, drained
4 (12- to 16-inch) metal skewers

1. Rinse pork shoulder under cold running water, and pat dry with paper towels. Cut into 1-inch cubes.

2. To a 1-gallon, reclosable plastic bag, add vegetable oil, vinegar, garlic, kosher salt, basil, and oregano. Seal and shake the bag to mix. Add roast, press out air, seal the bag, and refrigerate 4 hours or overnight.

3. Fire up the grill:

> ***For a charcoal grill:*** Open the bottom vents. Ignite 6 quarts or 2½ pounds charcoal briquettes or hardwood charcoal. When the coals are hot, set up for a one-level medium-heat fire (so you can hold your hand 5 inches above the cooking rack for only 4 to 5 seconds).
>
> ***For a gas grill:*** Turn each burner to high and ignite. Cover the grill. When hot, set all the burners to medium heat, except turn the center burner off.

4. While the grill heats, remove the bag from the refrigerator, and pour marinade into a small saucepan. Place saucepan over medium heat, bring to a low boil, simmer 5 minutes, stirring occasionally, and remove from heat.

5. Thread pork cubes, pepper pieces, and pineapple chunks alternately onto metal skewers. *On a charcoal grill:* Brush skewered pork, peppers, and pineapple with heated marinade, and grill 20 to 30 minutes over coals, turning often and brushing frequently with reheated marinade, until pork is cooked or until an instant-read thermometer when inserted into the center of a pork cube registers 150°F. *On a gas grill:* Brush skewered pork, peppers, and pineapple with heated marinade, and grill 25 to 35 minutes over heat, covered, turning often and brushing frequently with reheated marinade, until pork is cooked or until an instant-read thermometer when inserted into the center of a pork cube registers 150°F. Serve on skewers.

Barbecue Banter

To oil your grill rack, moisten a paper towel and rub oil on the rack before you put it on the grill. Or you can moisten a paper towel with oil and, wearing a fireproof mitt, use tongs to rub oil from the towel onto the grill.

Fire-Eater Pork and Corn Skewers

1¾- to 2-lb. pork tenderloin

1 (12-oz.) bottle full-flavored beer

2 large or 3 medium ears fresh or frozen corn, husk and silk removed and cut into 12 (¾-inch-thick) rounds

1 TB. hot paprika

1½ tsp. ground cayenne

1½ tsp. sweet paprika

1½ tsp. granulated garlic

1 tsp. salt

1 tsp. granulated sugar

6 flat metal skewers

1 large onion, peeled, stem and root ends cut off, and cut into chunks

2 medium green red bell pepper, stem ends cut off, seeds and ribs discarded, and cut into 1-inch squares

Vegetable oil spray

Serves: 6
Prep time: 60 minutes, plus 2 to 4 hours to marinate
Cook time: 14 to 18 minutes
Serving size: 1 kabob

1. Rinse pork tenderloin under cold running water, and pat dry with paper towels. Cut into 1-inch cubes.

2. Pour beer into a 1-gallon, reclosable plastic bag. Add cut-up pork and corn, press out air, seal the bag, and refrigerate 2 to 4 hours.

3. In a small bowl, stir together hot paprika, cayenne, sweet paprika, granulated garlic, salt, and sugar until combined.

4. Fire up the grill:

> *For a charcoal grill:* Open the bottom vents. Ignite 6 quarts or 2½ pounds charcoal briquettes or hardwood charcoal. When the coals are hot, set up for a one-level medium-heat fire (so you can hold your hand 5 inches above the cooking rack for only 4 to 5 seconds).
>
>
>
> *For a gas grill:* Turn each burner to high and ignite. Cover the grill. When hot, set all the burners to medium heat, except turn center burner off.

5. While the grill heats, remove pork and corn from the refrigerator and drain, discarding beer. Separate corn from pork cubes, covering and reserving corn. Place pork in a clean plastic bag, add spice mixture to the bag, seal, and shake to coat pork. Transfer pork to a pan, and let coated pork cubes sit, covered, at room temperature for about 20 minutes.

6. Divide pork cubes, corn, onion, and red and green bell peppers into 6 portions, thread them onto skewers, and spray kabobs with vegetable oil. *On a charcoal grill:* Grill kabobs, uncovered, over coals for 14 to 16 minutes, turning kabobs every few minutes to grill evenly on all sides, until meat is barely white at its center with clear juices or until an instant-read thermometer when inserted into the center of the pork registers 150°F. *On a gas grill:* Grill, covered, for 16 to 18 minutes, turning once halfway through until meat is barely white at its center with clear juices or until an instant-read thermometer when inserted into the center of the pork registers 150°F. Serve kabobs on skewers.

Flame Point

Do not place a hot grill cover on carpet, grass, or your wood deck. Also, never touch a grill's heat source or the grill to see if they're hot. (That's what thermometers are for!)

Part 6

Seafood: Finfish and Shellfish

You may feel a little hesitant about grilling finfish because you've heard it can be tricky. Let me tell you: it's not any trickier than grilling any other food, as long as you read and follow the tried-and-true methods for doing so. You'll end up more concerned about where to get the best and freshest finfish than how you're going to handle it on your grill.

Shellfish such as shrimp might seem tough to grill, too, but they're not. Shrimp's hard outer shell, like that on a lobster or even the harder shells on calms and mussels, protects it like a firewall protects your computer. You can almost blacken a shrimp's shell on the grill and then peel it off to find moist, pure white, tasty shrimp underneath.

Grilled Finfish

In This Chapter

◆ What to look for when purchasing fresh fish
◆ Tips on determining fish cooking time
◆ Ways to keep your fish from sticking

I grew up with a family who almost never ate fish. My mother hated fish (except for canned tuna) and shellfish (except for the rarely consumed shrimp). It took marrying a woman who loved fish and shellfish and who was used to getting up on dark mornings to go fishing with her dad in the cool clear waters of Northern Wisconsin for me to develop a taste for fish. She took my hand and showed me how great fish and shellfish could taste.

Today, I love all sorts of finfish and shellfish and, although it was harder to learn how to grill fish properly (without it sticking or falling apart) and shrimp (their visit above the glowing coals should be brief), I now enjoy both quite often. In this and the next chapter, I share recipes and ideas gleaned from 25 years of learning to appreciate and love finfish and shellfish, especially on the grill.

Telling If a Fresh Fish Is *Really* Fresh

A truly "fresh" whole fish should, well … look fresh. That means the eyes should be clear, not red or sunken, and the gills should be bright red and display a glossy surface sheen (as a fish ages in the display case, it loses its sheen, too).

Trust your nose. A fresh fish should smell fresh. It will smell like fish, but not "fishy." If the fish came from the ocean, it should have a scent reminiscent of seawater. When you press the fish's flesh, whether whole or fillet, it should offer resistance; if it's soft, it's old.

Timing Is Everything

The main reason my mother disliked fish so much was because it made her house "smell fishy." Later in my life, Asian friends who loved all kinds of seafood and had been eating it all their lives explained that cooking fish far past the point of being done produces the odor my mother found so offensive.

As I learned to cook finfish and shellfish, I found that there's a general rule to determine how long it should cook: "10 minutes to the inch," measured at the thickest part. So no matter how it's being prepared—fried, baked, sautéed, broiled, grilled, or poached—a 1-inch-thick fish fillet should take 10 total cooking minutes. Or a ½-inch-thick fish should take about 5 total cooking minutes.

Don't Get Stuck!

Fish can easily stick to your grill rack, and because fish has a less-firm structure than steak, it can break apart easily when you try to get it unstuck. The best way to deal with this potential problem is to avoid it. The only way I know to do that is to oil the grill rack well before putting a fish on it, oil the fish before it hits the grill, and if necessary, re-oil the grill before turning the fish over.

You could also use nonstick baskets with small holes to confidently grill your fish in. The basket keeps your fish from becoming part of the fire instead of part of your dinner.

The best way to oil a grill is to pour 2 or more tablespoons vegetable oil into a saucer or salad plate, fold a paper towel into quarters, soak the paper towel in the oil, place the grill rack on the grill, and with tongs, oil the rack with the oil-saturated paper towel. It is ill-advised to spray a vegetable spray on a hot grill to oil it, because the oil in the spray could catch fire and climb up the spray to the can.

When it comes to preparing fish, the one thing that's not written in stone is the ease of substituting one fish for another. As long as the fish is similar in thickness to the dimension a recipe indicates, a cod can stand in for halibut or perch or sea bass. It's more important that the fish is fresh than it be a specific species.

Lemon and Mustard–Glazed Halibut Steaks

Serves: 4
Prep time: 5 minutes
Cook time: 8 to 12 minutes
Serving size: 1 halibut steak

4 (6- to 8-oz., about 1-inch-thick) fresh or frozen and thawed halibut steaks

2 TB. unsalted butter

2 TB. fresh lemon juice (from 1 lemon)

1 TB. Dijon mustard

2 tsp. chopped fresh basil leaves or ½ tsp. dried basil, crumbled

Salt

Fresh-ground black pepper

1. Fire up the grill:

> *For a charcoal grill:* Open the bottom vents. Ignite 6 quarts or 2½ pounds charcoal briquettes or hardwood charcoal. When the coals are hot, set up for a one-level medium-heat fire (so you can hold your hand 5 inches above the cooking rack for only 4 to 5 seconds).
>
> *For a gas grill:* Turn each burner to high and ignite. Cover the grill. When hot, set the burners to medium heat.

2. While the grill heats, rinse halibut under cold running water and pat dry with paper towels.

3. In a small saucepan, heat butter, lemon juice, Dijon mustard, and basil over low heat until butter melts, stirring together. Brush both sides of halibut with seasoned butter and season with salt and pepper.

4. *On a charcoal grill:* Oil the grill rack well. Grill halibut over coals, uncovered, for 8 to 12 minutes or until fish flakes easily when tested with a fork, *gently* turning once halfway through and brushing occasionally with seasoned butter. The fish is done when it flakes easily when prodded with a fork or knife in the thickest part. *On a gas grill:* Oil the grill rack well. Place halibut on the grill rack over heat, cover, and follow as directed for a charcoal grill. Serve.

Flame Point

Never, never (did I mention never?) use spray vegetable oil to oil hot grill racks. The oil could flame up and travel up the spray to the can and explode. Only use vegetable oil spray to oil fish, meat, poultry, or vegetables headed for the grill.

Orange and Dill-Scented Sea Bass

4 (5- to 6-oz., about ¾-inch-
thick) fresh or frozen and
thawed sea bass fillets

2 TB. chopped fresh dill

2 TB. olive oil

½ tsp. salt

¼ tsp. ground white pepper

4 large oranges, cut into
¼-inch slices

1 orange, cut into wedges

4 fresh dill sprigs (optional)

Serves: 4
Prep time: about 12 minutes
Cook time: 9 to 11 minutes
Serving size: 1 fillet

1. Fire up the grill:

> *For a charcoal grill:* Open the bottom vents. Ignite 6 quarts or 2½ pounds charcoal briquettes or hardwood charcoal. When the coals are hot, set up for a one-level medium-heat fire (so you can hold your hand 5 inches above the cooking rack for only 4 to 5 seconds).
>
> *For a gas grill:* Turn each burner to high and ignite. Cover the grill. When hot, set the burners to medium heat.

2. While the grill heats, rinse sea bass under cold running water, and pat dry with paper towels.

3. In a small bowl, stir together dill, olive oil, salt, and white pepper. Brush both sides of fish with dill mixture.

4. *On a charcoal grill:* Oil the grill rack well. Arrange a bed of orange slices on the grill rack directly over coals. Arrange fish on top of orange slices, cover, and grill for 9 to 11 minutes or until it flakes easily when prodded with a fork or knife in the thickest part. (do not turn fish). *On a gas grill:* Oil the grill rack well. Arrange orange slices on the grill rack directly over heat. Place fish on top of oranges, cover, and follow as directed for a charcoal grill. Squeeze juice from orange wedges over grilled fish, and garnish with dill sprig (if using). Serve.

Barbecue Banter

When squeezed, Valencia oranges produce a great-tasting, very flavorful, sweet juice. They're much better for juicing than those oranges labeled "juice" oranges.

Pecan-Crusted Red Snapper Fillets

Serves: 4
Prep time: 25 minutes
Cook time: 5 to 10 minutes
Serving size: 1 fillet

4 (6- or 8-oz., ½- to ¾-inch-thick at the thickest part) fresh or frozen and thawed red snapper fillets (with skin)

2 TB. unsalted butter, softened

⅓ cup finely chopped pecans

2 TB. fine dry breadcrumbs

1 TB. chopped fresh parsley

1 tsp. grated lemon zest

2 cloves garlic, peeled and minced or pushed through a garlic press

¼ tsp. salt

⅛ tsp. fresh-ground black pepper

Dash ground cayenne

Chopped fresh parsley (optional)

Lemon wedges

1. Fire up the grill:

   > *For a charcoal grill:* Open the bottom vents. Ignite 6 quarts or 2½ pounds charcoal briquettes or hardwood charcoal. When the coals are hot, set up for a one-level medium-heat fire (so you can hold your hand 5 inches above cooking rack for only 4 to 5 seconds).
   >
   > *For a gas grill:* Turn each burner to high and ignite. Cover the grill. When hot, set the burners to medium heat.

2. While the grill heats, rinse snapper fillets under cold running water, and pat dry with paper towels.

3. In a small saucepan, heat butter, pecans, breadcrumbs, parsley, lemon zest, garlic, salt, pepper, and cayenne over medium heat until butter melts. Cook, stirring, for 3 to 4 minutes. Remove from heat.

4. *On a charcoal grill:* Oil the grill rack well. Place fish, skin side down, directly over coals. Evenly divide and spoon pecan mixture on top of fish; spread slightly. Grill, covered with vent open all the way, until fish flakes easily when prodded with a fork or knife in the thickest part, allowing about 5 minutes per ½-inch thickness of fish (do not turn). *On a gas grill:* Oil the grill rack well. Follow as directed for a charcoal grill.

5. Using a wide spatula, transfer snapper to dinner plates or a serving platter. Sprinkle snapper with additional snipped parsley (if desired), and serve with lemon wedges.

Barbecue Banter

When grating lemon zest (or any citrus fruit), use a very light pressure so you don't go too deep and also grate the white part of the peel. This white part of the peel—the pith—is quite bitter. The oils in the peel help boost the flavor. That's what you want.

Fennel and Lemon–Crusted Tuna Steaks

2 (about 1-lb., 1-inch-thick) tuna steaks

1 TB. plus 1 tsp. crushed fennel seeds

1 TB. plus 1 tsp. grated lemon zest

1 tsp. kosher salt

Olive oil spray

Lemon wedges

Serves: 4
Prep time: 10 to 12 minutes, plus 1 to 4 hours to marinate
Cook time: 10 minutes
Serving size: ½ steak

1. Rinse tuna steaks under cold running water, and pat dry with paper towels.

2. In a small bowl, stir together crushed fennel seeds, lemon zest, and kosher salt until combined. Rub both sides of each steak with seasoning mixture, wrap steaks in plastic, and refrigerate for 1 to 4 hours before grilling.

3. Fire up the grill:

> *For a charcoal grill:* Open the bottom vents. Ignite 6 quarts or 2½ pounds charcoal briquettes or hardwood charcoal. When the coals are hot, set up for a two-level fire: one side high heat (so you can hold your hand 1 to 2 inches above the cooking rack for only 1 to 2 seconds) and the other medium heat (so you can hold your hand 1 to 2 inches above cooking rack for only 4 to 5 seconds).
>
> *For a gas grill:* Turn each burner to high and ignite. Cover the grill. When hot, leave half the burners on high heat, and set the other half on medium heat.

4. While the grill heats, remove steaks from the refrigerator and let them sit, covered, at room temperature for about 30 minutes.

5. Just before grilling, spray or brush steaks well with oil. *On a charcoal grill:* Oil the grill rack well. Place steaks on the grill, uncovered, over high heat for 2 minutes per side. Move steaks to medium heat, and continue cooking for an additional 2 to 3 minutes per side, leaving a pink center. If there's any resistance when you first turn fish, re-oil the grate. *On a gas grill:* Oil the grill rack well. Sear both sides of steaks over high heat, uncovered, for 2 minutes each. Finish grilling, covered, over medium heat for 4 to 5 minutes, turning once midway.

6. Cut steaks in half, and serve immediately with lemon wedges.

Barbecue Banter

Fennel seeds add a nice, light anise (licorice) flavor note. To crush them, run them through a pepper mill set for coarse grind or in an electric spice grinder.

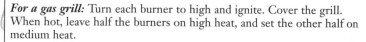

Swordfish Kabobs

Serves: 4
Prep time: 2½ hours (including marinating)
Cook time: about 8 minutes
Serving size: 1 steak

1½ lb. (1-inch-thick) swordfish steaks, skin discarded

1 cup finely chopped fresh parsley

2 cloves garlic, peeled and minced or pushed through a garlic press

2 tsp. ground cumin

2 tsp. sweet paprika

Scant ½ tsp. salt or to taste

¼ tsp. dried hot red pepper flakes

Lemon wedges

1. Rinse swordfish steaks under cold running water, and pat dry with paper towels. Cut into 1-inch cubes.

2. In a large mixing bowl, stir together parsley, garlic, cumin, paprika, salt, and red pepper flakes until combined. Add swordfish cubes to the bowl, toss to coat, and marinate, covered and chilled, stirring occasionally, for 2 hours.

3. Fire up the grill:

> *For a charcoal grill:* Open the bottom vents. Ignite 6 quarts or 2½ pounds charcoal briquettes or hardwood charcoal. When the coals are hot, set up for a one-level medium-heat fire (so you can hold your hand 5 inches above the cooking rack for only 4 to 5 seconds).
>
> *For a gas grill:* Turn each burner to high and ignite. Cover the grill. When hot, set the burners to medium heat.

Flame Point

If left on the grill too long, most fish will toughen up and become rubbery. That's especially true of swordfish. Watch the fish carefully during cooking to ensure you don't overcook it.

4. Thread swordfish cubes evenly on metal skewers, leaving about ¼-inch space in between each cube. *On a charcoal grill:* Oil the grill rack well. Grill swordfish on the grill rack over coals, uncovered, turning once, until just cooked through, about 8 minutes total or until fish flakes easily when prodded with a fork or knife in the thickest part. *On a gas grill:* Follow as directed for a charcoal grill, except close grill cover during grilling. Serve on skewers, passing plate of lemon wedges.

Brined and Grilled Dill-Scented Salmon

4 (6- to 8-oz.) pieces salmon fillet (not tail portion), with skin

2 cups water

¾ cup firmly packed light brown sugar

¼ cup plus 2 TB. kosher salt

1½ TB. granulated sugar

½ cup chopped fresh dill

1 TB. olive oil

Serves: 4
Prep time: 18 to 20 minutes, plus 1 hour to brine
Cook time: 8 to 10 minutes
Serving size: 1 fillet

1. Rinse salmon fillets under cold running water, and pat dry with paper towels.

2. Add water, brown sugar, kosher salt, and sugar to a blender. Cover and blend until sugar dissolves, stopping after every 10 seconds to check. Pour brine from the blender container into a 13×9-inch glass or ceramic baking dish, and stir in dill. Marinate salmon, skin-side up, in brine in baking dish, chilled, 1 hour. Do not turn salmon over, and do not brine longer than indicated.

3. Fire up the grill:

> *For a charcoal grill:* Open the bottom vents. Ignite 6 quarts or 2½ pounds charcoal briquettes or hardwood charcoal. When the coals are hot, set up for a one-level medium-low-heat fire (so you can hold your hand 5 inches above the cooking rack for only 5 to 6 seconds).
>
> *For a gas grill:* Turn each burner to high and ignite. Cover the grill. When hot, set the burners to medium-low heat.

4. Remove salmon from brine, and pat dry with paper towels. Discard brine.

5. *On a charcoal or gas grill:* Oil the grill rack well. Grill salmon, uncovered, over coals or heat, starting with skin-side up and turning once, until just cooked through and skin is crisp, about 8 to 10 minutes total. Serve.

Barbecue Banter

Farm-raised salmon doesn't contain as much of the healthy omega-3 fats as wild-caught salmon. Also farm-raised salmon have red dye added to their food to make them as red as wild-caught salmon.

Salmon with Zucchini Relish

Serves: 6
Prep time: 25 to 30 minutes, plus 1 hour for relish to marinate
Cook time: 20 to 30 minutes
Serving size: ⅙ fillet

2 TB. chopped onion

2 TB. distilled white vinegar

2 TB. water

1 tsp. granulated sugar

2 TB. chopped fresh parsley

1 tsp. salt

1 medium zucchini or summer squash, ends trimmed and coarsely chopped (1¼ cups)

1 (2-lb.) large salmon fillet (king, sockeye, coho, or Atlantic; *not* pink or chum)

2 TB. olive or vegetable oil

¼ to ½ tsp. dried dill weed

¼ tsp. fresh-ground black pepper

1. In a medium stainless-steel or glass bowl, stir together onion, vinegar, water, sugar, parsley, and ½ teaspoon salt until salt and sugar dissolve. Add zucchini and stir until coated. Cover and refrigerate at least 1 hour but no longer than 8 hours. Drain relish before serving.

2. Fire up the grill:

 For a charcoal grill: Open the bottom vents. Ignite 6 quarts or 2½ pounds charcoal briquettes or hardwood charcoal. When the coals are hot, set up for a one-level high-heat fire (so you can hold your hand 5 inches above the cooking rack for only 1 to 2 seconds).

 For a gas grill: Turn each burner to high and ignite. Cover the grill. When hot, leave the burners on high heat.

3. While the grill heats, rinse salmon fillet under cold running water, and pat dry with paper towels. Place fillet, skin side up, on a 24-inch piece of heavy-duty aluminum foil. Brush skin generously with oil, turn fish over, brush flesh generously with oil, season with dill weed, remaining ½ teaspoon salt, and pepper, and wrap foil securely around fish.

4. *On a charcoal grill:* Place fish on the grill rack over coals, cover, open cover vents fully, and grill 20 to 30 minutes or until fish flakes easily when prodded with a fork or knife in the thickest part. *On a gas grill:* Follow as directed for a charcoal grill. Serve fish, passing relish.

 **Barbecue Banter**
Always look for young, small zucchini when shopping. Older, large zucchini have large seeds and are not as naturally sweet.

Anise-Scented Skewered Salmon

2 (1 lb.) skinless salmon fillets

½ cup olive oil

2 TB. chopped fresh dill or 2 tsp. dried dill

2 TB. Sambuca or other anise-flavored liqueur or brandy

½ tsp. salt

½ tsp. fresh-ground black pepper

2 lemons, sliced

Sprigs fresh parsley or dill

Lemon wedges

4 (12- to 16-inch) flat metal skewers

Serves: 4
Prep time: 25 minutes, plus 30 minutes to marinate
Cook time: 8 to 10 minutes
Serving size: ½ fillet

1. Rinse salmon fillets under cold running water, and pat dry with paper towels. Cut salmon fillets into strips about 1 inch wide by 3 inches long.

2. In a large bowl, stir together olive oil, fresh or dried dill, Sambuca, salt, and pepper until combined. Add salmon strips, and toss to combine. Cover and refrigerate for 30 minutes, tossing once or twice.

3. Fire up the grill:

> *For a charcoal grill:* Open the bottom vents. Ignite 6 quarts or 2½ pounds charcoal briquettes or hardwood charcoal. When the coals are hot, set up for a one-level medium-heat fire (so you can hold your hand 5 inches above cooking rack for only 4 to 5 seconds).
>
> *For a gas grill:* Turn each burner to high and ignite. Cover the grill. When hot, set the burners to medium heat.

4. Remove salmon from marinade and *reserve* marinade. Thread salmon strips onto metal skewers, accordion fashion, alternating with lemon slices. *On a charcoal grill or gas grill:* Oil the grill rack well. Grill skewers on the grill rack above coals or heat, turning frequently and brushing once at the beginning with reserved marinade (discarding after that point), until salmon is cooked through, 8 to 10 minutes. Remove from the grill to dinner plates or a platter, and garnish with parsley or dill sprigs and lemon wedges. Serve.

Grill Guide

Reserve or **reserving** means to set aside because it will be used again shortly. It's a single word that says "Don't throw this away!"

Grilled Fresh Salmon Patty Sandwiches

Serves: 4
Prep time: 25 to 30 minutes, plus 30 minute to refrigerate
Cook time: 8 to 10 minutes
Serving size: 1 sandwich

1 (1½-lb.) boneless, skinless salmon fillet

⅓ cup fresh breadcrumbs

2 TB. cold water

1 TB. minced shallot or onion

1 TB. fresh lemon juice (from ½ a lemon)

1 TB. Dijon mustard

½ tsp. fresh-ground black pepper

1 small red onion, stem and root ends trimmed, and sliced crosswise into thin rounds

1½ TB. unseasoned rice vinegar

4 good-quality sandwich buns, split

Bottled or homemade Zippy Tartar Sauce (recipe in Chapter 7)

8 fresh spinach leaves

1. Rinse salmon fillet under cold running water, and pat dry with paper towels.

2. With a large knife, cut salmon into strips, cutting crosswise, and chop salmon until it's the texture of raw hamburger meat. Transfer chopped salmon to a large bowl, and add breadcrumbs, water, shallot, lemon juice, Dijon mustard, and pepper. With a dinner fork, stir and fold until mixed together well; avoid compacting. Divide mixture into 4 equal portions, and form into bun-size patties. Cover and refrigerate for 30 minutes.

3. While patties chill, in a medium stainless-steel or glass mixing bowl, combine onion and rice vinegar and toss well. Set aside for about 30 minutes, stirring frequently.

4. Fire up the grill:

   For a charcoal grill: Open the bottom vents. Ignite 6 quarts or 2½ pounds charcoal briquettes or hardwood charcoal. When the coals are hot, set up for a one-level medium-heat fire (so you can hold your hand 5 inches above the cooking rack for only 4 to 5 seconds).

   For a gas grill: Turn each burner to high and ignite. Cover the grill. When hot, set the burners to medium heat.

5. *On a charcoal grill:* Oil the grill rack well. Grill chilled salmon patties on the grill rack over coals, covered, cover vents opened all the way, turning once, until just opaque throughout, about 4 to 5 minutes on each side. During last few minutes of grilling, place buns, cut-side down, on the outer edges of the rack to

Barbecue Banter

It's important to rinse spinach leaves in several changes of cold water. Spinach is grown in very sandy soil, and that sand can get trapped in the spinach's crinkly leaves.

To get ⅓ cup fresh breadcrumbs, process 1 slice of bread in a food processor until it reaches the desired crumby-ness.

lightly toast. *On a gas grill:* Oil grill rack well. Grill chilled salmon patties on the grill rack over heat, covered; follow as directed for a charcoal grill.

6. To make sandwiches, spread tartar sauce over cut sides of toasted buns. Place a few spinach leaves on each bun bottom, place grilled patty on top of spinach, top with an equal amount of drained onions, add bun tops, and serve.

South-of-the-Border Fish in Foil

4 (.6- to 7-oz., ½- to ¾-inch-thick) fresh or frozen and thawed cod fillets

1 medium-ripe tomato, core and seeds removed, and coarsely chopped (about ¾ cup)

3 or 4 green onions, trimmed and thinly sliced (about ⅓ cup)

¼ cup sliced pimiento-stuffed green olives

2 TB. fresh lemon juice (from 1 lemon)

2 tsp. *capers*

1 clove garlic, peeled and minced or pushed through a garlic press

¼ tsp. salt

⅛ tsp. fresh-ground black pepper

Lemon wedges

Serves: 6
Prep time: about 40 minutes
Cook time: 15 to 20 minutes
Serving size: 1 fillet (packet)

1. Rinse cod fillets under cold running water, and pat dry with paper towels.

2. In a medium stainless-steel or glass mixing bowl, stir together tomato, onions, olives, lemon juice, capers, garlic, salt, and pepper until combined.

3. Fire up the grill:

> **For a charcoal grill:** Open the bottom vents. Ignite 6 quarts or 2½ pounds charcoal briquettes or hardwood charcoal. When the coals are hot, set up for a one-level medium-heat fire (so you can hold your hand 5 inches above the cooking rack for only 4 to 5 seconds).
>
> **For a gas grill:** Turn each burner to high and ignite. Cover the grill. When hot, set the burners to medium heat.

Grill Guide

Capers are pickled and bottled olive-green flower buds with a slightly bitter flavor. When purchasing, look for the smallest capers available, because they're sweeter.

4. While the grill heats, place each cod fillet on a 12-inch square of heavy-duty aluminum foil, lightly sprayed with vegetable oil to keep fish from sticking. Spoon equal amounts of tomato mixture onto each fillet, season with salt and pepper, and wrap foil securely around fish.

5. *On a charcoal grill:* Grill foil packets seam side up on the grill rack over coals, covered, cover vents fully open, 15 to 20 minutes, until fish flakes easily with fork (you'll have to open one packet to check, being careful of steam). *On a gas grill:* Grill foil packets seam-side up on the grill rack over heat, covered, and follow as directed for a charcoal grill. Be careful when opening packets because the hot steam will billow out. Serve fish in packets, passing lemon wedges.

Chapter 20

Shellfish

In This Chapter

- Tips for finding fresh shellfish
- Shellfish cooking hints
- Cook's tip: stock up on skewers!
- Shrimp sizes and count

Having spent the first two decades of my life eschewing seafood of all kinds, it makes sense that it took me a while before I got a handle on finfish, whether they came from fresh or saltwater. For a time, it all seemed mysterious.

When I finally felt confident that I had at least a basic understanding of how to purchase and prepare finfish, I dove into shellfish—now there's a seahorse of a different color! Be honest, how many people look at a crab, lobster, or clam in its natural habitat and say, "Does that greenish spiny thing look delicious"? Let's get real for moment: a cooked, shell-free, bright red shrimp draped over a cocktail glass looks wonderful, but that same shrimp with its beady little eyes and insect-looking legs scampering in the water didn't look mouth-watering to me.

Generally, shellfish take more time to prepare than finfish. If you've tried to open a fresh clam or oyster, you know what I mean. Fortunately, we don't have to open scallop shells to have scallops or dress shrimp before we can start to grill them. Whatever effort it may take, it's well worth it. Few things are as delicious as a properly cooked lobster or shrimp that's spent just the right amount of time on the grill.

Telling If Shellfish Is *Really* Fresh

It's almost impossible to buy shrimp in the United States that hasn't been frozen … and for the most part, that's a good thing. These days, shrimp are frozen on the shrimp boat nearly as soon as they're caught. When "fresh" shrimp arrives at the fish store or supermarket, they arrive frozen in blocks. They are then thawed, frequently under running cold water, and placed on crushed ice in the display case.

As with fish, when shopping for fresh shrimp, look for shrimp with a clean sheen to them, translucent gray or gray/green shells, and no visible freezer burn. If you lightly squeeze a shrimp, it should offer resistance; soft shrimp is old. Fresh shrimp should pass the sniff test, too. It should smell sweet and not "fishy" or like ammonia.

Always purchase clams and mussels live. If you tap an open clam or mussel shell, it should snap shut. If it stays open, throw it away. Also be wary of shellfish with cracked or broken shells. When you grill clams or mussels, if the shell doesn't open by the time the rest have, throw it away. Clams and mussels should smell fresh and briny, a lot like the ocean from which they came.

Beware of Overcooking Shellfish

Almost all shellfish cooks quickly; the "10 minutes to the inch" rule standard with fish does not apply here. Whether in or out of the shell, shrimp turn bright red when grilled and should offer definite resistance when pressed. Clams and mussel shells will pop open a minute or two before they're done. Because scallops are almost all water and protein with almost no fat, they should grill quickly and turn opaque white and, again, offer resistance when pressed.

Do your best to not overcook shellfish because overcooked shellfish is very dry and tough—definitely not good.

Wood Skewers Are Your Friends

Bamboo skewers, soaked in warm water for 30 minutes, are the best way to handle shrimp on the grill. A pound of shrimp can equal 20 to 40 shrimp. If you grill them unskewered, you'll have a hard time turning the first one over in time after getting the last one on the grill. With 5 to 8 shrimp on a skewer, it takes little time to lay them on the grill or pick them all up and turn them quickly.

I like to force the head and tail of a shrimp together and then insert the bamboo skewer through both. Shrimp naturally curl when cooked, so this skewering technique holds that shape nicely and looks good on the plate.

I've also become a fan of nonstick, stir-fry grill pans with holes all over. The holes are sized just right to keep everything but the smallest shrimp or bay scallop from falling through. If you're going to the trouble to get a fire going on the grill, a stir-fry grill pan makes that effort worthwhile.

Is a "Jumbo Shrimp" an Oxymoron?

Shrimp are sold by the count per pound; that is how many of a certain size shrimp make up 1 pound. The following table lists the sizes of shrimp and count for each.

Shrimp	Count Per Pound
Extra colossal	Under 10
Colossal	10 to 15
Extra jumbo	16 to 20
Jumbo	21 to 25
Extra large	26 to 30
Large	31 to 35
Medium large	36 to 42
Medium	43 to 50
Small	50+

So if 1 pound shrimp contained 21 to 25 shrimp, they can be called Jumbo. Each one of those shrimp weighs less than 1 ounce, but legally it's a "Jumbo."

Asian-Spiced Grilled Shrimp

Serves: 4
Prep time: about 30 minutes
Cook time: 6 to 8 minutes
Serving size: 3 shrimp as appetizer

1 lb. colossal (about 12 per lb.) shrimp, shells attached

5 TB. dry white wine

3 TB. soy sauce

2 TB. Oriental sesame oil

1½ TB. clover honey

1½ TB. sesame seeds

1 TB. Chinese hot chili sauce

2 cloves garlic, peeled and minced or pushed through a garlic press

2 green onions, trimmed and finely chopped

¾ tsp. grated fresh ginger

½ tsp. Chinese five-spice powder

1. Peel and *devein* shrimp, leaving tails attached. Rinse under cold running water and reserve.

2. To a 1-gallon, reclosable plastic bag, add wine, soy sauce, sesame oil, honey, sesame seeds, Chinese hot chili sauce, garlic, green onions, ginger, and Chinese five-spice powder. Seal the bag, and shake until combined. Add shrimp, push out air, seal the bag, and refrigerate at least 30 minutes or up to 2 hours.

3. Fire up the grill:

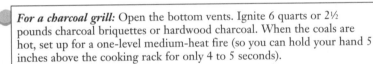

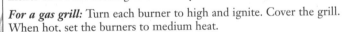

For a charcoal grill: Open the bottom vents. Ignite 6 quarts or 2½ pounds charcoal briquettes or hardwood charcoal. When the coals are hot, set up for a one-level medium-heat fire (so you can hold your hand 5 inches above the cooking rack for only 4 to 5 seconds).

For a gas grill: Turn each burner to high and ignite. Cover the grill. When hot, set the burners to medium heat.

4. Remove shrimp from marinade; strain marinade, discarding solids. Transfer marinade to a small saucepan, place over medium heat, bring to a low boil, reduce heat to low, and simmer at least 5 minutes until marinade becomes syrupy.

5. *On a charcoal grill:* Oil the grill rack well. Grill shrimp on the grill rack over coals 3 or 4 minutes per side until cooked through, brushing frequently with glaze. *On a gas grill:* Oil the grill rack well. Grill shrimp on the grill rack over heat, covered, and follow as directed for a charcoal grill. Evenly divide among serving plates and serve.

Grill Guide

To **devein** shrimp is to remove the small black vein that runs down a shrimp's back. It can be tedious work, but shrimp deveiners work well and quickly if the shrimp's shell has been removed. If you don't have the tool, run the point of a small sharp knife down a peeled shrimp's back, open, remove the vein, and discard.

Simple Charbroiled Shrimp

1 lb. jumbo (21 to 25 per lb.) shrimp

1 cup olive oil

½ cup chopped fresh parsley

2 TB. fresh lemon juice

2 cloves garlic, peeled and minced or pushed through a garlic press

1 tsp. kosher salt

Serves: 4
Prep time: 13 to 15 minutes, plus at least 2 hours to marinate
Cook time: 6 to 8 minutes
Serving size: 5 to 6 shrimp

1. Peel and devein shrimp, leaving tails attached. Rinse under cold running water, pat dry with paper towels, and place in a casserole dish.

2. In a medium-size stainless-steel or glass bowl, stir olive oil, parsley, lemon juice, garlic, and kosher salt together until combined. Pour over shrimp, stir to coat, cover, and refrigerate for at least 2 hours, stirring occasionally.

3. Fire up the grill:

> *For a charcoal grill:* Open the bottom vents. Ignite 6 quarts or 2½ pounds charcoal briquettes or hardwood charcoal. When the coals are hot, set up for a one-level medium-heat fire (so you can hold your hand 5 inches above the cooking rack for only 4 to 5 seconds).
>
> *For a gas grill:* Turn each burner to high and ignite. Cover the grill. When hot, set the burners to medium heat.

4. Remove shrimp from refrigerator and drain, reserving marinade. Boil marinade for 5 minutes, and use as a baste. *On a charcoal grill:* Using a nonstick, stir-fry grill pan, grill shrimp in pan over coals for 3 minutes per side or until cooked through, brushing frequently with marinade. *On a gas grill:* Using a nonstick, stir-fry grill pan, grill shrimp in pan on the grill rack over heat, uncovered, and follow as directed for a charcoal grill. Evenly divide grilled shrimp among serving plates and serve.

Barbecue Banter

As an alternative to using the grill, especially if you don't have one, the shrimp can be threaded onto skewers (either metal or bamboo) and grilled over coals or heat for the same amount of time, basting throughout. Serve them on the skewers.

Shrimp Satay

Serves: 6 to 8 as an appetizer or 4 as an entrée

Prep time: 30 minutes, plus 1 hour to marinate

Cook time: 6 minutes

Serving size: 4 to 6 shrimp as appetizers, 9 shrimp as entrée

36 extra-large shrimp (about 1½ lb.), peeled and deveined

2 TB. soy sauce

2 TB. (light) molasses

2 TB. fresh lime juice (from 1 lime)

2 TB. firmly packed light brown sugar

3 cloves garlic, peeled and minced or pushed through a garlic press

1½ tsp. ground coriander

3 TB. vegetable oil

18 bamboo or wooden skewers soaked in warm water for 30 minutes

1. Rinse shrimp under cold running water, drain, and blot dry with paper towels. Set aside while you prepare marinade.

2. In a large bowl, whisk soy sauce, molasses, lime juice, brown sugar, garlic, coriander, and 1 tablespoon oil until blended and sugar dissolves. Add shrimp, and toss to coat. Cover and marinate, in the refrigerator, for 1 hour.

3. Fire up the grill:

> *For a charcoal grill:* Open the bottom vents. Ignite 6 quarts or 2½ pounds charcoal briquettes or hardwood charcoal. When the coals are hot, set up for a one-level high-heat fire (so you can hold your hand 5 inches above the cooking rack for only 1 to 2 seconds).
>
> *For a gas grill:* Turn each burner to high and ignite. Cover the grill. When hot, leave the burners on high heat.

Barbecue Banter

Dark and blackstrap molasses work well in some things, but not here because the flavors are too strong and almost bitter. Light molasses provides plenty of flavor and no bitterness.

4. Drain shrimp, discard marinade, and thread shrimp onto skewers, 2 shrimp on each. *On a charcoal grill:* Oil the grill rack well. Grill shrimp on the hot grate, turning with tongs, until nicely browned on the outside and firm and pink inside, about 3 minutes per side. Brush shrimp once or twice with remaining oil during grilling. *On a gas grill:* Oil the grill rack well. Follow as directed for a charcoal grill, except cover.

5. Transfer sates to serving plates or a platter, and serve immediately.

Garlic-Skewered Shrimp

2 lb. jumbo (21 to 25 per lb.) shrimp

16 to 20 large whole cloves garlic, peeled

⅓ cup olive oil

¼ cup tomato sauce

2 TB. red wine vinegar

1½ tsp. dried basil, crumbled

3 large cloves garlic, peeled and minced or pushed through a garlic press

½ tsp. salt

½ tsp. ground cayenne

12 wood skewers, soaked in warm water for 30 minutes

Serves: 6
Prep time: 30 minutes. plus 1 hour to marinate
Cook time: 6 to 8 minutes
Serving size: 2 skewers with 7 to 8 shrimp

1. Peel and devein shrimp, leaving tails attached. Rinse shrimp under cold running water, and pat dry with paper towels.

2. Drop whole garlic cloves into a saucepan of rapidly boiling water and boil for 3 minutes. Drain well, and set aside.

3. In a large bowl, stir together olive oil, tomato sauce, vinegar, basil, minced garlic, salt, and cayenne. Add shrimp and toss to coat evenly. Cover and refrigerate for about 30 minutes, tossing once or twice.

4. Fire up the grill:

> *For a charcoal grill:* Open the bottom vents. Ignite 6 quarts or 2½ pounds charcoal briquettes or hardwood charcoal. When the coals are hot, set up for a one-level medium-heat fire (so you can hold your hand 5 inches above the cooking rack for only 4 to 5 seconds).
>
> *For a gas grill:* Turn each burner to high and ignite. Cover the grill. When hot, set the burners to medium heat.

5. Remove shrimp from marinade. There will be a little marinade remaining in bowl; reserve it. Thread 2 shrimp and 1 garlic clove alternately onto skewers: bend each shrimp almost in half, so the large end nearly touches the smaller tail end. Insert the skewer just above the tail, so it passes through the body twice. Follow 2 shrimp with a garlic clove.

6. *On a charcoal grill:* Oil the grill rack well. Grill skewers on grill rack over coals, uncovered, turning them frequently and brushing them once at the beginning with reserved marinade, discarding remaining marinade after doing so, until shrimp become pink, 6 to 8 minutes. *On a gas grill:* Oil the grill rack well. Follow as directed for a charcoal grill, except close the cover.

Barbecue Banter

Hundreds of different olive oils are available today. To know which one is best for you, check out magazines that specialize in testing different products (olive oils being just one) and give their opinions. Many of these organizations do not accept advertising and, therefore, cannot be influenced by advertising in judging the products.

Grilled Lobster Tails

Serves: 4
Prep time: 13 to 15 min-utes
Cook time: 8 to 10 min-utes
Serving size: 1 lobster tail

4 (8- to 10-oz.) lobster tails (thawed if frozen)

Salt to taste

Fresh-ground black pepper to taste

Unsalted butter, melted

Lemon wedges (optional)

1. Fire up the grill:

> *For a charcoal grill:* Open the bottom vents. Ignite 6 quarts or 2½ pounds charcoal briquettes or hardwood charcoal. When the coals are hot, set up for a one-level medium-heat fire (so you can hold your hand 5 inches above the cooking rack for only 4 to 5 seconds).
>
> *For a gas grill:* Turn each burner to high and ignite. Cover the grill. When hot, set the burners to medium heat.

Barbecue Banter

When purchasing lobster tails, buy from a reputable store, prefer-ably one that also sells fresh seafood. Talk to the fish person to find out which of the frozen tails will work best on your grill. It probably won't hurt to also ask for grilling suggestions.

2. While the grill heats, with sharp poultry shears or strong scis-sors, cut either side of the "flat belly shell" (it's on the opposite side of the tail that will turn red when grilled) and remove. Rinse lobster tails under cold running water, and pat dry with paper towels. Season with salt and pepper.

3. *On a charcoal grill:* Oil the grill rack well. Arrange lobster tails on the grill rack over coals, shell-side down. Brush generously with melted butter, and grill, covered, with the vent open halfway, 8 to 10 minutes or until lobster meat turns opaque white. (Do not turn tails over, as all the juices accumulated there will run out.) *On a gas grill:* Oil the grill rack well. Follow as directed for a charcoal grill. With tongs, carefully remove tails from the grill, place on serving plates or a platter, and serve, passing additional melted butter and lemon wedges (if using).

Crab Legs with Mustard Sauce

1 cup mayonnaise

2 TB. half-and-half

3½ tsp. dry mustard (preferably Colman's)

2 tsp. Worcestershire sauce

1 tsp. steak sauce

⅛ tsp. salt

3 lb. frozen king crab legs, thawed

½ cup unsalted butter, melted

Lemon wedges

Serves: 4		
Prep time: 15 minutes		
Cook time: 10 minutes		
Serving size: ¼ crab legs		

1. In a medium stainless-steel or glass mixing bowl, use a wire whisk to whisk together mayonnaise, half-and-half, dry mustard, Worcestershire sauce, steak sauce, and salt until smooth and combined. Cover and chill until needed.

2. Fire up the grill:

> *For a charcoal grill:* Open the bottom vents. Ignite 6 quarts or 2½ pounds charcoal briquettes or hardwood charcoal. When the coals are hot, set up for a one-level medium-heat fire (so you can hold your hand 5 inches above the cooking rack for only 4 to 5 seconds).
>
> *For a gas grill:* Turn each burner to high and ignite. Cover the grill. When hot, set the burners to medium heat.

3. While the grill heats, rinse crab legs under cold running water, and pat dry with paper towels. Carefully cut crab legs lengthwise in half through shell with a sharp knife or poultry shears, leaving narrow parts of legs whole.

4. *On a charcoal grill:* Oil the grill rack well. Place crab legs, shell sides down, on the grill, and brush with butter. Cover, open cover vent halfway, and grill 10 minutes or until shells turn red and crabmeat turns white and firm. *On a gas grill:* Oil the grill rack well. Follow as directed for a charcoal grill. Serve crab legs with mustard sauce and lemon wedges.

Barbecue Banter

I recommend using half-and-half in the mustard sauce in this recipe to keep the fat and calories reasonable. If you want to be totally decadent, substitute light or heavy whipping cream for the half-and-half.

Grilled and Marinated Mussels

Serves: 8
Prep time: 50 minutes
Cook time: 6 minutes
Serving size: 7 mussels plus marinade

6 large shallots, peeled and ends trimmed

8 large cloves garlic, peeled

½ bunch fresh parsley (flat leaf preferred), leaves only, rinsed and spun in a lettuce spinner

1 cup extra-virgin olive oil

½ cup unseasoned rice wine vinegar

¼ cup coarse mustard

Salt to taste

Fresh-ground black pepper to taste

56 fresh "live" (no more than 4 days old) New Zealand green-lipped or best local mussels (1½ to 2 lb.; preferably cultivated), with shells tightly closed

Warm, grilled, good-quality French bread

1. To the bowl of a food processor, with the steel blade in place, add shallots, garlic, and parsley, and chop, pulsing, until chopped fine but not puréed. Add processed shallot mixture to a medium mixing bowl, and stir in olive oil, vinegar, and mustard. Taste and adjust salt and pepper if necessary. Cover.

2. Fire up the grill:

> *For a charcoal grill:* Open the bottom vents. Ignite 6 quarts or 2½ pounds charcoal briquettes or hardwood charcoal. When the coals are hot, set up for a one-level high-heat fire (so you can hold your hand 5 inches above the cooking rack for only 1 to 2 seconds).
>
> *For a gas grill:* Turn each burner to high and ignite. Cover the grill. When hot, leave the burners on high heat.

3. While the grill heats, clean mussels by scrubbing them with a brush under cold water and scraping off any barnacles with a paring knife. If a mussel's beard is still attached, remove it by pulling it from tip to hinge or cutting it off with a knife.

4. When ready to grill, tap any mussels with open shells, and discard any that don't close by themselves. *On a charcoal grill:* Spread mussels on the grill rack, and grill, covered, with cover vent halfway open, 3 to 6 minutes or until shells open. Shortly after each mussel opens, remove it from the grill with tongs and place in a large, stainless-steel mixing bowl. After 6 minutes, remove and discard any unopened mussels. *On a gas grill:* Follow as directed for a charcoal grill. Pour marinade over mussels, stir and toss to coat, cover, and refrigerate for 24 hours, stirring and tossing occasionally. Serve with warm French bread to mop up any marinade remnants.

Barbecue Banter

Select live mussels with tightly closed shells, and give them the "sniff test." They should smell pleasantly briny. Pass on any or all with "off" odors. At home, pour any liquid off the mussels, place them in a bowl, cover with a clean, wet towel, and refrigerate immediately. (Some may open in your refrigerator for a quick "breath"; do not worry about this). Always grill mussels on the same day you purchase them.

Grilled Clams on the Half Shell

5 TB. unseasoned rice vinegar

3 TB. peanut oil

1 tsp. Asian sesame oil

½ tsp. grated fresh ginger

1 green onion, white and green parts, trimmed and thinly sliced

½ fresh jalapeño pepper, stem end trimmed, seeds and ribs discarded, and minced

¼ tsp. salt

⅛ tsp. ground cumin

1 to 2 cups coarse salt

24 small hard-shelled clams (2½ lb.) such as littlenecks (less than 2 inches wide), scrubbed well

Serves: 4	
Prep time: 45 minutes	
Cook time: 8 to 10 minutes	
Serving size: 6 clams	

1. To a pint jar, add vinegar, peanut oil, Asian sesame oil, ginger, green onion, jalapeño pepper, salt, and cumin. Screw on cover, and shake vigorously until combined.

2. Fire up the grill:

> *For a charcoal grill:* Open the bottom vents. Ignite 6 quarts or 2½ pounds charcoal briquettes or hardwood charcoal. When the coals are hot, set up for a one-level medium-heat fire (so you can hold your hand 5 inches above the cooking rack for only 4 to 5 seconds).
>
> *For a gas grill:* Turn each burner to high and ignite. Cover the grill. When hot, set the burners to medium heat.

3. Cover a tray with a ½-inch layer of coarse salt to hold clams in place for serving.

4. Grip 1 clam in a kitchen towel with its "hinge" facing toward you. Working with a bowl to catch any clam liquor, slide a clam knife between the two shells at a point opposite hinge, and rotate clam, sliding the knife between the shells, until the knife reaches the hinge. Cut through the hinge, being careful to avoid hitting the center of clam. Open shells, sliding the knife along the underside of the top shell to detach it from clam. Pull off the top shell and discard, keeping clam in the bottom shell, and slide the knife under clam to loosen, catching as much clam liquor as possible in the bowl.

5. *On a charcoal or gas grill:* Using tongs, arrange opened clams in 1 layer on the grill rack over coals or heat, and spoon some reserved liquor over the top. When clam liquor reaches a boil, grill, uncovered, until just cooked through, 3 to 4 minutes. Carefully transfer clams with tongs to platter, and drizzle with ginger dressing. Serve, passing dressing.

Barbecue Banter

Not all jalapeño peppers are created equal; some are hotter than others. When preparing to grill with jalapeño peppers, cut off a tiny little square of pepper, and taste it to know how hot—or not—it is. If it's hotter than you anticipated, you can put out the fire by chewing on a little bread.

Scallop and Mushroom Brochettes

Serves: 4 to 6
Prep time: 30 minutes, plus 30 minutes to marinate
Cook time: 6 to 8 minutes
Serving size: 1 skewer

2 lb. (20 to 30) fresh or frozen and thawed sea scallops

1 lb. large fresh button mushrooms, wiped clean with a damp paper towel

¼ cup extra-virgin olive oil

2 TB. fresh lemon juice (from ½ a large lemon)

1 tsp. dried tarragon, crumbled

1 clove garlic, peeled and minced or pushed through a garlic press

½ tsp. salt

¼ tsp. fresh-ground black pepper

2 limes, cut into ¼-inch-thick slices

6 metal kabob skewers

1. Remove and discard the small, flat muscle or "foot" usually attached to the side of each scallop. Remove and discard mushroom stems, rinse under cold water, and pat dry with paper towels.

2. In a large stainless-steel or glass mixing bowl, whisk together oil, lemon juice, tarragon, garlic, salt, and pepper until combined. Add scallops and mushrooms, and toss to coat evenly. Cover and refrigerate for 30 minutes, tossing once or twice.

3. Fire up the grill:

> *For a charcoal grill:* Open the bottom vents. Ignite 6 quarts or 2½ pounds charcoal briquettes or hardwood charcoal. When the coals are hot, set up for a one-level medium-heat fire (so you can hold your hand 5 inches above the cooking rack for only 4 to 5 seconds).
>
> *For a gas grill:* Turn each burner to high and ignite. Cover the grill. When hot, set the burners to medium heat.

4. Remove scallops and mushrooms from marinade; reserving marinade. Alternate scallops and mushrooms with lime slices onto 6 skewers. *On a charcoal grill:* Arrange skewers over coals on the grill rack. Grill, turning frequently and brushing once at the beginning with reserved marinade (discarding remaining marinade), until scallops are just cooked through, 6 to 8 minutes. *On a gas grill:* Follow as directed for a charcoal grill, except close cover.

 Lean Note

Overcooking scallops makes them tough and dry. One pound of scallops contains a mere 3.5 fat grams. If that doesn't seem too impressive, understand that 1 pound equals 454 grams. If they printed it on a scallop package (which they don't), scallops could legally be considered more than 99 percent fat free. There's 0 carbohydrate in a scallop and a scallop is 88 percent water.

Part 7

Everything Else

The recipes you'll find in Part 7 make grilling fun and even more delicious than cooking hamburgers or hot dogs. Until recently, not many folks thought about laying bread or bread dough over the flames of a hot fire. But you can easily make your own pizza dough (or not, your choice), lay it over hot coals, and in a short time have grilled pizza. To make your grilled pizza even better, you can even grill the toppings before making and grilling the finished pizza.

But there's more: fresh corn-on-the-cob, brushed with melted butter and seasoned with salt and pepper, hot off the grill is a summer treat no one should miss. It is, in fact addictive. ("Hi, my name's Don and I love grilled corn." "Hi, Don.") Corn's not the only grillable vegetable, though. By the end of Part 7, you'll know how to grill broccoli, red and green tomatoes, zucchini, garlic, sweet potatoes, and more.

And I didn't forget dessert! Check out the recipes for grilled bananas, peaches, nectarines, apples, and even peanut butter s'mores. Wow!

Chapter 21

Grilled Pizza and Breads

In This Chapter

- ◆ Grilling pizzas and other breads
- ◆ Selecting your pizza toppings: sauces, cheese, etc.
- ◆ Grilling over gas vs. charcoal

When most folks think about grilling, they think of hot dogs, hamburgers, steaks, or maybe "shrimp on the barbie." Few think of pizza or the Italian appetizer bruschetta or a genuinely *grilled* cheese sandwich. But you can make all these on a grill.

Grilling Bread and Pizza

Until recently, even I never thought about cooking pizza, or any bread, for that matter on a grill. But as you'll notice if you try the recipes in this chapter, each of these breads has a far better flavor from the grill than a toaster, skillet, or oven could ever impart. And using your grill as an oven helps keep your kitchen very cool during hot summer months.

Homemade vs. Premade Crust

Because I like simplicity and ease, I recommend buying a premade, ready-for-the-oven pizza crust for grilling instead of making a crust from scratch. But occasionally, when I have the time, I enjoy making a scratch pizza crust, especially because it tastes so much better than a premade crust.

If you've made bread before, you'll have no trouble making a scratch pizza crust because a pizza crust is actually a flat bread (which is why you'll use bread flour). If you've never made a yeast-raised dough in your life, don't be disappointed if your first scratch crust doesn't work the way you hoped. It takes time and experience—and a failure or two—before making perfect yeast dough becomes natural and easy.

Sauces

You can use a variety of sauces for your pizza. True, at your supermarket, you'll find some bottled and canned pizza sauces that are not half bad. Then, if you move down the aisle a bit, you'll come to a large wall of tomato-based spaghetti sauces. Many of these make excellent pizza sauces, too.

Or for something really simple: open some canned Italian plum tomatoes; squeeze out the juice from the tomatoes; and place them on a crust with salt, pepper, and dried basil. Something as simple as this can be the foundation for a very good grilled pizza.

Say "Cheese"

Mozzarella cheeses—the quintessential pizza cheese—comes in different forms and fat levels. The best mozzarella cheese for pizza is part–skim milk mozzarella. Whole-milk mozzarella has a high fat content and makes a smoother, creamier mozzarella cheese. Fresh mozzarella or buffalo mozzarella (fresh mozzarella cheese made from the whole milk of water buffalo, which are not related to American bison, erroneously called buffalo) taste great in a salad, but won't work well on grilled pizza.

Several other cheeses besides mozzarella work great in combination with mozzarella for topping pizza. Grated provolone works extremely well and brings a slightly smoky flavor. Grated Parmesan cheese adds a depth of flavor that mozzarella can't come close to matching. Some folks like to mix brick and mozzarella cheeses 50/50 to top a pizza. All these cheeses also make your grilled pizza something really special.

What cheeses don't work on a pizza? Creamy cheeses, such as American or high-butterfat content cheese. They taste good, no doubt about it, but they spread and run when they melt—right off a pizza's edge!

The Right Bread for the Job

As already mentioned, when making grilled pizza, you can use premade pizza crust or make your own. When you're grilling other breads, however, it's more important to give some thought to the kind and quality you use.

If you're making a grilled cheese sandwich on the grill, you don't want to use namby-pamby white bread. A good-quality, sandwich-style bread works great. Bread for bruschetta or garlic bread should come from a bakery, if at all possible. Supermarkets with their own, on-premises bakery are a distant, but doable second choice.

Gas vs. Charcoal

Because a gas grill has control knobs, you can easily adjust the heat levels—much more easily than on a charcoal grill, which requires moving hot coals around to change heat levels.

However, a charcoal grill heightens the flavor of anything that you grill on it, especially if you toss on some damp wood chips, more so than a gas grill.

Breads and pizza cook quickly on a grill, so you have to watch them like a hawk—but because breads cook quickly, you'll only need a small amount of time.

Classic Italian Bruschetta

Serves: 6 to 8
Prep time: 40 minutes
Cook time: 8 to 10 minutes
Serving size: 3 to 4 bruschetta

1 lb. fresh plum tomatoes, rinsed, peeled, cored, seeded, and minced

½ cup packed fresh basil leaves, minced

½ tsp. dried oregano, crumbled

3 TB. olive oil plus additional for brushing bread

2 medium cloves garlic, peeled and minced, or pushed through a garlic press

¼ tsp. fresh-ground black pepper

1 tsp. salt

1 loaf crusty, country-style Italian bread, or French baguette, sliced ½-inch thick

1 or 2 large garlic cloves, peeled and sliced in half crosswise

1. Fire up the grill:

 For a charcoal grill: Open the bottom vents. Ignite 6 quarts or 2½ pounds charcoal briquettes or hardwood charcoal. When the coals are hot, set up for a one-level medium-heat fire (so you can hold your hand 5 inches above cooking rack for only 4 to 5 seconds).

 For a gas grill: Turn each burner to high and ignite. Cover the grill. When hot, set the burners to medium heat.

2. In a small bowl, stir together tomatoes, basil, oregano, olive oil, garlic, black pepper, and salt until combined.

3. *On a charcoal or gas grill:* Grill about ⅓ sliced bread, uncovered, on the grill rack over coals until lightly toasted and golden, about 1 or 2 minutes. With tongs, quickly turn over bread, and toast the other side. Remove toasted bread slices from the grill. Repeat twice more with remaining bread.

4. Brush one side of toasts lightly with additional oil, rub them with garlic halves, and top with 1 or 2 teaspoons tomato mixture. Serve.

Barbecue Banter

Plum tomatoes are far meatier than regular tomatoes and give off much less water when cut up, reducing the chance of "soggy" bruschetta.

Grilled Basil and Cheese Pizza

1 recipe Basic Pizza Dough
(recipe follows)

¼ cup canned pizza sauce

Kosher salt

Fresh-ground black pepper

3 to 4 garlic cloves, peeled
and thinly sliced

16 fresh basil leaves

⅔ cup shredded or diced
mozzarella cheese

Serves: 8 as appetizer, *2 to 4 as entrée*
Prep time: 12 to 14 minutes plus 1¾ hours to prepare dough
Cook time: 12 to 14 minutes
Serving size: 2 slices as appetizer, 8 or 4 slices as entrée

1. Fire up the grill:

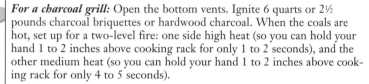

> *For a charcoal grill:* Open the bottom vents. Ignite 6 quarts or 2½ pounds charcoal briquettes or hardwood charcoal. When the coals are hot, set up for a two-level fire: one side high heat (so you can hold your hand 1 to 2 inches above cooking rack for only 1 to 2 seconds), and the other medium heat (so you can hold your hand 1 to 2 inches above cooking rack for only 4 to 5 seconds).

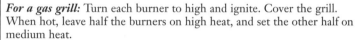

> *For a gas grill:* Turn each burner to high and ignite. Cover the grill. When hot, leave half the burners on high heat, and set the other half on medium heat.

2. *On a charcoal grill:* Arrange coals in a double layer on one side and in a single layer on the other.

3. Generously oil a circular baking sheet, and place one disc of dough on it. Carefully stretch out dough into a 12- to 14-inch-diameter circle. (It doesn't have to be perfect. Your first pizza doughs will probably be a lot like mine: strange looking. Don't worry; practice makes perfect, and it's not how it looks, but how it tastes.) Stretch out the other piece of dough.

4. With your first dough, use both hands to carefully lift dough circle from the baking sheet. Lay it onto the grill over the hottest part of the fire. In 1 to 2 minutes, the underside of that dough will be done; look for the top to puff slightly. Using tongs or two spatulas, turn over dough and move it to the medium-heat side of the grill.

5. Spoon on 2 tablespoons pizza sauce, and with the back of a spoon, spread sauce around as evenly as possible out to the dough's edge. Season with kosher salt and pepper, distribute ½ garlic, arrange ½ basil leaves on sauce, and then sprinkle with ½ cheese.

6. Using spatulas, slide pizza back over to the hotter part of the grill, rotating to ensure even cooking. Cover the grill, opening vents all the way. Grill until dough's underside is slightly blackened and cheeses melts, 2 to 4 minutes.

7. Remove pizza from the grill, place it on a cutting board, cut, and serve while you repeat the procedure again with second stretched-out dough.

Basic Pizza Dough

<table>
<tr><td>

*Serves: enough for
2 (12- to 14-inch)
diameter pizzas*

Prep time: about 30 minutes, plus 1¼ hours to rise

Serving size: ¼ to ½ of each pizza dough

</td></tr>
</table>

¾ cup warm water (105°F to 115°F)

1 (¼-oz.) pkg. active dry yeast

2 tsp. granulated sugar

2 tsp. kosher salt

1 TB. whole-wheat flour

2 TB. extra-virgin olive oil, plus more for the bowl

1¾ cups all-purpose or bread flour, plus more for work surface

1. Pour warm water into a large mixing bowl, add yeast and sugar, and stir to dissolve. Let sit 5 minutes. Stir in salt, whole-wheat flour, and olive oil. Gradually stir in enough all-purpose or bread flour to form a dough that comes away from the sides of the bowl.

2. Knead dough on a floured work surface (I use my kitchen counter), in a food processor, or in a mixer fitted with a dough hook, until smooth and elastic. (If dough is sticky, add flour 1 tablespoon at a time, and then knead until no longer sticky.) Dough should be soft and pliable, not sticky. This takes about 6 to 8 minutes.

3. Lightly oil a clean, large bowl. Place dough in the bowl, and brush top of dough with oil. Cover bowl loosely with plastic wrap. Let dough rise in a warm, draft-free spot until doubled in bulk, about 1¼ hours. Punch down dough, divide it into 2 equal pieces, and shape each piece into a ball. Cover loosely with plastic wrap, and let dough sit on the counter for 15 minutes.

4. Now use the dough in any of your favorite pizza dough recipes—why not try it in Grilled Basil and Cheese Pizza, earlier in this chapter?

Barbecue Banter

Active dry yeast packets are stamped with a date; after that date, they may not work well. Whenever I decide to make a yeast dough, I discard the old yeast hibernating in my refrigerator and go buy some new yeast. To make certain it's as fresh as I can possibly get, I look for a date stamp as far in the future as possible.

Middle Eastern–Style Pizza

12 oz. ground lamb

1 (8-oz.) can tomato sauce

1 clove garlic, peeled and minced, or pushed through a garlic press

¼ tsp. ground allspice

1 (10-oz.) pkg. refrigerated pizza dough

2 plum tomatoes, rinsed, cored, seeded, and thinly sliced crosswise into rounds

½ cup chopped green sweet bell pepper

½ cup crumbled *feta cheese* (2 oz.)

¼ cup minced fresh mint

Serves: 4
Prep time: 30 minutes
Cook time: 13 to 15 minutes
Serving size: ¼ pizza

1. In a large skillet, cook ground lamb over medium heat until meat is no longer pink, breaking up clumps with a fork. Drain well, and stir in tomato sauce, garlic, and allspice. Set aside.

2. Lightly coat a 12-inch pizza pan with nonstick cooking spray. With your fingers, pat refrigerated pizza dough onto the prepared pan.

3. Fire up the grill:

> *For a charcoal grill:* Open the bottom vents. Ignite 6 quarts or 2½ pounds charcoal briquettes or hardwood charcoal. When the coals are hot, set up for a one-level medium-heat fire (so you can hold your hand 5 inches above cooking rack for only 4 to 5 seconds) and place briquettes in a ring all the way around the edge of the grill.
>
> *For a gas grill:* Turn each burner to high and ignite. Cover the grill. When hot, set one burner on low heat and the rest to medium heat.

4. *On a charcoal grill:* Place pizza crust in the pan on the grill rack over the coals and grill, uncovered, for 5 minutes. Turn over crust, spread with sauce, and top with tomatoes and bell pepper. Return pizza to the grill, cover, open cover vent fully, and grill for 8 to 10 minutes or until pizza is heated through, checking occasionally to be sure crust doesn't overbrown. *On a gas grill:* place pizza crust in the pan on the grill rack over low heat, cover, and follow the charcoal grilling directions. Carefully remove pizza from the grill. Sprinkle with feta cheese and mint, cut into slices, and serve.

Grill Guide

You can't beat good **feta cheese** for flavor. Feta is traditionally made from sheep's milk or sheep's and goat's milk, but it now can also be made with cow's milk. This sensational Greek cheese is salty and sharp with a creamy texture that almost melts in your mouth. Take the time to find good quality feta cheese—it's worth it.

Grilled Italian Sausage Pizza

Serves: 4
Prep time: 45 minutes
Cook time: 8 to 10 minutes
Serving size: ½ pizza

1 cup chopped canned plum tomatoes, drained

½ cup chopped fresh basil

1 clove garlic, peeled and minced, or pushed through a garlic press

½ tsp. salt

12 oz. uncooked sweet or hot Italian link sausage

1 medium onion, peeled and cut into ½-inch slices

1 green sweet bell pepper, seeds and ribs discarded, and cut into 1-inch strips

4 (7-inch) pkg. prebaked pizza crusts

1 cup shredded mozzarella cheese (4 oz.)

½ cup grated Parmesan cheese

1. In a small bowl, stir together tomatoes, basil, garlic, and salt. Set aside.

2. Fire up the grill:

For a charcoal grill: Open the bottom vents. Ignite 6 quarts or 2½ pounds charcoal briquettes or hardwood charcoal. When the coals are hot, set up for a one-level medium-heat fire (so you can hold your hand 5 inches above cooking rack for only 4 to 5 seconds).

For a gas grill: Turn each burner to high and ignite. Cover the grill. When hot, set the burners to medium heat.

Barbecue Banter

You're probably familiar with pork Italian sausage. But have you ever tried Italian sausage made with turkey or chicken? No? Then by all means try it. They're similarly priced, if cost is a concern.

3. *On a charcoal grill:* Arrange the coals around a centered drip pan. Place sausage on the grill rack over the drip pan. Cover, open cover vent, and grill for 12 minutes. Turn sausage. Put onion and sweet pepper on an oiled grill basket, and place on the grill directly over the coals. Cover and grill for 8 to 12 minutes more or until sausage juices run clear and vegetables are tender, turning vegetables over once halfway through grilling. *On a gas grill:* Follow the charcoal grilling directions, except don't use a drip pan. Remove sausage and vegetables from the grill. Thinly slice sausage, and set aside.

4. *On a charcoal or a gas grill:* Place pizza crusts on the grill directly over the coals or heat. Cover and grill crust for 3 minutes and turn. Divide mozzarella cheese, tomato mixture, sausage, onion, and sweet pepper among pizza crusts. Sprinkle with Parmesan cheese, cover, and grill about 5 minutes more or until heated through and cheese melts. Serve.

Stone-Grilled Smoky Pita Bread Pizza (Gas Grill Only)

2 cups wood chips (oak or mesquite)

4 (8-inch) round pita breads

6 TB. bottled or canned pizza sauce

Salt

Fresh-ground black pepper

1¼ tsp. dried basil, crumbled

1 large sweet green or red bell pepper, seeds and ribs discarded, and cut into thin slices

1 (6-oz.) can mushrooms, drained and squeezed

12 black olives, sliced

6 oz. grated part-skim mozzarella cheese

Serves: 4		
Prep time: 16 to 20 minutes		
Cook time: 8 to 10 minutes		
Serving size: 1 pita pizza		

1. Lay out a piece of heavy-duty foil 12×18 inches. Place wood chips in the center of the foil, forming into a rectangle of equal height. Lift up two opposing sides of foil, bring together, and fold until reaching chips. Fold the ends underneath. Poke about a dozen holes into the top of the foil packet. Remove one of the cooking grates from the gas grill, place packet as near as possible to the flames on one end of the grill, and replace the cooking grate. (If your grill comes with different directions for producing smoke, follow the manufacturer's directions.)

2. Open the gas source, and, one at a time, turn each burner on high, igniting each immediately before going on to the next. Place a pizza stone on the cooking grate on the side away from the smoke packet. Leave the burners under the smoke packet on high; adjust the burners under the pizza stone to low. Cover the grill, allowing it to heat up, about 15 minutes.

3. While the grill heats, prepare pizza: lay out all 4 pita breads. Spread 1½ tablespoon pizza sauce over each pita. Lightly dust each with salt, pepper, and ¼ teaspoon basil. Distribute bell peppers, mushrooms, and olives evenly among pizzas. Equally divide and distribute grated cheese over pizzas.

4. Adjust the grill: if the smoke packet is producing smoke, turn those burners to medium. Uncover the grill, place 2 pizzas (or all 4 if they fit) on the stone. Close the grill cover, and grill 8 to 10 minutes or until cheese melts and turns golden.

5. Remove pizza from stone, cut into wedges, and serve. Follow your grill's directions for shutdown, and allow the stone to cool completely before removing it from the grill.

 Barbecue Banter

You can purchase pizza stones from a variety of sources. They come round, square, and rectangular and vary in price. My round pizza stone cost less than $12, and I've owned it for 3 years.

"Grilled" Grilled Cheese Sandwich

Serves: 4
Prep time: 15 minutes
Cook time: about 7 minutes
Serving size: 1 sandwich

8 slices good-quality white sandwich bread

Salted butter, softened

8 (¾-oz.) slices American or processed cheddar cheese

Sweet paprika

Bread and butter pickle slices

1. Fire up the grill:

> **For a charcoal grill:** Open the bottom vents. Ignite 6 quarts or 2½ pounds charcoal briquettes or hardwood charcoal. When the coals are hot, set up for a one-level medium-heat fire (so you can hold your hand 5 inches above cooking rack for only 4 to 5 seconds).
>
> **For a gas grill:** Turn each burner to high and ignite. Cover the grill. When hot, set the burners to medium heat.

Barbecue Banter

Good-quality white sandwich bread isn't that easy to find these days. Sure, you can always buy gummy, white, too-sweet white bread. But sandwich bread is drier, more firm, far less sweet, and stands up to toasting over a fire better than any other white bread (except for French).

2. *On a charcoal grill:* Place all 8 bread slices over the coals and grill until golden. Remove bread from the grill. Lightly butter toasted bread sides. Place 2 cheese slices on each of 4 toasted bread slices, and top with bread slices, toasted-side facing cheese. Lightly sprinkle all 4 sandwich tops with paprika. Place sandwiches over coals, paprika side down. Lightly sprinkle sandwich tops with paprika. Cover the grill, open the cover vents fully, and grill 2 minutes or until sandwiches are golden. Uncover the grill, turn over sandwiches, and grill 2 minutes more or until sandwiches are golden. *On a gas grill:* Follow the charcoal grilling directions except place bread and sandwiches over heat. Remove sandwiches from the grill, spread both sides of sandwiches very lightly with butter, and serve garnished with pickle slices.

Grilled Garlic Bread

1 (16-oz.) large loaf crusty
French or sourdough bread

3 TB. extra-virgin olive oil

1 large or 2 medium whole
cloves fresh garlic, peeled

1 large or 2 medium ripe
tomatoes

Kosher salt

½ tsp. dried basil, crumbled

Serves: 4 to 6
Prep time: about 10 min-utes
Cook time: 4 to 5 min-utes
Serving size: ¼ to ⅙ loaf

1. Fire up the grill:

   For a charcoal grill: Open the bottom vents. Ignite 6 quarts or 2½ pounds charcoal briquettes or hardwood charcoal. When the coals are hot, set up for a one-level medium-heat fire (so you can hold your hand 5 inches above cooking rack for only 4 to 5 seconds).

   For a gas grill: Turn each burner to high and ignite. Cover the grill. When hot, set the burners to medium heat.

2. While the grill heats, slice bread lengthwise. Brush cut sides of each bread half with olive oil.

3. *On a charcoal grill:* Place bread, cut sides down, over the coals and grill, uncovered, for 2 to 3 minutes or until golden. Slice off bottom of garlic cloves, and rub garlic over both halves of toasted bread.

4. Slice tomatoes in half and scrub over toasted and garlic-seasoned bread. Season bread with kosher salt and basil. Return bread to the grill, crust side down, and warm about 2 minutes. *On a gas grill:* Follow the charcoal grilling directions, except place bread over heat. Remove bread from the grill, slice, and serve.

Barbecue Banter

Garlic is seasonal, even though you may see it in the produce section year round. If your garlic has grown little green shoots from the clove's ends, you don't have to discard it. Those shoots are bitter, though, and you don't want to eat them. To remove the shoots, split a clove in half lengthwise, and with the sharp point of a knife, pry the green shoot out of the clove. It should essentially pop right out. Discard the shoot, and treat the garlic clove as you usually would.

Texas Toast

Serves: 4
Prep time: 5 minutes
Cook time: 4 to 6 minutes
Serving size: 1 toast

4 TB. unsalted butter, softened

4 slices good-quality white bread, about 1-inch thick

½ tsp. seasoned salt or garlic salt

1. Fire up the grill:

> *For a charcoal grill:* Open the bottom vents. Ignite 6 quarts or 2½ pounds charcoal briquettes or hardwood charcoal. When the coals are hot, set up for a one-level medium-heat fire (so you can hold your hand 5 inches above cooking rack for only 4 to 5 seconds).
>
> *For a gas grill:* Turn each burner to high and ignite. Cover the grill. When hot, set the burners to medium heat.

2. *On a charcoal or gas grill:* Brush the grill rack with vegetable oil. Grill bread over coals or heat, uncovered, for 4 to 6 minutes, turning once, until golden brown. Remove bread from the grill, spread both sides of toasted bread slices with butter. Sprinkle with seasoned salt and serve.

Barbecue Banter _____

You'd think it would be better to butter the bread before putting it on the grill, wouldn't you? Well, I tried that and was very disappointed. The butter melted almost immediately when it hit the grill, then dripped onto the hot coals. The coals flamed up, charring the bread instead of toasting it. In the end, instead of nice brown grill marks, the finished toast had black grill marks.

Chapter 22

Sides: Slaws and Salads

In This Chapter

- Serving up sensational sides
- Getting hints on preparing pasta, veggies, and beans for salads
- Understanding how the best oil pulls a salad together

Grilling or barbecuing out in the backyard isn't nearly as good without the side dishes that go along with it. Sure, you can buy them at the supermarket, but those are rarely as good as the ones you can make fresh at home.

Perfect Grilled Meal Accompaniments

What do you serve alongside a grilled meal? Think about the salads you find in your supermarket's deli section. The pasta salads, bean salads, and the slaws—these all work well alongside a grilled steak or chicken, or a hamburger and hot dog.

But of course you can make them better at home. In the following sections, I give you some tips on doing just that.

Cabbage and Slaws

Most folks hate cooked cabbage and think it "stinks up" the house while it cooks. But shred it, combine it with carrots or other vegetables, dress it nicely, and voilà—nearly everyone loves it.

When you first make and combine a slaw, it looks thick and creamy. Give it a day in the refrigerator, and all of a sudden a white moat of liquid surrounds an island of slaw. What happened? The sugar and salt in the dressing caused the cabbage and other vegetables to give off water. Just tip the bowl, holding the slaw back, and drain off the extra water. Add a tablespoon or two mayonnaise and remix. Ta-da—fresh-looking and fresh-tasting slaw.

Preparation Tips: Potatoes and Pasta for Salads

Making your own pasta and potato salad is easy, but keep these preparation rules in mind.

Always boil potatoes in their skins; this keeps them from falling apart in the water. After the potatoes are cooked and cooled and they firm up, you can then peel them, if desired, and cut the potato into pieces. I like to leave the skins on potatoes I use in potato salads because I like the skin's color, texture, and healthy fiber. Also, it's a good idea to add a teaspoon of salt and a tablespoon of vinegar to the water to help keep the potatoes from falling apart.

I've really come to like Yukon Gold potatoes for potato salad, even though for years I used to make it from red potatoes. Boiled Yukon Gold potatoes have the perfect characteristics for potato salad: they're not too sticky, they have a terrific flavor, and their golden color adds visual appeal. Some folks like to use boiled russet potatoes, but I'll stand by Yukons.

After cooking pasta for a salad to the desired tenderness, rinse the pasta under cold water. Do this for two reasons: to cool it down for the salad and to wash the sticky carbohydrates off so the pasta doesn't stick together in a lump.

Beans: Fresh, Canned, or Both?

Cooking dried beans for a bean salad is almost unnecessary. Canned beans are so good today (well, most of them) that it's easier and takes less time to open a can, rinse off the beans, and work them into the salad.

It's different for fresh beans, though. Canned green beans have been cooked during the canning process, so you want to be sure to cook fresh beans, too, before tossing them into a salad. Just cook fresh beans for 4 to 5 minutes in rapidly boiling water, and then plunge them into a bowl of ice water to produce bright-green beans with a terrific flavor and texture. This holds true for any fresh bean.

The Right Oil

If I'm making salad dressing, the right oil for the job is almost always olive oil. It's got a great flavor and, because it's high in monounsaturated fat (the good stuff) and low in saturated fat (the bad stuff), it's actually very good for you, too. If you're not cooking with it but instead making a dressing, always use a good-quality, extra virgin olive oil. (Extra-virgin olive oil is made from the first pressing and is the purest and the most sweet.)

Red and Green Slaw

Serves: 6 to 8
Prep time: 25 minutes, plus 1 hour to refrigerate
Serving size: ½ cup

1 small head (about 1½ lb.) green cabbage

¼ head (about 6 oz.) red cabbage

Ice water

1 cup mayonnaise

4 TB. fresh lemon juice (from 1 large lemon)

¼ cup granulated sugar

½ tsp. salt

¼ tsp. fresh-ground black pepper

4 ribs celery, finely chopped

6 green onions, finely chopped, with some of green tops

1 medium carrot, peeled and shredded

1. Shred green and red cabbages into a large mixing bowl, and cover with ice water. Chill 1 hour. Drain thoroughly. (Or spin dry in a salad spinner.)

2. In a large bowl, whisk together mayonnaise, lemon juice, sugar, salt, and pepper until combined. Add cabbages, celery, onion, and carrot to the bowl. Using a large rubber spatula, stir and fold until vegetables are coated with dressing. Refrigerate, covered, 1 hour before serving.

Barbecue Banter

Hate the strings on celery? Never fear; they're easy to remove. Break the top of a rib off backward toward the string side, and pull down. The piece you break is still attached to the strings. It acts like a little handle that you can use to quickly pull out the strings. Turn the rib around and do the same from the bottom up. Chances are excellent that you'll have removed all the chewy strings.

Cabbage Slaw with Raisins, Apples, and Peanuts

½ cup seedless raisins

¼ cup hot water

1 cup mayonnaise

2 TB. distilled white vinegar

1 TB. granulated sugar

½ tsp. salt

¼ tsp. fresh-ground black pepper

½ large head (about 1½ lb.) cabbage, shredded

2 large apples, peeled, cored, and chopped

½ cup chopped salted roasted peanuts

Serves: 10 to 12
Prep time: 35 minutes
Serving size: ½ cup

1. In a small bowl, soak raisins in hot water until they soften and plump, about 20 minutes. Drain thoroughly.

2. While raisins soak, in a large mixing bowl, stir or whisk together mayonnaise, white vinegar, sugar, salt, and pepper. Add cabbage, apples, peanuts, and soaked and drained raisins. Toss salad with dressing, cover, and chill. Toss salad again before serving.

Barbecue Banter

By putting raisins into hot water for a time, they actually rehydrate, plump up, and get soft. They also seem sweeter.

Old-Fashioned Classic Potato Salad

4 lb. (equal-size) Yukon Gold potatoes

¼ cup plus 2 TB. cider vinegar

2 tsp. salt

1½ cups chopped celery (from 4 medium stalks)

1 cup chopped white onion (from 1 large)

4 large hard-boiled eggs, peeled and chopped

2 cups mayonnaise

Serves: 12
Prep time: about 60 minutes
Cook time: 20 to 30 minutes
Serving size: ½ cup

Lean Note

You can easily trim 2,400 calories and 224 fat grams from this old-time salad by substituting an equal amount of low-fat mayonnaise for regular mayonnaise.

1. In a 3-quart saucepan, cover potatoes with salted cold water by 2 inches and simmer, uncovered, until just tender, about 15 to 25 minutes, depending on size of potatoes, or until easily pierced by a fork. Drain in a colander, and cool until they can be comfortably handled.

2. While potatoes cool, whisk together vinegar and salt in a large bowl just until salt is dissolved.

3. When potatoes are cool enough to handle, peel and cut them into 1-inch pieces, and add them to vinegar mixture as you cut them. Toss gently with a rubber spatula to combine. Let potatoes cool to room temperature and then add celery, onion, hard-boiled eggs, and mayonnaise, and stir gently to combine. Taste and adjust seasoning. Serve at room temperature or chilled.

Macaroni and Cheese Salad

Serves: 12
Prep time: about 30 minutes
Cook time: 5 to 7 minutes
Serving size: ½ cup

1 (8-oz.) pkg. elbow macaroni

1 TB. olive oil

4 oz. medium cheddar cheese, shredded (about 2 cups)

½ cup frozen baby peas, thawed

½ medium-large sweet onion or other mild onion, peeled and diced

1 medium green bell pepper, seeds and ribs discarded, and diced

1 cup mayonnaise

¼ cup jarred roasted red peppers, drained well and chopped

3 TB. sweet pickle relish

2 TB. sour cream

Pinch ground white pepper

Barbecue Banter

When frozen baby peas come to room temperature, they look and taste as if they've already been cooked. If you cook and cool them at that point, they'll actually be overcooked. They taste fresher and sweeter if left uncooked.

1. Cook macaroni according to the package directions. Drain macaroni, rinse and drain under cold water, transfer it to a large bowl, and toss with olive oil. Add cheese, peas, onion, green bell pepper, mayonnaise, red bell peppers, pickle relish, sour cream, and white pepper. With a large rubber spatula, stir and fold until vegetables are coated with dressing.

2. Refrigerate salad, covered, for at least 1 hour for flavors to develop. Serve chilled.

Delicatessen-Style Macaroni Salad

8 oz. dry macaroni

¾ cup mayonnaise

3 TB. sweet pickle relish

3 TB. finely chopped sweet onion

½ tsp. salt

1 cup fresh or frozen and thawed baby peas

4 hard-boiled eggs, peeled and chopped

½ cup thinly sliced celery

¼ cup finely chopped green bell pepper

Serves: 12
Prep time: 40 minutes (includes hard boiling and chilling eggs)
Cook time: 5 to 7 minutes
Serving size: ½ cup

1. Cook macaroni according to the package directions. Drain well, rinse, and cool.

2. In a medium mixing bowl, whisk together mayonnaise, pickle relish, onion, and salt until combined. Add baby peas, hard-boiled eggs, celery, bell pepper, and cooled macaroni. With a large rubber spatula, stir and fold until vegetables are coated with dressing. Chill well before serving.

Barbecue Banter _____

If it's summer and you have a local farmer's market, check out its red sweet bell peppers. In the winter, red sweet bell peppers are very expensive and don't actually justify the cost, unless color is important in your dish. In the summer, red peppers, which are actually ripe green peppers, are sweeter and less expensive—sometimes the same prices as green peppers.

'Dem Devil Eggs

6 large eggs

¼ cup mayonnaise

1 tsp. Dijon mustard

⅛ tsp. ground cayenne

Salt

Fresh-ground black pepper

Sweet paprika

Serves: 12
Prep time: 25 minutes
Cook time: 15 minutes
Serving size: 1 deviled egg

1. In a 3-quart heavy saucepan, cover eggs with cold water by 1½ inches. Bring to a rolling boil over high heat, partially covered. Reduce heat to low, and simmer eggs, covered completely, for 30 seconds. Remove the saucepan from heat, and

Barbecue Banter

Ever see hard-boiled eggs with a green ring around the yolk? That green ring is caused by cooking the eggs at too high a temperature for too long.

let it stand, covered, 15 minutes. Transfer eggs with a slotted spoon to a bowl of ice and cold water to stop the cooking, and let stand 5 minutes.

2. Peel eggs and halve lengthwise. Carefully remove yolks and mash in a bowl with a fork. Add mayonnaise, mustard, and cayenne, and stir with fork until smooth. Season with salt and black pepper to taste.

3. Using a spoon, mound yolk mixture into whites, smoothing with the back of the spoon. Dust eggs with paprika, cover, and refrigerate until needed.

Chapter 23

Grilled Veggies

In This Chapter

- ◆ Grilling more than just meat: veggies!
- ◆ Deciding on which veggies you can grill—and which you shouldn't

I was skeptical when I first thought of grilling vegetables. Grilled onions and mushrooms? Yes, they work. Grilled corn-on-the-cob works, too. But aside from these veggies, what other produce is grillable? I mean grilled green beans? Grilled peas? Some things seemed to be better left alone.

Grill It Up!–Or Not?

After I started experimenting with veggies on the grill, I found my initial thoughts were correct—some vegetables are not meant to be cooked on the grill. However, I also discovered some are quite delicious when they're grilled.

To save you the same experimentation time, the following table lists grillable veggies versus the save-this-for-the-raw-veggie-tray produce.

Good-to-Grill Veggies	Not-So-Good-to-Grill Veggies
Asparagus, broccoli, fennel, cauliflower, cabbage, celery hearts, corn-on-the-cob, eggplant, endive, jicama, leeks, mushrooms, sweet peppers, sweet and white potatoes, some winter squash, summer squash (zucchini), green onions, tomatoes	String beans, brussels sprouts, chard, iceberg lettuce, okra, turnips, shell beans (lima beans, kidney beans, etc.)

To Precook or Not to Precook?

Some vegetables take a long time to cook, so they work better on the grill if you precook them on the stove first. Carrots, because they're so dense, benefit from some time in boiling water before heading for the grill. Also sweet potatoes and white potatoes both benefit from precooking before grilling.

In the nondense category, celery, zucchini, and sweet peppers are more than 90 percent water. They'll do just fine hitting the grill without any precooking.

Grilled Corn-on-the-Cob—Husks On

6 ears fresh corn, husks on   **Salt**
4 oz. (1 stick) melted butter   **Fresh-ground black pepper**

Serves: 6
Prep time: 15 minutes
Cook time: 15 minutes
Serving size: 1 ear of corn

1. Fire up the grill:

   > *For a charcoal grill:* Open the bottom vents. Ignite 6 quarts or 2½ pounds charcoal briquettes or hardwood charcoal. When the coals are hot, set up for a one-level medium-heat fire (so you can hold your hand 5 inches above cooking rack for only 4 to 5 seconds).
   >
   > *For a gas grill:* Turn each burner to high and ignite. Cover the grill. When hot, set the burners to medium heat.

2. Pull husks back and down from corn, but keep them attached at the base. Pull off silks and discard. Push husks back around ears, and soak in cold water for 10 minutes.

3. *On a charcoal or gas grill:* oil the grill rack well. Drain corn and grill (in husks), uncovered, over the coals or heat, turning every 2 minutes, for 15 minutes. Remove corn from the grill, pull husks back and off, and discard. Serve immediately, passing melted butter, salt, and pepper.

Barbecue Banter

It may be worth the effort to head for your local farmer's market or roadside stand to pick up fresh corn for tonight's grilled dinner. From the moment an ear of corn is picked, the sugar in the kernels begins to turn to starch (losing sweetness). The shortest time between pickin' and grillin' produces a significantly superior result.

Grilled Corn-on-the-Cob—Husks Off

Serves: 6
Prep time: 5 minutes
Cook time: 10 to 14 minutes
Serving size: 1 ear corn

6 ears fresh corn, husks and silks removed

Melted butter

Salt

Fresh-ground black pepper

1. Fire up the grill:

> *For a charcoal grill:* Open the bottom vents. Ignite 6 quarts or 2½ pounds charcoal briquettes or hardwood charcoal. When the coals are hot, set up for a one-level medium-heat fire (so you can hold your hand 5 inches above cooking rack for only 4 to 5 seconds).
>
> *For a gas grill:* Turn each burner to high and ignite. Cover the grill. When hot, set the burners to medium heat.

2. Brush ears of corn lightly with melted butter.

3. *On a charcoal grill:* oil the grill rack well. Grill corn over coals, uncovered, turning every 2 minutes and brushing with more butter after about 10 minutes, until some of the kernels turn golden brown. *On a gas grill:* oil the grill rack well. Grill corn over heat for 12 to 14 minutes, turning once midway and brushing with butter, until some of the kernels turn golden brown.

4. Remove from the grill and brush corn again with butter. Serve hot, passing salt and pepper at the table.

Barbecue Banter

Older corn-on-the-cob—as opposed to fresh-picked from the field corn—actually tastes better after it's cooked by boiling. But that's not so for grilling. The grill actually makes old corn worse by drying it out. If you know you don't have the freshest corn, soak the ears in cold water for 10 to 15 minutes before taking them to the grill.

Snappy Broccoli and Olives

2 cups water

3½ cups broccoli florets

¾ cup large pitted black olives

2 TB. chopped fresh flat-leaf parsley

2 TB. red wine vinegar

2 TB. olive oil

5 cloves garlic, peeled and minced, or pushed through a garlic press

½ tsp. crushed red pepper flakes

Salt

4 (12-inch) round metal skewers

Serves: 4 side dishes
Prep time: 15 minutes, plus 10 minutes to marinate
Cook time: 6 to 8 minutes
Serving size: 1 skewer, about 1 cup

1. Fire up the grill:

> *For a charcoal grill:* Open the bottom vents. Ignite 6 quarts or 2½ pounds charcoal briquettes or hardwood charcoal. When the coals are hot, set up for a one-level medium-heat fire (so you can hold your hand 5 inches above cooking rack for only 4 to 5 seconds).
>
> *For a gas grill:* Turn each burner to high and ignite. Cover the grill. When hot, set the burners to medium heat.

2. In a large saucepan, bring water to a boil. Add broccoli florets, and simmer, covered, for 2 minutes. Rinse florets under cold water and drain well.

3. In a medium mixing bowl, combine broccoli and olives.

4. In another small bowl, whisk together parsley, wine vinegar, oil, garlic, red pepper flakes, and salt. Pour marinade over broccoli and olives, and marinate at room temperature for 10 minutes, stirring occasionally. Remove broccoli and olives from marinade, reserve marinade.

5. On long metal skewers, alternately thread broccoli florets and olives.

6. *On a charcoal grill:* oil the grill rack well. Grill kabobs on the rack, uncovered, directly over coals for 6 to 8 minutes or until broccoli is lightly browned and tender, turning occasionally, and brushing with reserved marinade. *On a gas grill:* place kabobs on the grill rack over heat, cover, and follow the charcoal grilling directions. Remove kabobs from the grill and serve.

Barbecue Banter

Broccoli stems can be as tasty as broccoli florets. Getting them to that point takes a little effort, though. Using a sharp paring knife, remove the hard, tough outer layer from the broccoli's stem. Underneath that tough exterior lies a pale green interior that's sweet. When it's cut up into ¾-inch pieces and cooked as long as florets, it's just as tender and flavorful.

Pepper and Summer Squash Skewers

Serves: 4
Prep time: 30 minutes, plus 30 minutes to marinate
Cook time: 8 to 10 minutes
Serving size: 1 skewer

1½ lb. (about 4 medium or 6 small) green zucchini or yellow summer squash, or small *patty pan squash* cut crosswise into 1-inch long pieces

1 large green sweet bell pepper, stem and core with seeds removed, cut into 1-inch squares

1 large red sweet bell pepper, stem and core with seeds removed, cut into 1-inch squares

⅓ cup olive oil

2 TB. red wine vinegar

1 clove garlic, peeled and minced, or pushed through a garlic press

½ tsp. dried thyme, crumbled

½ tsp. salt

¼ tsp. fresh-ground black pepper

10 to 12 large fresh (white) button mushrooms, stems discarded and wiped clean with a damp paper towel

1. In a large stainless-steel or glass bowl, whisk together olive oil, wine vinegar, garlic, thyme, salt, and black pepper. Add vegetables and mushrooms, and toss to combine. Let stand for 30 minutes, tossing occasionally.

2. Fire up the grill:

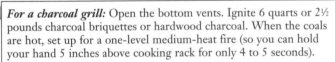
> *For a charcoal grill:* Open the bottom vents. Ignite 6 quarts or 2½ pounds charcoal briquettes or hardwood charcoal. When the coals are hot, set up for a one-level medium-heat fire (so you can hold your hand 5 inches above cooking rack for only 4 to 5 seconds).
>
>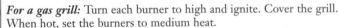
> *For a gas grill:* Turn each burner to high and ignite. Cover the grill. When hot, set the burners to medium heat.

3. Remove vegetables from marinade, reserving marinade. Thread bell pepper chunks, squash pieces, and mushrooms alternately onto the skewers.

4. *On a charcoal grill:* oil the grill rack well. Arrange the skewers on the rack over the coals and grill, uncovered, turning occasionally and brushing with reserved marinade, until lightly browned, 8 to 10 minutes. *On a gas grill:* follow charcoal grilling directions except close the grill cover. Remove skewers from the grill and serve.

Grill Guide

Patty pan squash looks like a patty with scalloped edges. The younger and smaller they are, the sweeter and more tender. I discovered patty pan squash late in life, but I've sure made up for it during the last few summers.

Grilled Acorn Squash with Honey, Garlic, and Butter

2 (1-lb.) *acorn squash*

4 TB. clover (or other mild) honey

4 TB. unsalted butter, melted

1 tsp. kosher salt

½ tsp. fresh-ground black pepper

1 clove garlic, peeled and minced, or pushed through a garlic press

Serves: 4
Prep time: 20 minutes
Cook time: 65 minutes
Serving size: ½ squash

1. Fire up the grill:

   For a charcoal grill: Open the bottom vents. Ignite 6 quarts or 2½ pounds charcoal briquettes or hardwood charcoal. When the coals are hot, set up for a one-level high-heat fire (so you can hold your hand 1 to 2 inches above cooking rack for only 1 to 2 seconds).

   For a gas grill: Turn each burner to high and ignite. Cover the grill. When hot, set the burners to medium heat.

2. Using a large, sharp knife, cut squash in half lengthwise. Scrape out seeds with a spoon's edge and discard. Pierce squash flesh with a fork (without piercing the skin) in several areas.

3. In a small bowl, stir together honey, butter, kosher salt, pepper, and garlic.

4. *On a charcoal grill:* oil the grill rack well. Grill squash, cut side down, over the coals until grill marks show, about 10 minutes. Turn squash 90 degrees and grill 10 minutes. Turn over squash and fill with honey mixture. Grill squash, away from the coals, covered, with cover vent halfway open, for 45 minutes or until fork-tender. *On a gas grill:* follow the charcoal grilling directions, except for cover vent. Remove squash from the grill and serve.

Grill Guide

Acorn squash is a winter squash, as opposed to zucchini, which is a summer squash. Summer squash have thin, tender skins and interiors and can be eaten raw. Winter squash have hard, tough skin and hard interiors that are unpleasant to eat raw and require long cooking to become tender.

Grilled Tomatoes with Gorgonzola Cheese

Serves: 4 as appetizer
Prep time: 20 to 25 minutes
Cook time: about 9 minutes
Serving size: 3 tomato halves

8 large fresh basil leaves

2 small cloves garlic, peeled and minced or pushed through a garlic press

3 TB. extra-virgin olive oil

3 tsp. balsamic vinegar

½ tsp. salt, plus more to taste

½ tsp. fresh-ground black pepper, plus more to taste

6 large plum tomatoes (1½ lb. total), cored and halved lengthwise

5 oz. *Gorgonzola cheese,* crumbled (1 cup)

6 Romaine lettuce leaves, thinly sliced crosswise

1. Fire up the grill:

> *For a charcoal grill:* Open the bottom vents. Ignite 6 quarts or 2½ pounds charcoal briquettes or hardwood charcoal. When the coals are hot, set up for a one-level high-heat fire (so you can hold your hand 1 to 2 inches above cooking rack for only 1 to 2 seconds).
>
> *For a gas grill:* Turn each burner to high and ignite. Cover the grill. When hot, set the burners to medium heat.

Grill Guide

Gorgonzola cheese is an Italian cow's milk cheese that dates back to the ninth century. You might recognize it when you see it because of its veins of blue/green mold running through it; it's similar to Roquefort cheese, but creamier and with greener mold.

2. Finely chop 6 basil leaves. In a large stainless-steel or glass bowl, stir together basil with garlic, olive oil, balsamic vinegar, salt, and pepper to taste. Add tomatoes and toss to coat.

3. *On a charcoal grill:* oil the grill rack well. Transfer tomatoes to the grill with a slotted spatula, reserving dressing in the bowl. Grill, covered, with the cover vent halfway open turning over once with spatula, just until lightly browned, about 4 minutes total. Arrange tomatoes, cut sides up, in a small nonaluminum pan, and sprinkle with Gorgonzola cheese. Place the pan with the tomatoes on the grill, cover, and grill until cheese melts, about 5 minutes. *On a gas grill:* oil the grill rack well. Transfer tomatoes to the grill with a slotted spatula, reserving dressing in the bowl. Grill, covered, turning over once with spatula, just until lightly browned, about 4 to 5 minutes total. Arrange tomatoes, cut sides up, in a small nonaluminum pan, and sprinkle with cheese. Place the pan with the tomatoes on the grill, cover, and grill until cheese melts, about 5 minutes.

4. While tomatoes grill, thinly slice remaining basil leaves and add to reserved dressing. Add lettuce leaves, salt, and pepper, and toss well. Divide lettuce and dressing among 4 plates, and top with tomatoes. Serve immediately.

Grilled Zucchini

4 to 5 medium zucchini or summer squash (about 2 lb.), rinsed, ends trimmed and cut into ¾-inch thick pieces

2 to 3 TB. olive oil

Dried basil, crumbled

Salt

Fresh-ground black pepper

Serves: 4
Prep time: 15 minutes
Cook time: 8 to 10 minutes
Serving size: about ¾ cup

1. Fire up the grill:

> *For a charcoal grill:* Open the bottom vents. Ignite 6 quarts or 2½ pounds charcoal briquettes or hardwood charcoal. When the coals are hot, set up for a one-level high-heat fire (so you can hold your hand 1 to 2 inches above cooking rack for only 1 to 2 seconds).
>
> *For a gas grill:* Turn each burner to high and ignite. Cover the grill. When hot, set the burners to medium heat.

2. Line a small metal baking pan with a piece of foil. Place sliced zucchini on the foil, cut side up.

3. Pour olive oil into a saucer. Brush oil on zucchini's cut surfaces, and season with basil, salt, and pepper to taste. Turn over zucchini and repeat.

4. *On a charcoal grill:* oil the grill rack well. Using a pair of tongs, place zucchini slices on the grill rack over the coals, and grill 4 to 5 minutes or until golden brown. Using the tongs, turn over zucchini or summer squash slices and grill 4 to 5 minutes or until golden brown. *On a gas grill:* follow the charcoal grilling directions, except place over heat and close cover while grilling. Remove zucchini from the grill and serve immediately.

Variation: Consider making kabobs, alternating 1 pound cleaned and trimmed fresh mushrooms of roughly equal size (using 2 bamboo skewers instead of 1 to keep them from spinning when turning). Brush with oil, dust with seasonings, and grill as directed for zucchini.

Barbecue Banter

Select fresh, un-bruised, undamaged zucchini or summer squash that feels firm when squeezed. The squash should not be too large, because the larger squash gets, the older it is. The older the squash, the less sweet its flavor and the more mature and tougher its seeds.

Country Vegetable Mix

Serves: 5 as a side
Prep time: 18 to 20 minutes
Cook time: 20 minutes
Serving size: about 1 cup

2 fennel bulbs, fronds and stems removed, root end cut off rinsed under cold water and sliced (about 1½ cups)

1 cup peeled and sliced carrots

½ lb. green beans, trimmed (about 2 cups)

1 medium onion, peeled and cut into thin wedges

½ tsp. salt

¼ tsp. coarse-ground black pepper

2 TB. *extra-virgin olive oil*

2 TB. snipped fresh basil leaves or 2 tsp. dried basil, crumbled

1. Fire up the grill:

 For a charcoal grill: Open the bottom vents. Ignite 6 quarts or 2½ pounds charcoal briquettes or hardwood charcoal. When the coals are hot, set up for a one-level high-heat fire (so you can hold your hand 1 to 2 inches above cooking rack for only 1 to 2 seconds).

 For a gas grill: Turn each burner to high and ignite. Cover the grill. When hot, set the burners to medium heat.

Grill Guide _____

Extra-virgin olive oil is made only from the first pressing of the olives. It is almost sweet, is low in acid, and has a beautiful green or green/gold color. Successive olive pressings produce less flavorful, lighter in color, and more acidic oil.

2. In a large bowl, toss together fennel, carrots, green beans, and onion until mixed.

3. Fold a 36×18-inch piece of heavy-duty foil in half to make an 18-inch square. Place vegetables in the center of the foil, season vegetables with salt and pepper, and drizzle with olive oil. Bring opposing edges of the foil up, and seal with a double fold. Fold remaining edges together to completely enclose vegetables, leaving space for steam.

4. *On a charcoal grill:* grill the foil packet directly over the coals, covered, with cover vents half open, about 20 minutes or until vegetables are crisp-tender. *On a gas grill:* follow the charcoal grilling directions, except for cover vent. Open the foil packet carefully, as steam will billow out. Stir basil leaves into vegetables. Taste and adjust seasonings as necessary, and serve.

Grill-Roasted Garlic

6 firm fresh garlic heads
Olive oil
Salt

Fresh-ground black pepper
Sliced warm French bread

Serves: 6
Prep time: 10 minutes
Cook time: 45 to 50 minutes
Serving size: 1 garlic head

1. Fire up the grill:

For a charcoal grill: Open the bottom vents. Ignite 6 quarts or 2½ pounds charcoal briquettes or hardwood charcoal. When the coals are hot, set up for a one-level high-heat fire (so you can hold your hand 1 to 2 inches above cooking rack for only 1 to 2 seconds).

For a gas grill: Turn each burner to high and ignite. Cover the grill. When hot, set the burners to medium heat.

2. With a sharp knife, cut off top of garlic heads, just exposing raw garlic clove tips. Brush with olive oil. Place each garlic head on a piece of 6×6-inch heavy-duty foil. Bring the sides of the foil up to form a cup-shaped packet, leaving the top of the packet open. Season garlic with salt and pepper to taste.

3. *On a charcoal grill:* place garlic head packets away from the coals, close the grill cover, open the cover vent halfway, and grill-roast for 45 to 50 minutes or until cloves are tender and easily pierced with a knife. *On a gas grill:* follow the charcoal grilling directions, except for the cover vent. Remove packets from the grill. Serve, passing sliced warm French bread to smear garlic on.

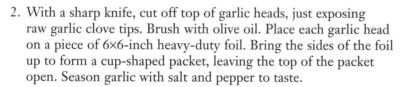

Barbecue Banter

Raw garlic has a pungent flavor and is almost never eaten just by itself. Roasting garlic, whether in an oven or on a grill, mellows and sweetens the flavor. Roasted garlic cloves are so soft they can be squeezed out of their skins and spread, like soft butter, on bread. Try making mashed potatoes adding a whole head (without the skins, of course) of roasted and mashed garlic cloves.

Grilled Sweet Potatoes and Apples

Serves: 4
Prep time: 30 to 35 minutes
Cook time: 20 to 25 minutes
Serving size: 1 cup sweet potato and 4 apple wedges

2 medium sweet potatoes, peeled and cut into 1-inch cubes

1 tsp. finely shredded lemon zest

¼ tsp. ground cinnamon

⅛ tsp. salt

⅛ tsp. fresh-ground black pepper

2 medium cooking apples (McIntosh or Rome Beauty), cored and cut into ⅛s

⅓ cup pure maple syrup

1. Fire up the grill:

   > *For a charcoal grill:* Open the bottom vents. Ignite 6 quarts or 2½ pounds charcoal briquettes or hardwood charcoal. When the coals are hot, set up for a one-level medium-heat fire (so you can hold your hand 1 to 2 inches above cooking rack for only 4 to 5 seconds).
   >
   > *For a gas grill:* Turn each burner to high and ignite. Cover the grill. When hot, set the burners to medium heat.

Barbecue Banter

Sweet potatoes and potatoes are not related, contrary to popular belief. And yams and sweet potatoes, although often referred to interchangeably, are two entirely different plants. Sweet potato varieties can have white, yellow, red, purple, or brown skins, and the flesh inside can range in color from white to orange-red.

2. In a medium saucepan, cook sweet potatoes, covered, in a small amount of boiling water for 10 minutes. Drain and cool.

3. In a small bowl, stir together maple syrup, lemon peel, cinnamon, salt, and black pepper. Set aside.

4. Fold a 36×18-inch piece of heavy foil in half to make an 18-inch square. Place sweet potatoes and apple pieces in the center of the foil. Drizzle maple syrup mixture over potatoes and apples. Bring the opposing edges of the foil up and seal with a double fold. Fold the remaining edges together to completely enclose potatoes and apples, leaving space for steam.

5. *On a charcoal grill:* grill foil packet directly over the coals, covered, with cover vents half open, about 20 to 25 minutes or until apples are tender. *On a gas grill:* follow the charcoal grilling directions, except for cover vent. Open the foil packet carefully, as steam will billow out. Taste, adjust seasoning if necessary, and serve.

Grilled Fruits and Desserts

In This Chapter

- ◆ Grilling fresh fruit
- ◆ Peeling and coring tips

Dessert—it's always my favorite part of the meal! But can you grill dessert? Yes you can, but it can be a little tricky because so many desert components can't be grilled. Can you imagine grilling a block of chocolate? What a mess! And you can't grill ice cream. But you can grill fruits and toppings for ice cream or frozen yogurt.

Why Grill Fresh Fruit?

You've worked hard enough on the rest of the meal, so grilling dessert should be simple. Luckily, you can easily grill fruit chunks and coat them with a tasty glaze.

When it's ripe, fruit is all ready to eat, so grilling fruit is easy and quick. The grill just kisses the fruit and caramelizes some of the fruit's natural sugar, heightening its natural flavor.

Fruit Peeling and Coring Tricks

To help you get that fruit on the grill faster, try these handy peeling and coring tricks:

- ◆ If you're grilling pears or apples, first cut them in half lengthwise and then use a melon baller tool to quickly and neatly cut out the core.
- ◆ To remove the peel from peaches or apricots, plunge them into boiling water for 30 seconds and immediately into ice water. The peel should slip right off.
- ◆ For peeling pineapples, check out a pineapple peeler, which removes the rough skin and core in one move.

Decadent Grilled Banana Sundaes

¼ **cup coconut, toasted**

¼ **cup sliced almonds, toasted**

3 large firm bananas

1 TB. unsalted butter, melted

2 tsp. orange juice, not from concentrate

½ **cup caramel ice cream topping**

¼ **tsp. ground cinnamon**

1 pt. vanilla ice cream

Serves: 4
Prep time: 40 minutes
Cook time: 4 to 5 minutes
Serving size: 1 sundae

1. Preheat the oven to 350°F. Spread coconut and almonds on a baking sheet and bake for about 7 minutes, or until golden and fragrant; let cool.

2. Fire up the grill:

> *For a charcoal grill:* Open the bottom vents. Ignite 6 quarts or 2½ pounds charcoal briquettes or hardwood charcoal. When the coals are hot, set up for a one-level medium-heat fire (so you can hold your hand 5 inches above the cooking rack only 4 to 5 seconds).
>
> *For a gas grill:* Turn each burner to high and ignite. Cover the grill. When hot, set the burners to medium heat.

3. Peel bananas, cut in half lengthwise, and then cut each piece in half crosswise. (You'll have 12 pieces.) Place bananas on a plate or tray. In a small bowl, stir together butter and 1 teaspoon orange juice. Brush butter-juice mixture over all sides of bananas.

4. *On a charcoal grill*: oil the grill rack well. Grill bananas over heat, uncovered, for 4 minutes or until heated through, turning over halfway through grilling. *On a gas grill*: place bananas on the grill rack over heat. Cover and follow the charcoal grilling directions.

5. In a heavy, medium saucepan stir together caramel topping and remaining orange juice. Heat caramel mixture on grill rack alongside bananas directly over coals or heat (or on kitchen stovetop) until mixture boils, stirring frequently. Stir in cinnamon. Add bananas to sauce, and stir gently to coat.

6. To serve, spoon sauce and bananas over scoops of ice cream. Sprinkle with coconut and almonds, and serve immediately.

Barbecue Banter

Green bananas have tough skins and are hard, flavorless, and starchy inside. As a banana ripens (bananas are one of the few fruits that actually "ripen" off the tree), the skin changes to bright yellow, to dull yellow, and then to brown black. As the fruit ripens, the inside flesh gets softer and sweeter.

Grilled Apricot Cobbler

Serves: 4
Prep time: 45 minutes
Cook time: 6 to 8 minutes on the grill, 30 minutes in the oven
Serving size: ¼ cobbler

1½ lb. (about 18 to 20) fresh apricots, sliced into halves and pitted

4 TB. unsalted butter, melted

7 TB. plus 3 tsp. granulated sugar

1 TB. plus ¾ cup all-purpose flour

1½ tsp. fresh lemon juice (from ½ lemon)

⅛ to ¼ tsp. pure almond extract

¾ tsp. baking powder

¼ tsp. baking soda

¼ tsp. salt

2 TB. cold unsalted butter, cut into bits

½ cup buttermilk, well-shaken

1. Fire up the grill:

> *For a charcoal grill:* Open the bottom vents. Ignite 6 quarts or 2½ pounds charcoal briquettes or hardwood charcoal. When the coals are hot, set up for a one-level medium-heat fire (so you can hold your hand 5 inches above the cooking rack only 4 to 5 seconds).
>
> *For a gas grill:* Turn each burner to high and ignite. Cover the grill. When hot, set the burners to medium heat.

2. Lay apricot halves on a foil-lined cookie sheet. Brush both sides of each apricot half with melted butter. *On a charcoal or gas grill:* oil the grill rack well. Using tongs, place apricot halves on the grill rack over the coals or heat, and grill 3 to 4 minutes or until grill-marked. Turn over apricots and repeat. Remove grilled apricots to a tray and cool.

3. For filling: toss together grilled apricots, 7 tablespoons sugar, 1 tablespoon flour, lemon juice, and almond extract in a 9-inch glass or ceramic pie plate and let stand until juicy, about 30 minutes.

4. Place the oven rack in the middle position and begin heating the oven to 400°F.

5. For topping: in a medium bowl stir together remaining ¾ cup flour, baking powder, baking soda, salt, and 1 teaspoon sugar. Cut remaining 2 tablespoons butter into small bits, and blend it in with your fingertips, a pastry blender, or a dinner fork until mixture resembles coarse meal. Stir in buttermilk with a fork just until combined (do not overmix).

Barbecue Banter

Apricots are members of the rose family and are closely related to plums, peaches, cherries, and almonds. It's not always easy to get good, fresh apricots, but even though their season is fairly short, it's well worth it to find good apricots.

6. Drop rounded tablespoons of dough over apricots, leaving spaces in between to allow topping to expand. Sprinkle dough with remaining 3 teaspoons sugar.

7. Bake cobbler until topping is golden, about 30 minutes. Cool slightly, about 15 minutes, and serve warm.

Grilled Fresh Peach Sundaes

2 medium almost-ripe peaches, halved lengthwise, pitted, and peeled

1 TB. unsalted butter, melted

2 TB. clover (or other mild) honey

⅛ tsp. ground nutmeg

1 pint (2 cups) vanilla ice cream or vanilla frozen yogurt

1 cup fresh blueberries, rinsed under cold water and patted dry with paper towels

1 cup sliced strawberries

¼ cup crushed gingersnap cookies (use a food processor)

Serves: 4
Prep time: about 25 minutes
Cook time: 8 to 10 minutes
Serving size: 1 sundae

1. Fire up the grill:

> *For a charcoal grill:* Open the bottom vents. Ignite 6 quarts or 2½ pounds charcoal briquettes or hardwood charcoal. When the coals are hot, set up for a one-level medium-heat fire (so you can hold your hand 5 inches above the cooking rack only 4 to 5 seconds).
>
> *For a gas grill:* Turn each burner to high and ignite. Cover the grill. When hot, set the burners to medium heat.

2. Brush cut sides of peaches with melted butter.

3. *On a charcoal grill:* oil the grill rack well. Grill peaches, uncovered, directly over medium coals for 8 to 10 minutes or until tender, turning and brushing once with honey halfway through. *On a gas grill:* place peaches on grill over heat, cover, and follow charcoal directions.

4. To serve, sprinkle cut sides of peaches with nutmeg. Place 1 peach half, cut side up, in each dessert dish. Top each half with ½ cup ice cream (or yogurt), some blueberries, and strawberries. Sprinkle with crushed gingersnaps and serve.

Barbecue Banter

Peaches are really nectarines with fuzzy skin. For grilling, choose peaches or nectarines that are fully ripe but still firm.

Whiskey-Flavored Grilled Caramel Apples

Serves: 6
Prep time: 25 minutes
Cook time: 8 to 11 minutes
Serving size: 1 skewer

10 TB. unsalted butter

1 cup firmly packed light brown sugar

¼ tsp. ground cinnamon

¼ cup bourbon or other whiskey

6 TB. whipping cream

6 medium-size apples (such as Golden Delicious, Gala, Braeburn, or Empire) peeled, cored, and cut into 1-inch-thick wedges

1. Fire up the grill:

> *For a charcoal grill:* Open the bottom vents. Ignite 6 quarts or 2½ pounds charcoal briquettes or hardwood charcoal. When the coals are hot, set up for a one-level medium-heat fire (so you can hold your hand 5 inches above the cooking rack only 4 to 5 seconds).
>
> *For a gas grill:* Turn each burner to high and ignite. Cover the grill. When hot, set the burners to medium heat.

2. In a heavy saucepan over medium heat, stir together 4 tablespoons butter, brown sugar, cinnamon, and bourbon. Bring mixture to a boil, and boil for 2 minutes, stirring frequently. Remove syrup from heat, and stir in whipping cream. (Be very careful, as cream will spatter and steam as it hits the very hot sauce.)

3. In a small saucepan, over medium heat melt remaining 6 tablespoons butter. Thread apples onto metal skewers, and then brush apples with melted butter.

4. *On a charcoal grill:* oil the grill rack well. Grill apples, uncovered, over coals for 8 to 10 minutes, turning at least once, until tender. In the last 1 to 2 minutes of grilling, baste apples with some sauce. *On a gas grill:* grill, covered, grilling for 9 to 11 minutes, turning once midway and basting with some sauce.

5. Divide apples among individual serving bowls. Drizzle additional sauce over apples, and serve immediately.

Barbecue Banter

Always be careful when cooking with alcohol. Before the alcohol cooks off, it can catch fire when hot and allowed near an open flame. In a dessert like this, the alcohol cooks off (evaporates), leaving only terrific flavor notes.

Pineapple, Nectarine, and Banana Kabobs

1 (8-oz.) carton low-fat vanilla yogurt

1 tsp. finely shredded lime zest

1 TB. plus 2 tsp. fresh lime juice (from ½ large lemon)

¼ tsp. ground cinnamon

1 small fresh pineapple, peeled and cored

2 large ripe, firm, nectarines or peeled peaches, pitted

2 medium-ripe, firm bananas

6 (6- to 8-inch) bamboo skewers, soaked in warm water for 30 minutes

1 TB. unsalted butter, melted

Serves: 6
Prep time: 25 minutes, plus 30 minutes to soak bamboo skewers
Cook time: 6 to 8 minutes
Serving size: 1 kabob

1. In a small bowl, stir together yogurt, lime zest, 1 tablespoon lime juice, and cinnamon. Cover and chill.

2. Fire up the grill:

> *For a charcoal grill:* Open the bottom vents. Ignite 6 quarts or 2½ pounds charcoal briquettes or hardwood charcoal. When the coals are hot, set up for a one-level medium-heat fire (so you can hold your hand 5 inches above the cooking rack only 4 to 5 seconds).
>
> *For a gas grill:* Turn each burner to high and ignite. Cover the grill. When hot, set the burners to medium heat.

3. Cut prepared pineapple into 1-inch-thick slices and then quarter slices. Cut nectarines into wedges. Cut bananas into chunks. Alternately thread pieces of fruit on the skewers.

4. In a small bowl, stir together melted butter and remaining 2 teaspoons lime juice. Brush over kabobs.

5. *On a charcoal grill:* oil the grill rack well. Grill kabobs, uncovered, directly over the coals for 6 to 8 minutes or until heated through, turning once or twice. *On a gas grill:* follow the charcoal grilling directions, except close cover. Remove kabobs from the grill, place on serving plates, drizzle sauce over kabobs, and serve.

Barbecue Banter

Pineapple is an excellent fruit for grilling. Try grilling 1-inch-thick fresh pineapple rings. When they're golden, serve the rings with a touch of light brown sugar sprinkled over them.

Grilled Fruit with Minted-Honey Sauce

Serves: 3 to 6
Prep time: 16 to 18 minutes, plus 30 minutes to soak bamboo skewers
Cook time: about 5 minutes
Serving size: 1 or 2 skewers

¾ cup reduced-fat sour cream

1½ TB. clover (or other mild) honey

1 TB. fresh lime juice

1½ TB. finely chopped fresh mint leaves

2 firm-ripe plums, pits removed, and each cut into 8 wedges (16 pieces total)

2 firm-ripe peaches, pits removed, and each cut into 8 wedges (16 pieces total)

½ ripe small pineapple (¾ lb.), peeled, cored, and cut into 1-inch pieces (16 pieces total)

8 (8-inch) wooden or bamboo skewers, soaked in warm water 30 minutes

1. Fire up the grill:

 For a charcoal grill: Open the bottom vents. Ignite 6 quarts or 2½ pounds charcoal briquettes or hardwood charcoal. When the coals are hot, set up for a one-level medium-heat fire (so you can hold your hand 5 inches above the cooking rack only 4 to 5 seconds).

 For a gas grill: Turn each burner to high and ignite. Cover the grill. When hot, set the burners to medium heat.

2. In a small bowl, stir together sour cream, honey, lime juice, and mint; chill.

3. Thread fruit onto the skewers, alternating 2 plum wedges, 2 peach quarters, and 2 pineapple chunks on each skewer. *On a charcoal grill*: oil the grill rack well. Grill fruit directly over the coals, uncovered, turning once, until browned and slightly softened, about 5 minutes total. *On gas grill*: follow the charcoal grilling directions, except grill over heat. Serve fruit on skewers and pass sauce.

Barbecue Banter

You can use plums on the grill, but you can also substitute *pluots,* a tasty cross between apricots and plums with a smooth skin, or *apriums,* the same cross with a fuzzy skin. They both contain more sugar than their non-crossed counterparts.

Peanut Butter S'Mores

32 graham cracker squares

1 cup smooth peanut butter

2 Hershey's milk chocolate bars, divided into 16 squares

16 marshmallows (plus a few extra for any that may fall into fire)

8 (18-inch) metal skewers

Serves: 8		
Prep time: about 18 to 20 minutes		
Cook time: Varies		
Serving size: 2 s'mores		

1. Fire up the grill:

> *For a charcoal grill:* Open the bottom vents. Ignite 6 quarts or 2½ pounds charcoal briquettes or hardwood charcoal. When the coals are hot, set up for a one-level medium-heat fire (so you can hold your hand 5 inches above the cooking rack only 4 to 5 seconds).
>
> *For a gas grill:* Turn each burner to high and ignite. Cover the grill. When hot, set the burners to medium heat.

2. Spread 16 graham cracker squares with peanut butter, and press a square of milk chocolate in the center of each.

3. Slide a marshmallow onto the end of each skewer. *On charcoal grill or a gas grill:* remove the grill and have guests hold the skewers as close to the coals or heat as possible, turning from time to time to toast marshmallows evenly. When marshmallows are toasted, slide them off the skewer onto a graham cracker with milk chocolate square pressed into peanut butter. Top with plain graham cracker. Repeat with remaining 8 marshmallows.

Barbecue Banter

Regular graham crackers work better for s'mores than honey graham crackers or low-fat graham crackers. Also if you spray the metal skewer with vegetable oil before putting the marshmallow on, it will release more easily when you want to finally slide it off. And think about what peanut butter you're using. Natural peanut butter sounds good, but the oil usually separates from the puréed peanut and it's hard to bring it back together. It's better to use smooth peanut butter than crunchy, too. Smooth, reduced-fat peanut butter works well with s'mores.

Glossary

al dente   Italian for "against the teeth." Refers to pasta (or other ingredient such as rice) that is neither soft nor hard, but just slightly firm against the teeth. This, according to many pasta aficionados, is the perfect way to cook pasta.

all-purpose flour   Flour that contains only the inner part of the wheat grain. Usable for all purposes from cakes to gravies.

allspice   Named for its flavor echoes of several spices (cinnamon, cloves, nutmeg), allspice is used in many desserts and in rich marinades and stews. Allspice is a defining flavor of Jamaican jerk.

almonds   Mild, sweet, and crunchy nuts that combine nicely with creamy and sweet food items.

andouille sausage   A sausage made with highly seasoned pork chitterlings and tripe, and a standard component of many Cajun dishes.

arugula   A spicy-peppery garden plant with leaves that resemble a dandelion and have a distinctive—and very sharp—flavor.

baby back ribs   Small pork ribs cut from the top of a young hog's center loin section. Baby backs are considered especially juicy and tender.

bake   To cook in a dry oven. Dry-heat cooking often results in a crisping of the exterior of the food being cooked. Moist-heat cooking, through methods such as steaming, poaching, etc., brings a much different, moist quality to the food.

balsamic vinegar   Vinegar produced primarily in Italy from a specific type of grape and aged in wood barrels. It is heavier, darker, and sweeter than most vinegars.

barbecue   Generally refers to grilling done outdoors over an open charcoal or wood fire as well as to the equipment on which the food is grilled. More specifically it refers to cooking meat slowly and for a long time over a low heat fire, brushed at the end with sauce (barbecue sauce).

barbecue sauce   A frequently sweet, sometimes tart, and always spicy sauce used to baste meats, poultry, or seafood. It is also used as a table sauce or condiment for grilled foods.

basil   A flavorful, almost sweet, resinous herb delicious with tomatoes and used in all kinds of Italian or Mediterranean-style dishes.

baste   To keep foods moist during cooking by spooning, brushing, or drizzling with a liquid.

beat   To quickly mix substances.

beef back ribs   The portion remaining after a rib roast is boned. Sometimes the ends of the ribs are cut from the full rib and are called short ribs.

beef boneless top loin steak   Sometimes called New York strip steak; cut from the top loin and very tender and flavorful.

beef Porterhouse steak   A crosscut steak containing part of the tenderloin and part of the top loin. It is similar to a T-bone steak except it's thicker and the proportion of the tenderloin to the top loin is greater.

Belgian endive   A plant that resembles a small, elongated, tightly packed head of romaine lettuce. The thick, crunchy leaves can be broken off and used with dips and spreads.

black pepper   A biting and pungent seasoning, freshly ground pepper is a must for many dishes and adds an extra level of flavor and taste.

blend   To completely mix something, usually with a blender or food processor, more slowly than beating.

blue cheese   A blue-veined cheese that crumbles easily and has a somewhat soft texture, usually sold in a block. The color is from a flavorful, edible mold that is often added or injected into the cheese.

boil   To heat a liquid to a point where water is forced to turn into steam, causing the liquid to bubble. To boil something is to insert it into boiling water. A rapid boil is when a lot of bubbles form on the surface of the liquid.

bouillon   Dried essence of stock from chicken, beef, vegetable, or other ingredients. This is a popular starting ingredient for soups as it adds flavor (and often a lot of salt).

braise   To cook with the introduction of some liquid, usually over an extended period of time.

breadcrumbs   Tiny pieces of crumbled dry bread. Breadcrumbs are an important component in many recipes and are also used as a coating, for example with breaded chicken breasts.

brie   A creamy cow's milk cheese from France with a soft, edible rind and a mild flavor.

brine   A highly salted, often seasoned, liquid used to flavor and preserve foods. To brine a food is to soak, or preserve, it by submerging it in brine. The salt in the brine penetrates the fibers of the meat and makes it moist and tender.

brochette   French term for "kabob," food cooked on a skewer.

briquettes (or **charcoal briquettes**)   Square, pillow-shaped fuel made from compressed pulverized/powdered charcoal, anthracite coal for long burning, limestone to create white ash, starch as binders, and sawdust and sodium nitrate for quick lighting.

brisket   Cut of meat located between the fore shank and the plate and directly below the chuck, composed of layers of meat and fat. A whole brisket can be cut into two pieces: a flat, oblong "back half" or "flat half," which is leaner than "front half" or "point cut."

broil   To cook in a dry oven under the overhead high-heat element.

broth   *See* stock.

brown   To cook in a skillet, turning, until the food's surface is seared and brown in color.

brown rice   Whole-grain rice including the germ with a characteristic pale brown or tan color; more nutritious and flavorful than white rice.

bruschetta (or **crostini**)   Slices of toasted or grilled bread with garlic and olive oil, often with other toppings.

Cajun cooking   A style of cooking that combines French and Southern characteristics and includes many highly seasoned stews and meats.

capers   Usually sold preserved in jars, capers are the flavorful buds of a Mediterranean plant. The most common size is *nonpareil* (about the size of a small pea); others are larger, including the grape-size caper berries produced in Spain.

caramelize   To cook sugar over low heat until it develops a sweet caramel flavor. The term is increasingly gaining use to describe cooking vegetables (especially onions) or meat in butter or oil over low heat until they soften, sweeten, and develop a caramel color.

caraway   A distinctive spicy seed used for bread, pork, cheese, and cabbage dishes. It is known to reduce stomach upset, which is why it is often paired with, for example, sauerkraut.

cardamom   An intense, sweet-smelling spice, common to Indian cooking, used in baking and coffee.

cayenne   A fiery spice made from (hot) chili peppers, especially the cayenne chili, a slender, red, and very hot pepper.

celery salt   Celery salt is a blend of ground celery seeds and table salt. You've probably tasted it in tuna salad without knowing it.

charcoal (or **lump charcoal**)   Sold in bags similar to briquettes. Pure charcoal is carbonized wood with no additives that might impart unwanted flavors to food cooked over it. It usually comes in the naturally irregular shapes of the real wood from which it is made. Bags of lump charcoal are usually marked with the name of the wood it was made from, like hickory, oak, or mesquite.

charcoal grate   A rack that holds lump charcoal or charcoal briquettes in the grill's firebox.

charcoal grill   A grill that uses lump charcoal or charcoal briquettes as its principal fuel.

cheddar   The ubiquitous hard cow's milk cheese with a rich, buttery flavor that ranges from mellow to sharp. Originally produced in England, cheddar is now produced worldwide.

chevre   French for goat's milk cheese, chevre is a typically creamy-salty soft cheese delicious by itself or paired with fruits or chutney. Chevres vary in style from mild and creamy to aged, firm, and flavorful. *Artisanal* chevres are usually more expensive and sold in smaller quantities; these are often delicious by themselves. Other chevres produced in quantity are less expensive and often more appropriate for combining with fruit or herbs.

chickpeas (also **garbanzo beans**)   A yellow-gold, roundish bean that's the base ingredient in hummus. Chickpeas are high in fiber and low in fat, making this a delicious and healthful component of many appetizers and main dishes.

chilis (also **chiles**)   Any one of many different "hot" peppers, ranging in intensity from the relatively mild ancho pepper to the blisteringly hot habañero.

chili powder   A seasoning blend that includes chili pepper, cumin, garlic, and oregano. Proportions vary among different versions, but they all offer a warm, rich flavor.

chimney starter   A sheet-metal cylinder-shaped container used to start a charcoal fire.

Chinese five-spice powder   A seasoning blend of cinnamon, anise, ginger, fennel, and pepper.

chives   A member of the onion family, chives grow in bunches of long leaves that resemble tall grass or the green tops of onions. Chives provide a light onion flavor to any dish. They're very easy to grow and are often grown in gardens.

chop To cut into pieces, usually qualified by an adverb such as "*coarsely* chopped," or by a size measurement such as "chopped into ½-inch pieces." "Finely chopped" is much closer to mince.

chorizo A spiced pork sausage eaten alone and as a component in many recipes.

chutney A thick condiment often served with Indian curries made with fruits and/or vegetables with vinegar, sugar, and spices.

cider vinegar Vinegar produced from apple cider, popular in North America.

cilantro A member of the parsley family and used in Mexican cooking and some Asian dishes. Cilantro is what gives some salsas their unique flavor. Use in moderation, as the flavor can overwhelm. The seed of the cilantro is the spice coriander.

cinnamon A sweet, rich, aromatic spice commonly used in baking or desserts. Cinnamon can also be used for delicious and interesting entrées.

clove A sweet, strong, almost wintergreen-flavor spice used in baking and with meats such as ham.

coriander A rich, warm, spicy seed used in all types of recipes, from African to South American, from entrées to desserts.

Cornish game hen A small hybrid bird that usually yields a single serving. Although sometimes available fresh, they are most often found in the supermarket freezer section.

count In terms of seafood or other foods that come in small sizes, the number of that item that compose 1 pound. For example, 31 to 40 count shrimp are large appetizer shrimp often served with cocktail sauce; 51 to 60 are much smaller.

crimini mushrooms A relative of the white button mushroom but brown in color and with a richer flavor. The larger, fully grown version is the portobello. *See also* portobello mushrooms.

croutons Pieces of bread, usually between ¼ and ½ inch in size, that are sometimes seasoned and baked, broiled, or fried to a crisp texture. Popular in soups and salads.

crushed red pepper flakes A coarse seasoning made from whole, moderately hot, dried red chilies—everything but the stem. Instead of being seeded and ground to a powder like cayenne, the dried chilies are crushed, seeds and all.

cube To cut into squares a half-inch or larger.

cumin A smoky-tasting spice popular in Middle-Eastern and Indian dishes. Cumin is a seed; ground cumin seed is the most common form of the spice used in cooking.

curing A method of preserving uncooked foods, usually meats or fish, by either salting and smoking or pickling.

curry A general term referring to rich, spicy, Indian-style sauces and the dishes prepared with them. A curry will use curry powder as its base seasoning.

curry powder A ground blend of spices used as a basis for curry and a huge range of other Indian-influenced dishes. All blends are rich and flavorful. Some, such as Vindaloo and Madras, are notably hotter than others. Common ingredients include hot pepper, nutmeg, cumin, cinnamon, pepper, and turmeric. Some curry can also be found in paste form.

dash A few drops, usually of a liquid, released by a quick shake of, for example, a bottle of hot sauce.

devein To remove the dark vein from the back of a large shrimp with a sharp knife.

dice To cut into small cubes about ¼-inch square.

Dijon mustard Hearty, spicy mustard made in the style of the Dijon region of France.

dill A unique herb that is perfect for eggs, salmon, cheese dishes, and, of course, vegetables (pickles!).

direct grilling A method of quickly cooking food by placing it on a grill rack directly over the heat source.

dollop A spoonful of something creamy and thick, like sour cream or whipped cream.

dredge To cover a piece of food with a dry substance such as flour or corn meal.

drip pan A metal or disposable foil pan placed under food to catch drippings when grilling.

drizzle To lightly sprinkle drops of a liquid over food. Drizzling is often the finishing touch to a dish.

dry In the context of wine, a wine that contains little or no residual sugar, so it's not very sweet.

dry mustard A spice made by grinding yellow mustard seeds to a powder. It can be used to make mustard, when a liquid such as vinegar is added.

emulsion A combination of liquid ingredients that do not normally mix well beaten together to create a thick liquid, such as a fat or oil with water. Classic examples are salad dressings and mayonnaise. Creation of an emulsion must be done carefully and rapidly to ensure that particles of one ingredient are suspended in the other.

entrée The main dish in a meal. In France, however, the entrée is considered the first course.

extra-virgin olive oil *See* olive oil.

fennel   In seed form, a fragrant, licorice-tasting herb. The bulbs have a much milder flavor and a celerylike crunch and are used as a vegetable in salads or cooked recipes.

feta   This white, crumbly, salty cheese is popular in Greek cooking, on salads, and on its own. Traditional feta is usually made with sheep's milk, but feta-style cheese can be made from sheep's, cow's, or goat's milk. Its sharp flavor is especially nice with bitter, cured black olives.

file powder   Ground sassafras. Also sometimes referred to as *gumbo file powder* because it's usually used for gumbo. It delivers flavor and acts as a last-minute thickener.

fillet   A piece of meat or seafood with the bones removed.

fish basket   A grill-top metal frame that holds a whole fish intact, making it easier to turn.

flake   To break into thin sections, as with fish.

flank steak   A large, thin, fairly lean, boneless cut of beef.

flare-ups   Flames caused by fat dripping onto hot coals or lava rocks.

floret   The flower or bud end of broccoli or cauliflower.

flour   Grains ground into a meal. Wheat is perhaps the most common flour. Flour is also made from oats, rye, buckwheat, soybeans, etc. *See also* all-purpose flour; whole-wheat flour.

fold   To combine a dense and light mixture with a circular action from the middle of the bowl.

fructose   Sugar naturally found in fruit, slightly sweeter than table sugar.

fry   *See* sauté.

fusion   To blend two or more styles of cooking, such as Chinese and French.

garlic   A member of the onion family, a pungent and flavorful element in many savory dishes. A garlic bulb, the form in which garlic is often sold, contains multiple cloves. Each clove, when chopped, provides about 1 teaspoon garlic.

garlic press   A metal kitchen tool that squeezes or presses a peeled garlic clove through small holes, producing instantly what would otherwise take a minute or 2 with a knife and cutting board. If you cook with a lot of garlic, a garlic press can be a real time-saver.

garnish   An embellishment not vital to the dish but added to enhance visual appeal.

gas grill   A grill that uses gas from a propane tank or natural gas line for fuel.

giblet   A chicken's heart, liver, and gizzard.

ginger   Available in fresh root or dried, ground form, ginger adds a pungent, sweet, and spicy quality to a dish. It is a very popular element of many Asian and Indian dishes, among others.

glaze   To form a shiny, flavorful coating on food as it cooks, usually by basting it.

Gorgonzola   A creamy and rich Italian blue cheese. "Dolce" is sweet, and that's the kind you want.

grate   To shave into tiny pieces using a sharp rasp or grater.

grid   A latticework of metal rods that holds food on a grill; sometimes referred to as a grill grate.

grill basket   A hinged wire basket used to hold fish or vegetables for grilling.

grill rack   The metal grid upon which food to be grilled is placed.

grilling   Outdoor or indoor cooking methods in which food is placed on a metal grid, directly over the heat source, whether charcoal, wood, gas, or electric coil.

grind   To reduce a large, hard substance, often a seasoning such as peppercorns, to the consistency of sand.

Gruyère   A rich, sharp cow's milk cheese made in Switzerland. It has a nutty flavor.

handful   An unscientific measurement term that refers to the amount of an ingredient you can hold in your hand.

Havarti   A creamy, Danish, mild cow's milk cheese perhaps most enjoyed in its herbed versions such as Havarti with dill.

hibachi   A small, portable, uncovered grill, often made of cast iron.

hickory chips   Small chips of aromatic wood that are usually soaked in water and then tossed onto glowing coals during cooking to flavor the food with their smoke.

hoisin sauce   A sweet Asian condiment similar in consistency to ketchup made with soybeans, sesame, chili peppers, and sugar.

hot red pepper sauce   Bottled manufactured cooking and table sauce made from fresh or dried red hot chilies. Tabasco is the most commonly known brand.

horseradish   A sharp, spicy root that forms the flavor base in many condiments from cocktail sauce to sharp mustards. It is a natural match with roast beef. The form generally found in grocery stores is prepared horseradish, which contains vinegar and oil, among other ingredients. Use pure horseradish much more sparingly than the prepared version, or try cutting it with sour cream.

indirect grilling   Method of grilling food slowly, off to one side of the heat source, usually over a drip pan in a covered grill.

infusion A liquid in which flavorful ingredients such as herbs have been soaked or steeped to extract that flavor into the liquid.

Italian seasoning (also **spaghetti sauce seasoning**) The ubiquitous grocery store blend of dried herbs, which includes basil, oregano, rosemary, and thyme, is a useful seasoning for quick flavor that evokes the "old country" in sauces, meatballs, soups, and vegetable dishes.

jalapeño chili Extremely hot fresh chili pepper with a distinctive sharp flavor. A broad, tapering chili, usually dark green in color, although ripe red ones are occasionally available. When cutting or chopping, use kitchen or disposable gloves to protect your hands from the volatile chili oils if you have any cuts. Also, wash your hands liberally with warm, soapy water after handling chilies, and avoid touching your eyes.

julienne A French word meaning "to slice into very thin pieces."

kabob Pieces of meat, poultry, seafood, and/or vegetables threaded onto a skewer and grilled.

kalamata olives Traditionally from Greece, these medium-small long black olives have a smoky rich flavor, very different from run-of-the-mill canned black olives.

kettle grill A round charcoal grill with a heavy, round cover. It usually stands on three legs and can be used for either direct or indirect grilling, as well as barbecuing.

key limes Very small limes grown primarily in Florida known for their tart taste.

knead To work dough to make it pliable so it will hold gas bubbles as it bakes. Kneading is fundamental in the process of making yeast breads.

kosher salt A coarse-grained salt made without any additives or iodine used by many cooks because it does not impart a chemical flavor and dissolves easily.

lava rock A natural rock that results from volcanic lava and is used as an alternative to ceramic briquettes in gas or electric grills. It can be used many times, but it eventually needs to be replaced.

lemon zest The yellow part of the peel of a fresh lemon. The zest is packed with lemon oil and boosts the flavor of anything in which it's used. A standard box grater, using the next-to-the smallest grate, makes grating lemon or lime zest quick and easy. Be careful not to grate the white part under the zest, called the pith, as it's bitter.

lentils Tiny lens-shape pulses used in European, Middle Eastern, and Indian cuisines.

linguine A type of pasta that looks similar to spaghetti but instead of being round has two flat sides and has a meatier bite than spaghetti. If you can, use a whole-wheat blend linguine that has more healthy fiber than regular white pasta.

live-fire cooking Cooking over the flames and heat of a variety of fires, like charcoal, gas, or wood. The heat that rises up from the coal's and gas' flames seems almost alive.

lump charcoal   Carbon residue of wood that's been charred, usually in random shapes and is used for heat source in charcoal grills.

marinate   To soak meat, seafood, or other food in a seasoned liquid, called a marinade, which is high in acid content (usually from vinegar or lemon juice). The acids break down the muscle of the meat, making it tender and adding flavor.

marjoram   A sweet herb, a cousin of and similar to oregano, popular in Greek, Spanish, and Italian dishes.

medallion   A small round cut, usually of meat or vegetables such as carrots or cucumbers.

medium-done   The center of the meat should have a slightly pink or red color. The meat will be slightly firm and springy when pressed. If using a thermometer, it should register 160°F for medium.

medium-rare   The center of the meat should have a bright red color and be slightly springy when pressed. If using a thermometer, it should register 130-135°F for medium-rare.

medium-well   The center of the meat should have very little pink color and be firm and springy when pressed. If using a thermometer, it should register 170°F for medium-well.

meld   To blend and spread flavors over time in some dishes. Melding is often why recipes call for overnight refrigeration and also why some dishes taste better as leftovers.

mesclun   Mixed salad greens, usually containing lettuce and assorted greens such as arugula, cress, endive, and others.

mince   To cut into very small pieces smaller than diced pieces, about ⅛ inch or smaller.

mix   To combine ingredients in any way that distributes them evenly.

nutmeg   A sweet, fragrant, musky spice used primarily in baking.

olive oil   A fragrant liquid produced by crushing or pressing olives. Extra-virgin olive oil is the oil produced from the first pressing of a batch of olives; oil is also produced from other pressings after the first. Extra-virgin olive oil is generally considered the most flavorful and highest quality and is the type you want to use when your focus is on the oil itself.

olives   The fruit of the olive tree commonly grown on all sides of the Mediterranean. There are many varieties of olives but two general types: green and black. Black olives are also called ripe olives. Green olives are immature, although they are also widely eaten. *See also* kalamata olives.

oregano   A fragrant, slightly astringent herb used in Greek, Spanish, and Italian dishes.

oyster sauce   A thick Asian sauce made from ground oysters, salt, and water with a slightly sweet taste.

oxidation   The browning of fruit flesh that happens over time and with exposure to air. If you need to cut apples in advance, minimize oxidation by rubbing the cut surfaces with a lemon half. Oxidation also affects wine, which is why the taste changes over time after a bottle is opened.

paprika   A rich, red, warm, earthy spice available in sweet, mild, and hot forms that also lends a rich red color to many dishes. Hungarian and Spanish paprikas are preferable.

parboil   To partially cook in boiling water or broth. Parboiling is similar to blanching, although blanched foods are quickly cooled with cold water.

Parmesan   A hard, dry, flavorful cheese primarily used grated or shredded as a seasoning for Italian-style dishes.

parsley   A fresh-tasting green leafy herb used to add color and interest to just about any savory dish. Often it is used as a garnish just before serving.

pecans   Rich, buttery nuts native to North America. Their flavor, a terrific addition to appetizers, is at least partially due to their high unsaturated fat content.

peppercorns   Large, round, dried berries that are ground to produce pepper.

pickle   A food, usually a vegetable such as a cucumber, that has been pickled in brine.

pinch   An unscientific measurement term that refers to the amount of an ingredient— typically a dry, granular substance such as an herb or seasoning—you can hold between your finger and thumb.

pita bread   A flat, hollow wheat bread that can be used for sandwiches or sliced, pizza style, into slices. Pita bread is terrific soft with dips or baked or broiled as a vehicle for other ingredients.

pizza stone   Preheated with the oven, a pizza stone cooks a crust to a delicious, crispy, pizza-parlor texture. It also holds heat well, so a pizza removed from the oven on the stone will stay hot for as long as a half-hour at the table. Can also be used for other baking needs, including bread.

porcini mushrooms   Rich and flavorful mushrooms used in rice and Italian-style dishes.

portobello mushrooms   A mature and larger form of the smaller crimini mushroom, portobellos are brownish, chewy, and flavorful. They are trendy served as whole caps, grilled, and as thin sautéed slices. *See also* crimini mushrooms.

preheat   To turn on an oven, broiler, or other cooking appliance in advance of cooking so the temperature will be at the desired level when the assembled dish is ready for cooking.

purée   To reduce a food to a thick, creamy texture, usually using a blender or food processor.

red pepper flakes   Spice composed of coarsely ground flakes of dried red chilies, including seeds, which add moderately hot flavor to the foods they season.

reduce   To boil or simmer a broth or sauce to remove some of the water content, resulting in more concentrated flavor and color.

reserve   To hold a specified ingredient for another use later in the recipe.

rice vinegar   Vinegar produced from fermented rice or rice wine, popular in Asian-style dishes and different from rice wine vinegar.

ricotta   A fresh Italian cheese smoother than cottage cheese with a slightly sweet flavor.

roast   To cook something uncovered in an oven, usually without additional liquid.

Roquefort   A world-famous (French) creamy but sharp sheep's milk cheese containing blue lines of mold, making it a "blue cheese."

rosemary   A pungent, sweet herb used with chicken, pork, fish, and especially lamb. A little of it goes a long way.

rotisserie   The spit or long metal skewer that suspends and rotates food over a grill's heat source.

sage   An herb with a musty yet fruity, lemon-rind scent and "sunny" flavor. It is a terrific addition to many dishes.

salsa   A style of mixing fresh vegetables and/or fresh fruit in a coarse chop. Salsa can be spicy or not, fruit-based or not, and served as a starter on its own (with chips, for example) or as a companion to a main course.

salt, coarse or kosher   Coarse-grained salt whose crystals are well suited for use in dry marinades (rubs) for grilled foods.

satay (also **sate**)   A popular Southeast Asian dish of broiled skewers of fish or meat, often served with peanut sauce.

sauté   To pan-cook over lower heat than used for frying.

savory   A popular herb with a fresh, woody taste.

scoring   To cut shallow slashes into the surface of the meat with a very sharp knife, usually at 1-inch intervals on a diagonal in both directions so the slashes form diamond shapes across both sides of a piece of meat. Scoring aids in heating meat slightly faster and allows flavorings to enhance the meat below the surface.

Scoville scale   A scale used to measure the "hot" in hot peppers. The lower the Scoville units, the more mild the pepper. Ancho peppers, which are mildly hot, are about 3,000 Scovilles; Thai hot peppers are about 6,000; and some of the more daring peppers such as Tears of Fire and habañero are 30,000 Scovilles or more.

sear To quickly brown the exterior of a food over high heat to produce and heighten flavors (the Maillard effect) that would otherwise not occur without it. It has been scientifically proven that searing does not seal in juices, as was once believed.

sesame oil An oil, made from pressing sesame seeds, that is virtually tasteless if clear, and if seeds are toasted before pressing, aromatic and flavorful. Sesame oil has a low smoke point.

shallot A member of the onion family that grows in a bulb somewhat like garlic and has a milder onion flavor. When a recipe calls for shallot, use the entire peeled bulb. (They might or might not have cloves.)

shellfish A broad range of seafood, including clams, mussels, oysters, crabs, shrimp, and lobster. Some people are allergic to shellfish, so care should be taken with its inclusion in recipes.

shiitake mushrooms Large, dark brown mushrooms originally from the Far East with a hearty, meaty flavor that can be grilled or used as a component in other recipes and as a flavoring source for broth. They can be used either fresh or dried.

shred To cut into many long, thin slices.

short-grain rice A starchy rice popular for Asian-style dishes because it readily clumps for eating with chopsticks.

simmer To boil gently so the liquid barely bubbles.

skewers Thin wooden or metal sticks, usually about eight inches long, that are perfect for assembling kebabs, dipping food pieces into hot sauces, or serving single-bite food items with a bit of panache.

skillet (also **frying pan**) A generally heavy, flat-bottomed metal pan with a handle designed to cook food over heat on a stovetop or campfire.

skim To remove fat or other material from the top of liquid.

slice To cut into thin pieces.

soy sauce A dark brown liquid made from soybeans that has undergone a fermenting process. Soy sauces have a salty taste, but are lower in sodium than traditional table salt. Specific types of soy sauce are shoyu and tamari. Shoyu is a blend of soybeans and wheat. Tamari is made only from soybeans and is a byproduct of making miso.

starter fluid Petroleum-based liquid poured over coals to facilitate lighting, now generally discouraged because the fluid's fumes frequently violate air-quality control standards.

stir To mix ingredients until uniform consistency. Stir once in a while or occasionally, often for stirring frequently and continuously for stirring constantly.

stir-fry To cook small pieces of food in a wok or skillet over high heat, moving and turning the food quickly to cook all sides.

stock A flavorful broth made by cooking meats and/or vegetables with seasonings until the liquid absorbs these flavors. This liquid is then strained and the solids discarded. Stock can be eaten by itself or used as a base for soups, stews, sauces, risotto, or many other recipes.

tarragon A sweet, rich-smelling herb perfect with seafood, vegetables (especially asparagus), chicken, and pork.

T-bone steak Tender, flavorful cut of beef from the center of the short loin, containing a small T-shaped bone.

tenderloin Tenderest portion of the short loin of beef, veal, lamb, or pork.

teriyaki A delicious Japanese-style sauce composed of soy sauce, rice wine, ginger, and sugar. It works beautifully with seafood as well as most meats.

thyme A minty, zesty herb whose leaves are used in a wide range of recipes.

toast To heat something, usually bread, so it is browned and crisp.

toss To tumble ingredients lightly with a lifting motion (such as a green salad), usually to coat evenly with a sauce or dressing or mix with another food.

turbinado sugar Turbinado sugar looks like very light brown sugar; unlike brown sugar, though, it's free flowing but with larger crystals. It works better than any other form of sugar in a rub.

turmeric A spicy, pungent yellow root used in many dishes, especially Indian cuisine, for color and flavor. Turmeric is the source of the brilliant yellow color in many prepared mustards.

veal Meat from a calf, generally characterized by mild flavor and tenderness. Certain cuts of veal, such as cutlets and scaloppini, are well suited to quick-cooking.

venison Deer meat.

vents Holes in a grill cover or firebox that open and close. When open, air circulates through, increasing the heat of the fire.

vinegar An acidic liquid widely used as dressing and seasoning. Many cuisines use vinegars made from different source materials such as fermented grapes, apples, and rice. *See also* balsamic vinegar; cider vinegar; rice vinegar; white vinegar; wine vinegar.

walnuts Grown worldwide, walnuts bring a rich, slightly woody flavor to all types of food. For the quick cook, walnuts are available chopped and ready to go at your grocery store. They are delicious toasted and make fine accompaniments to cheeses.

water chestnuts   Actually a tuber, water chestnuts are a popular element in many types of Asian-style cooking. The flesh is white, crunchy, and juicy, and the vegetable holds its texture whether cool or hot.

whisk   To rapidly mix, introducing air to the mixture.

white mushrooms   Ubiquitous button mushrooms. When fresh, they will have an earthy smell and an appealing "soft crunch." White mushrooms are delicious raw in salads, marinated, sautéed, and as component ingredients in many recipes.

white vinegar   The most common type of vinegar found on grocery store shelves. It is produced from grain.

whole-wheat flour   Wheat flour that contains the entire grain.

wine vinegar   Vinegar produced from red or white wine.

wood chips or chunks   Natural hardwood materials added to a fire to impart smoky flavor to food as it cooks.

Worcestershire sauce   Originally developed in India and containing tamarind, this spicy sauce is used as a seasoning for many meats and other dishes.

zest   Small slivers of peel, usually from a citrus fruit such as lemon, lime, or orange.

zester   A small kitchen tool used to scrape zest off a fruit. A small grater also works well.

Sources and Resources

This may be Appendix B, but it's filled with "A" stuff. I figured that if you read the book, learned a lot, and really got into grilling and barbecue you might want to widen your vista a bit and learn more about both. That's why national, international, and local barbecue associations are listed first. These are groups of folks who *really* love grilling and barbecue. They know where the grilling and barbecue events and contests are throughout the year, in your state and probably in adjacent states. Drop them an e-mail, find out what they're up to, and see what happens.

Next I've added a suppliers section. Here you get information on how to contact companies that sell high-quality meat, sausage, and game, as well as spices, woods, equipment, and a couple general-information websites. You may not find all the following information useful, but something will jump out at you and grab your interest or attention and you'll be glad you read through this.

National, International, and Local Barbecue Associations

Arizona BBQ Society (ABS)
8510 N. Mulberry Place
Tucson, AZ 85704
back@mindspring.com
www.exit201.com/azbbq/bbqstart.htm

AZ BARBQ Cookers Association
Attention: Roland Regeon
635 W. Hazelwood Street
Phoenix, AZ 85013
602-277-7306
Fax: 602-388-9038
R2Chili@aol.com

California Barbecue Association (CBBQA)
Attention: Frank Boyer
21911 Bear Creek Way
Los Gatos, CA 95033-9497
408-354-4693
frankbbq@slip.net
www.cbbqa.com

Central Texas Barbecue Association (CTBA)
Attention: John Biles, Secretary
3401 Las Moras
Temple, TX 76502
254-778-1756
jbiles@vvm.com

East Texas Barbecue Cookers Association (ETBCA)
Attention: Donna Stanaland
114 Carlos Dews Road
Garrison, TX 75946
936-560-3545
donnak@netdot.com

Greater Omaha Barbecue Society (GOBS)
Attention: Lowell Wilhite
7474 Rogers Road
Omaha, NE 68124
402-592-0217 or 402-333-GOBS
BarBQBill@aol.com
www.novia.net/~cedmunds/gobs

Greater Wichita Barbecue Society
Attention: Russ West
2135 N. Riverside Boulevard
Wichita, KS 67203
316-264-5115

International Barbeque Cookers Association (IBCA)
PO Box 300556
Arlington, TX 76007-0556
817-469-1579
www.ibcabbq.org

Iowa Barbeque Society (IBS)
8838 Meredith Drive
Urbandale, IA 50322
515-223-2622
lewmiller1@prodigy.net
www.iabbq.org

Kansas City Barbecue Society (KCBS)
11514 Hickman Mills Drive
Kansas City, MO 64134
1-800-963-KCBS (1-800-963-5227) or
816-765-5891
Fax: 816-765-5860
kcbs@kcbs.us
www.kcbs.us

Lone Star Barbecue Society (LSBS)
Attention: Pat and Glenn Nicholas
PO Box 120771
Arlington, TX 76012-0771
817-261-9507
Fax: 817-795-1968
nich1@airmail.net
www.lonestarbarbecue.com

National Barbecue Association (NBBQA)
PO Box 9685
Kansas City, MO 64134
816-767-8311
nbbqa@nbbqa.org
www.nbbqa.org

The New England BBQ Society (NEBBQS)
The Burnt Ends
Attention: Bob Godwin
PO Box 97
No. Billerica, MA 01862-0097
nebbq@aol.com

North Texas Area BBQ Cookers Association (NTABCA)
PO Box 3024
Denton, TX 76201
817-382-1942

Pacific Northwest Barbecue Association (PNWBA)
PO Box 80267
Seattle, WA 98108
info@pnwba.com
www.pnwba.com

South Carolina Barbeque Association (SCBA)
PO Box 5841
Columbia, SC 29250
lhigh1@sc.rr.com
www.scbarbeque.com

Texas Gulf Coast BBQ Cooker's Association (TGCBCA)
Attention: Lon Babcock, Pit Boss
26611 Weir Way
Magnolia, TX 77355
713-356-6244
Fax: 281-356-9604)
lbabcock@tgcbca.org
www.tgcbca.org

Specialty Meats and Game

Aidells Sausage Company
1625 Alvarado Street
San Leandro, CA 94577
510-614-5450
Fax: 510-614-2287
info@aidells.com
www.aidells.com

Balducci's
334 East 11th Street
New York, NY 10003-7426
www.balduccis.com

Eurogrocer
304 Main Avenue, #363
Norwalk, CT 06851
1-800-490-8781
Fax: 201-505-8994
service@eurogrocer.com
www.eurogrocer.com

Seattle's Finest Exotic Meats
2245 148th Ave N.E.
Bellevue, WA 98007
425-641-1069 or 1-800-680-4375
www.exoticmeats.com

Herbs, Spices, and Hot Sauces

Kalustyan's
123 Lexington Avenue
New York, NY 10016
212-685-3451
Fax: 212-683-8458
sales@kalustyans.com
www.kalustyans.com

Mo Hotta Mo Betta
PO Box 1026
Savannah, GA 31402
1-800-462-3220
International: 912-748-1364
Fax: 1-800-618-4454
mohotta@mohotta.com
www.mohotta.com

Penzeys Spices
1-800-741-7787
Fax: 262-785-7678
www.penzeys.com

Spices etc.
PO Box 2088
Savannah, GA 31402
1-800-827-6373
spices@spicesetc.com
www.spicesetc.com

Suttons Bay Trading Company
1241 North Wells Street
Ft. Wayne, IN 46808
1-888-747-7423
customerservice@suttonsbaytrading.com
www.suttonsbaytrading.com

Equipment and Supplies

Barbecue Wood
PO Box 8163
Yakima, WA 98908
509-965-0123 or 1-800-DRYWOOD
(1-800-379-9663)
Fax: 509-965-3553
sales@bbqwoods.com
www.barbecuewood.com

Barbeques Galore
10 Orchard Road, Suite 200
Lake Forest, CA 92630
1-800-752-3085
Fax: 949-597-2434
CustomerService@BBQGalore.com
www.bbqgalore.com

Chef's Catalogue
5070 Centennial Boulevard
Colorado Springs, CO 80919-2402
1-800-884-2433
customerservice@ecare.chefscatalog.com
www.chefscatalog.com

Meat-Processing and Sausage-Making Supplies

Butcher and Packer Supply Company
www.butcher-packer.com

Grill Wizard Barbecue Grill Brush
www.grillwizard.com

Barbecue and Grilling Information

Barbecue'n on the Internet
www.barbecuen.com

Home BBQ
www.homebbq.com/duportal/home/default.asp

Texas Cooking Online
www.texascooking.com

Index

H

N

Check Out These
Best-Sellers

Grammar and Style
SECOND EDITION

Laurie E. Rozakis, Ph.D.

1-59257-115-8 • $16.95

Buying and Selling a Home
FOURTH EDITION

Shelley O'Hara and Nancy D. Lewis

1-59257-120-4 • $18.95

Being a Groom
SECOND EDITION

Jennifer Lata Rung and Mark Rung

0-02-864456-5 • $9.95

Learning Spanish
THIRD EDITION

Gail Stein

0-02-864451-4 • $18.95

Personal Finance in Your 20s & 30s
SECOND EDITION

Sarah Young Fisher and Susan Shelly

0-02-864374-7 • $19.95

Organizing Your Life
FOURTH EDITION

Georgene Lockwood

1-59257-413-0 • $16.95

Total Nutrition
FOURTH EDITION

Joy Bauer, M.S., R.D., C.D.N.

1-59257-439-4 • $18.95

Positive Dog Training

Pamela Dennison

0-02-864463-8 • $14.95

The Bible
THIRD EDITION

James Stuart Bell and Stan Campbell

1-59257-389-4 • $18.95

Calculus

W. Michael Kelley

0-02-864365-8 • $18.95

Music Theory
SECOND EDITION

Michael Miller

1-59257-437-8 • $19.95

The Perfect Resume
THIRD EDITION

Susan Ireland

0-02-864440-9 • $14.95

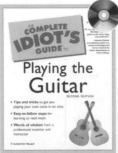

Playing the Guitar
SECOND EDITION

Frederick Noad

0-02-864244-9 • $21.95

MANGA ILLUSTRATED

John Layman and David Hutchison

1-59257-335-5 • $19.95

Knitting and Crocheting
SECOND EDITION
Illustrated

Barbara Breiter and Gail Diven

1-59257-089-5 • $16.95

More than *450 titles* available at
booksellers and online retailers everywhere